D1596581

INTERPRETIVE ACTS

INTERPRETIVE ACTS

In Search of Meaning

WENDELL V. HARRIS

CLARENDON PRESS · OXFORD

1988

Oxford University Press, Walton Street, Oxford OX2 6DP
Oxford New York Toronto
Delhi Bombay Calcutta Madras Karachi
Petaling Jaya Singapore Hong Kong Tokyo
Nairobi Dar es Salaam Cape Town
Melbourne Auckland
and associated companies in
Beirut Berlin Ibadan Nicosia

Oxford is a trade mark of Oxford University Press

Published in the United States
by Oxford University Press, New York

© Wendell V. Harris 1988

All rights reserved. No part of this publication may be reproduced,
stored in a retrieval system, or transmitted, in any form or by any means,
electronic, mechanical, photocopying, recording, or otherwise, without
the prior permission of Oxford University Press

British Library Cataloguing in Publication Data
Harris, Wendell
Interpretive acts : in search of meaning.
1. Speech acts (Linguistics)
2. Sociolinguistics
I. Title
401'.9   P40
ISBN 0-19-812959-9

Library of Congress Cataloging in Publication Data
Harris, Wendell V.
Interpretive acts.
1. Criticism. 2. Language and languages. 3. Speech acts (Linguistics)
4. Discourse analysis. I. Title.
PN81.H2846   1988   801'.95   87-24769
ISBN 0-19-812959-9

Set by Colset Private Ltd.
Printed in Great Britain by
Biddles Ltd.
Guildford and King's Lynn

*To colleagues everywhere engaged in
increasing understanding and
appreciation of the powers
of language*

Preface

For a good twenty years now, the humanities and social sciences have been preoccupied with the powers and limitations of language. During these years literary theory seems to have become peculiarly fascinated with what language cannot do, with the impossibility of language meaning what an individual intends it to mean, if indeed individuals can intend or mean. Among some of our most influential theorists, language, and therefore literature, has come to seem very much like Hiawatha's arrow—easy enough to shoot, but impossible to direct towards a target: 'It fell to earth I know not where.' One recalls a scene from *Henry IV*:

> GLENDOWER: I can call spirits from the vasty deep.
> HOTSPUR: Why so can I, or so can any man,
>   But will they come when you do call for them?

Within many academic halls this has been transmogrified into:

RHETORICIAN: Rhetoric makes communication effective.
POST-STRUCTURALIST SCEPTIC: Yes, but do you really think rhetoric can determine what you communicate?

It can indeed be plausibly argued that it is impossible for a child to learn the language. A mother points to a long-tailed furry object and says 'Cat.' How is the child to know whether the pointing arm, or finger, or the floor, or the mother herself is to be associated with the word 'cat'? Suppose the mother were to say while pointing, 'Look at the cat'. The situation is hardly improved: now the child must know the meaning of 'look' and 'at', the learning of which involves the same problem.

It can be plausibly argued that the very creation of language is impossible, for something like the situation just described would have been necessary for tree-swinging humanoid Ak to convey to his companion Ek that 'Wof' meant the-long-tailed-furry-big-toothed-thing-that-ate-Ik. It can be plausibly argued that words are wholly separated from the things they supposedly refer to, the presence of a word indeed generally affirming the absence of the thing referred to, so that *words* cannot in fact communicate knowledge about *things*. It can be further argued that since words refer only to other words, to determine the meaning of a word leads to infinite regress, and so we cannot in fact communicate anything to each other.

But language does exist and children do learn it; language does appear to be useful in communicating all sorts of things about extralinguistic objects and *almost* all the time we feel that we are successful in communicating with others who use the same language and that they are successful in communicating with us.

In reaction to the prevalence of theories of literature and language that question the possibility of stating anything, including presumably the very question of the possibility of communicating anything, I began to ask what sort of theory might be erected by asking not *whether* communication is possible, but, given that we do communicate, *how* this occurs. The multitude of issues that arose turned out to be not so much individually difficult as collectively daunting—given their complex interrelation, resolution of any one of them tended to presuppose the results of previous resolution of others. What finally seemed the order that would allow me to beg the fewest questions as I went along had to begin in a thicket of basic issues, not on a hill-top allowing a perspicuous survey.

Let me therefore here map the shape rather than the order of my argument, and set out the relationships between certain central conclusions while reserving the arguments for those conclusions. *First*, the essential difference between regarding a word as a unit of the total system of language (*langue*) and as a portion of discourse (*parole*) is that the second places it in context. If it is possible—*since* it is possible—for us to understand others and use language ourselves so that others understand us in a reasonably satisfactory way, the user and the interpreter must be paying careful attention to context. With exceptions rare enough to attract special attention, we discover from the probable context the sense and implications to assign each word. We thus know from the context whether to associate the word 'bridge' with a span over a river, a card game, or artificial teeth. E. D. Hirsch's distinction between the intended *meaning* of the author of a text and the many *significances* the text may have for the reader is very useful here, though my use of that terminology is not wholly parallel with Hirsch's. It seems to me that we gain in precision if we define *interpretation* as the reconstruction of *intended meaning* that attempts to take into account as far as possible the context in which the author assumed the anticipated audience would place the utterance or text. Such a definition makes explicit the author's need to calculate contexts that can or will occur to the audience. Since the author must make assumptions about the reader and the reader must make assumptions about those assumptions, interpretation can never be more than probable, but there is a great difference between saying that constructions of meaning can never be more than probable and saying that meaning is necessarily indeterminable. The definition I have adopted further suggests that *significance* results from analyses of the text or utterance in terms of contexts *not* presumed by the author.

Differences in context then also represent the effective differences between spoken and written language and between literature and non-literature. I will use 'discourse' as an umbrella term for all uses of language, whether utterances or written texts, 'author' for all users, and 'audience' for all interpreters.

Now to define 'meaning' and 'interpretation' in this way is to narrow both rather sharply. Much of what critics do, much of what the readers of a novel or hearers of a speech find it worthwhile to talk about, is excluded from 'meaning' as so defined. The fact is that we are rarely content with interpretation *per se*. However, an understanding of the possibility, process, and limits of the interpretation of meaning is crucial. First, all consideration of significance depends on the possibility of interpretation. Not only did Walter Pater presumably intend interpretable meanings in all that he wrote, but T. S. Eliot presumed that he understood those meanings before he attacked their significance; Hillis Miller presumably believed he understood not only Pater's meaning but Eliot's when he mentions Pater's influence on Eliot in opening an essay in which he assigns quite another significance to Pater's writing; you and I presume that we understand the meanings of all three as we comment on any one of them in terms of the others.

Second, though much of what interests us in a text arises from perceptions of significance, interpretation is a much more complicated matter than we tend to realize. When we speak of context we are speaking not of a single surrounding ambience but a multitude of interacting kinds of knowledge and awareness: I will be suggesting seven aspects or dimensions of context. Reconstruction of the author's assumptions about the interaction of these dimensions is an active process, not a passive absorption, which, I hope to show, is usefully described by a number of the concepts developed by speech-act theory. However, I will be modifying and adding to these to reflect the fact that the speech-act must be complemented by the interpretive act. In doing so I am attempting to make explicit what we do when we write or read, *not* to outline a method of interpretation different from that which we in fact routinely employ. I have in the past used the term 'ecological' to describe that active interpretation which recognizes that the context, like a physical environment, is made up of interacting forces. The term has not met with universal favour: it has been described as too 'wet', too 'botanical', and as confusingly derived. An alternative is 'koinonoetic', which captures the *commonality* of knowledge required in interpretation. I will be using both 'ecological' and 'koinonoetic'; some readers may prefer one, some the other.

Third, I hope to exhibit the importance of consciously distinguishing meaning from significance, interpretation from criticism. Doubtless much of what we think of as literary criticism clearly intertwines interpretation and critical analysis, but we frequently confuse our students, not seldom each other, and at least occasionally ourselves by not being sufficiently aware of, or willing to make, the distinction. Many a text will yield intriguing political, economic, psychological, philosophical, and/or ethical significances when considered in the appropriate—quite legitimate—contexts. But not to differentiate between those significances and the meanings that the author could with any probability have intended to convey leads to arguments conducted at cross-purposes. Critics in fact frequently assert that although an author did not intend such-and-such a meaning, the *text* nevertheless has that meaning. This is in effect to admit half the case I am making by distinguishing between authorial intentions and critical discoveries. Such critics of course generally deny the relevance or recoverability of meanings intended by the author: one of my major purposes is to counter such denials.

Finally, in analysing the process of interpretation and sketching the frontiers between meaning and the many other useful and fascinating things we do when we comment on human discourse, the complementarity of all sorts of critical and scholarly activities begins to emerge with special clarity. I am not sanguine enough to think that literary historians, New Critical explicators, cultural historians, rhetoricians, biographers, and structuralist, feminist, deconstructive, Marxist, and psychoanalytical critics will agree

with my assessment of their particular contributions to interpretation of meaning or critical analysis. But perhaps those who
privilege any one of these kinds of commentary will find some
cogency in what my approach suggests about the places of the others.

In exploring the act of interpretation I will be drawing on the
impressive amount of help to be found in the contemporary investigations of linguists, socio-linguists, rhetoricians, argument theorists, philosophers of language, and discourse analysts. I can only
point to, not stay to develop or debate, supporting evidence from
such allied endeavours. Nor has my purpose allowed me to be either
comprehensive or technically precise in my summaries of the contributions of various disciplines, sub-disciplines, and individuals.
Linguists, philosophers, rhetoricians, and traditional literary
scholars and critics will each find my summaries and examples of
relevant insights from their respective fields of expertise simplistic.
My goal, however, is to incorporate what is at present obvious in
these several fields into the broad outlines of a theory of interpretation the possibility of which, to judge by the present state of
commentary on literary and other texts, is very much less obvious.
My thorough indebtedness to J. L. Austin, H. P. Grice, E. D. Hirsch,
Charles Altieri, and Louise Rosenblatt in particular will be evident.
Though much in their work does not fit comfortably together, the
insights on which I draw are, I believe, in themselves quite compatible. The result is intended as a delineation of the boundaries of
interpretation, a survey of the interrelationships between interpretation and criticism, and a primer of literary commentary for
students. These intentions have required brief rehearsals of salient
aspects of certain reasonably familiar theories.

The reader will notice, possibly with annoyance, the frequency
with which I argue for the differentiation of concepts that have
become misleadingly conflated. I am sorry for it, but the sometimes
careless, sometimes wilful blurring of such distinctions has created
much of that intellectual murkiness in which all meaning comes to
seem equally obscure.

Authors of quoted passages and sponsors of specific insights are
identified in the text; page numbers are cited parenthetically
(together with the first initials of the title of the book or essay where
necessary); full publication details may be found in the References.

W. V. H.

Acknowledgements

I wish to acknowledge with pleasure and appreciation the leave from Northern Illinois University and Fellowship from the National Endowment for the Humanities that allowed me to begin reading in the history and theory of literary criticism a decade ago while pursuing another project, and the sabbatical leave from Pennsylvania State University and Guggenheim Fellowship that allowed me to write the present book.

Passages from W. B. Yeats's poems 'Shepherd and Goatherd' and 'Demon and Beast,' as published in *The Collected Poems of W. B. Yeats*, are used by permission of A. P. Watt Ltd. on behalf of Michael B. Yeats and Macmillan London Ltd., and are also used by permission of Macmillan Publishing Company (New York): 'Shepherd and Goatherd' from *The Collected Poems* by W. B. Yeats, copyright 1919 by Macmillan Publishing Company, renewed 1947 by Bertha Georgie Yeats, and 'Demon and Beast' from *13 Collected Poems* by W. B. Yeats, copyright 1924 by Macmillan Publishing Company, renewed 1952 by Bertha Georgie Yeats.

W. V. H.

Contents

In the point of fact, philosophy, baffled in its aims, has passed into criticism, and minds that a century ago might have been lost in searching into the mystery of knowledge and the roots of being, turn their whole gaze on the products of human thought, and the history of human endeavour. But the philosophers turning critics are apt to carry into the new study somewhat of the despair learned from the old, and, I repeat it, carefully avoid system. The deeper, therefore, their criticism delves, the more it becomes a labyrinth of confusion.

Eneas Sweetland Dallas, *The Gay Science* (1866), i. 31.

It appears to me that what we are very largely up to in practice, and to a considerable extent in theory, is the hardening of the mind into a set of unrelated methodologies without the controlling advantage of a fixed body of knowledge, a fixed faith, or a fixed purpose.

R. P. Blackmur, *The Lion and the Honeycomb* (1950), 178.

It is curious, considering the brilliance of the leading scholars in the field, how much critical theory today has relapsed into a confused and claustrophobic battle of methodologies, where, as in Fortinbras's campaign in *Hamlet*, the ground fought over is hardly big enough to hold the contending armies.

Northrop Frye, 'Literary and Linguistic Scholarship in a Postliterate World', *PMLA*, 99 (1984), 991.

1

Reality, Thought, and Language

Though theories of literature generally begin with definitions of literature, literature is constructed of language; language names the reports of our senses; and those reports arise out of some sort of interaction with what we normally call reality. So we must try to begin with reality, difficult as that is to do, and relate it properly to language at the outset. The alternatives are to drag reality in later when all other explanatory manœuvres fail, or pretend it isn't there at all. Beginning in this way will also require that we confront a number of traditional literary-critical questions in unaccustomed speculative company. Readers to whom this chapter seems either a rehearsal of the obvious or an exercise alien to literary theory will, I trust, withhold judgement until they have completed the second chapter.

1. Two Sources of Metaphysical Scepticism

The present preoccupation with language in the humanities is much less with the history and structural characteristics of language ('philosophy', 'grammar', and 'linguistics' as these have traditionally been known) than with a metaphysical questioning of the relationship between language and everything else that makes up experience. I use the term 'metaphysics' advisedly: to challenge metaphysical assumptions or deny the possibility of metaphysics are themselves metaphysical acts. The present extreme scepticism about the relationship between language and reality is a fresh assault on venerable philosophical problems.

One traditional source of radical doubt arises from the ancient questions of the extent to which human sense reports are the same from person to person and the extent to which human senses accurately reflect the reality they report. Thus one finds in the third century BC ten Pyrrhonian modes of withholding assent from propositions.

(1) The first mode results from the variety of animals, consequently for the possibility, in principle, of getting different representations about things.

(2) The second mode results from the diversity of men, who are different from one another and have therefore different sensations and representations.

(3) The third mode results from the diverse ways the organs of the senses are made up, which makes what is good for one be bad for another.

(4) The fourth mode results from the circumstances which determine the acceptance or rejection of a thing . . .

(5) The fifth mode results from the positions, distances and places of things, for example, the same thing may appear bigger or smaller depending on the distance from which we are looking at it.

(6) The sixth mode refers to mixtures which differ, because nothing comes pure to our senses but mixed with other elements.

(7) The seventh mode is based on the quantities and compositions of substances.

(8) The eighth mode results from the relationship between things (no thing can be perceived without being related to others).

(9) The ninth mode results from the frequency or rarity of things, for instance, the appearance of a comet, being quite a rare phenomenon, produces a great impression, whereas that of the sun, which is much more important, impresses nobody, being a common sight.

(10) The tenth mode derives from the relativity of behaviours, customs, laws, mystical beliefs, and dogmatic convictions.

(Dumitriu, i. 263.)

If the reference of words is to sense reports that may differ from each other and perhaps from that which stimulated them, we must eschew as misplaced a trust in the ability of language to treat of a reality behind sense reports.

A second traditional source of doubt looks back to fifth- and fourth-century BC Greek scepticism that questioned how any proof is possible since the premises of a syllogistic argument presumably are trustworthy only if they are the conclusions of previous syllogisms, and so on *ad infinitum*. That is, any logical demonstration must finally be grounded in indemonstrables lying outside the very deductive scheme upon which we depend for knowledge. Once the possibility of an adequate starting-point for any chain of syllogisms is questioned, the reliability of the connections between the language in which propositions are stated and the reality to which those propositions are presumed to refer becomes problematic.

Accurate thinking about the role of language requires that we distinguish between these two sources of dubiety. Their history since the Renaissance is roughly this: mankind's relation to reality was first discussed in terms of the accuracy of our notions of matter or brute reality, then in terms of the processes necessary to make the manipulation of thought a more accurate reflection of reality, and now in terms of how the language upon which thought depends can possibly relate to reality. That is, the locus of debate has moved from ontology to epistemology to semiotics. To the recognition that what we can know of reality depends on the limitations of our senses, we owe the long history of debates over whether the second-ary qualities of objects really exist and whether qualities of objects exist of which we are unaware. Evidently how one responds to such questions depends primarily on how one defines terms like 'qualities' and 'exist'. Happily the literary theorist need not enter this logomachy. As Kant saw long ago, since all we know and communi-cate about is grounded in sense reports, we need not attempt to penetrate behind sense reports to investigate the adequacy of lan-guage. The question that theorists of language and literature must face is the second: that of the relation of the language in which we assert propositions to the raw reports of our senses (to what C. S. Peirce called 'percepts', v. 53). A more contemporary mode of stating the problem would be that, whatever the adequacy of our sensory apparatus, we 'know' reality only to the extent that the continuous reports of our senses are translated into concepts. With-out such concepts the mind would presumably contain a mere chaos of reports; memory would be impossible as would the comparison of present sensations with past ones.

The theory of the relation of language (and therefore literature) to reality that I will urge is grounded in the currently converging con-clusions of a variety of fields: linguistics and socio-linguistics, dis-course and argument theory, the philosophy of language, and the sociology of knowledge. All point towards a constantly interactive, mutually defining system through which sensation, concepts, and language produce what we call perceptions, which in turn may generate new concepts. As I. A. Richards wrote in *The Philosophy of Rhetoric* (1936), 'A sensation would be something that was just *so*, on its own, a datum; as such we have none. Instead we have perceptions, responses whose character comes to them from the past as well as the present occasion.' (30.) E. H. Gombrich adopts the same frame of reference in speaking of perception as resulting from the 'interplay between expectation and observation,' so that a perception is a 'modification of an anticipation' (60, 172). The way in which these cumulatively interact in any one individual we may call 'experience'. I will attempt to maintain this distinction between sensations, perceptions, and experience, throughout.

In other words, it is impossible for us to assert what reality might be other than as it is reported by our senses (often highly indirectly, as in theories of high-energy physics) and impossible for us to communicate about that reality other than by language that has in some way already acted on it as surely as have our senses. One simply accepts that there is a *physical* realm of birth, death, brick walls, birds, mice, men and women, cakes and ale. These *natural facts* arise out of a 'brute reality' whose resistance to or satisfaction of our desires is reported by our senses; brute reality is that which most of us believe would exist whether there were sentient minds or not.

Such a definition attempts to side-step as far as possible the many metaphysical thought-traps whose successive modifications make up the greater part of the history of philosophy. The outer form of these traps is an expression of the first form of radical doubt, 'How would that which impacts on our senses be sensed by a being whose senses had none of the limitations we believe ours to have?' In such a formulation lurk terms whose very definitions require presuppositions innumerable. Fortunately, descriptions of brute or extralinguistics reality that claim all that is necessary for the purposes of literary theory are not far to seek:

I.A. RICHARDS. It is the whatever it is in which we live; and there we have to leave it; for to speak more of it is not to speak of it, but of the modes of our life in it. (*CI* 181.)

C.S. PEIRCE. . . . reality is insistency. That is what we mean by 'reality.' It is the brute irrational insistency that forces us to acknowledge the reality of what we experience . . . (vi. 340.)

KENNETH BURKE. . . . the *unanswerable opponent*, the opponent who cannot be refuted. (*PLF* 92.)

PETER BERGER *and* THOMAS LUCKMAN. It will be enough, for our purposes, to define 'reality' as a quality appertaining to phenomena that we recognize as having a being independent of our own volition (we cannot 'wish them away') and to define 'knowledge' as the certainty that phenomena are real and that they possess specific characteristics. (1.)

To this we may add Stephen Toulmin's modest mode of claiming that we know something at least about this reality:

The question we ask . . . whether any collection of sensory data *justifies* us in claiming knowledge about the world, does not call for entailments at all: the question is rather whether the evidence of our senses is always in fact rebuttable—whether the presumptions it creates are always in fact open to serious dispute—and to this question the answer is surely 'No.'   (250.)

In addition to natural facts we must also recognize *institutional facts*: marriage, insurance, government. And to avoid confusioń, I would add to these a *hypothetical* realm: that of scientific theory. Thus we have separate realms for cabbages, kings, and quarks. That we are able to communicate about such 'facts' in ways that allow predictive non-linguistic manipulation and reflect non-linguistic irrefragability (one cannot walk through brick walls, swallow cyanide with impunity, or jump twenty feet high) guarantees both that there exists something besides language and that language is indeed usefully communicative. The task interpretation faces is not the promulgation of the reasons language cannot function, but the investigation of the processes that makes it functional *despite* the curious fact that we can never establish a one-to-one correspondence between language and that to which it refers. Words frequently have several meanings and can always be used in new ways; words gain new meanings while old meanings are largely forgotten; words carry with them certain evaluative overtones and connotations which change over time; unpredictable figurative uses continually occur. That is why the whole of the senses, associations, and implications of a given word of which an author could be aware *may* be relevant to any particular instance of use. But interpretive theory must equally recognize that the relevance of any or all of these varies from case to case, and that in any instance some, probably most, of these possibilities will be wholly irrelevant to interpretation, however interesting their pursuit may be in itself.

2. *The Saussurian Revolution*

It is a commonplace that the foundation of contemporary theories of language has been derived from Ferdinand de Saussure (1857–1913). No set of insights into the nature of language is more widely acknowledged—unfortunately certain misunderstandings of the implications of these insights have also become widely established. Saussure's greatest influence has arisen out of four very important distinctions:

1. That between *langue*, the total system of signs and their relations in a natural language, and *parole*, instances of use or utterance of that language. 'If we could embrace the sum of word-images stored in the minds of all individuals,' wrote Saussure of *langue*, 'we could identify the social bond that constitutes language. It is a storehouse filled by the members of a given community through their active use of speaking, a grammatical system that has a potential existence in each brain, or, more specifically, in the brains of a group of individuals.' (13–14.) *Parole* on the other hand is the use of the resources of language in a particular instance by a particular individual.

2. That between the system of *langue* regarded synchronically (as a complete system existing at a given moment) and *langue* regarded diachronically (as changing throughout history).

3. That between the two components of any sign or word: the signifier (a sound pattern or written equivalent) and a signified (a division of what would otherwise be a chaos of present sensations and images of previous sensations to which it is arbitrarily related). 'Without language, thought is a vague, uncharted nebula,' wrote Saussure. 'The linguistic fact can therefore be pictured in its totality—i.e. language—as a series of continuous subdivisions [signifieds] marked off on both the indefinite plane of jumbled ideas . . . and the equally vague plane of sounds [signifiers] . . .' (112.)

4. That between the concept or signified and the sensations it marks off. This distinction is more implied than developed, but as soon as one accepts Saussure's dictum that 'the linguistic sign unites, not a thing and a name, but a concept and a sound image' (66), the naïve view of language as the fitting of names to pre-existing things 'out there' is for ever shattered.

The constituents of each of these pairs do not so much oppose as imply or complement each other. *Parole* would be impossible without the system of *langue*; *langue* could never arise or be maintained unless it supported the function of *parole*. If the system of *langue* were unchanging, there would be no need to distinguish the synchronic moment of its existence from the diachronic succession of such moments; on the other hand, diachronic changes represent a series of synchronic systems. One cannot think a signifier without a signified nor a signified without a signifier.

Now the confusions to which commentators on Saussure have been especially liable result from a common source: the tendency to think of *langue* as existing, like Plato's Ideas, quite insulated from the daily experience of men and women. In the first place, the arbitrariness of the 'bond between sound and idea' that Saussure stressed has been illegitimately extended to the relationship between a 'signified' and that portion of the jumble of ideas marked off by that signified. (George Watson's 'The Stacked Deck of Language' is a witty and incisive critique of misunderstandings of Saussure's place in the long tradition of the 'arbitrariness' of language.) It is obvious that the meaning of a sign can hardly be determined by its relationship to an extralinguistic reality since the sensations induced by that reality can only be discussed in terms of the signs that have already divided it up. It is equally obvious that we cannot get behind sensations and the language that names the concepts that divide up sensations in order to assess the accuracy with which language reflects the reality that is the source of the sensation. However, it does not follow (and Saussure nowhere states) that the process by which sensation is carved up is wholly arbitrary and unmotivated. Indeed, 'language' cannot *act* at all: it exists only as understood and used by human minds. The accurate statement is that the flow of sensation is divided up by concepts (signifieds) according to human purposes. Signifieds make distinctions, distinctions are made where useful, usefulness depends on purpose. We distinguish between mist, drizzle, and rain (in English) because it is useful to be able to do so. Keeping his distance from all theories of reality, Saussure never seems to have committed himself to any specific statement about the relationship between the sense-engendered chaos to which language gives order and the reality to which our sense respond. He was not making a metaphysical statement. Rather, when Saussure spoke of arbitrariness in language, he seems to have had in mind primarily the arbitrariness of diachronic changes in the signifier, that is, the unpredictability of phonetic changes like the great vowel shift.

Second, Saussure's concept of *langue* does *not* authorize the view that the meaning of words in discourse (*parole*), is indeterminable. When he describes *langue* as a 'system of interdependent terms in which the value of each term results solely from the simultaneous presence of others' (114), the term 'value' is equivalent to 'position in a system' and must be distinguished from 'meaning in the context of use'. Words do not remain suspended in the system of *langue*; they are used in particular contexts by human beings.

Third, Saussure's emphasis on the synchronic structure of *langue* was meant to counter linguists' historical concentration on the tracing of changes in language over time. We should not allow it to obscure the importance of constant change within *langue*, nor the fact that such change is not brought about by language somehow acting on itself, but rather by human activity acting on language. The system of *langue* has its existence only communally: 'The arbitrary nature of the sign explains in turn why the social fact alone can create a linguistic system. The community is necessary if values that owe their existence solely to usage and general acceptance are to be set up.' (113.) Linguistic changes must then be initiated through *parole* within the community and incorporated within the *langue* by the community. What the Anglo-Saxons called the 'word hoard' is not a stable repository.

Such changes are possible because, as Eric Lenneberg phrases it in *Biological Foundations of Language*, 'Strictly speaking, words are not labels of fixed and conventionally agreed upon classes of objects but modes of categorization; they characterize a productive, creative process . . .' (27). Adjustments within the *langue* do not occur by some mysterious 'structural' process that operates untouched by human minds. When the word 'blahs' entered the language, the boundaries of words like 'blues' or 'sulks' were altered. Users of the language recognized in the 'blahs' a psychological state that had been included in 'the blues' or 'the sulks' but which can be differentiated as being less focused on one's individual situation than the first and less prone to peevish outward expression than the second. Thus 'the blues' and 'the sulks' lose part of their territories to a more specific term. As 'scenario' widened its boundaries and came to mean 'one of several imagined sequences of events', a method of planning that might have been called 'considering contingencies' became 'imagining scenarios'. As long as 'scenario' continues to seem useful, contingency planning shrinks towards 'planning what to do if A, B, or C happens', and no longer includes 'if D happens, and we do E, someone else will respond with F, requiring us to do G'. On the other hand, if, as happened under the Nixon administration that popularized the term, the imagining of scenarios comes to be associated with a dishonest sort of cunning, the process is reversed and the range of 'scenario' shrinks. Changes in *langue* begin with changes in use, often initiated by events not primarily linguistic in nature.

Thus reality is 'known' through reality-induced concepts that are expressed by language; language can be used to shift the boundaries of concepts; shifting the boundaries of any concept initiates shifts of greater or lesser significance within the total system of language; the shifting of the boundaries of concepts alters to some extent our grasp of reality. Or, more precisely, *parole*, occurring in a set of contexts of use (which includes reality to the extent it is reflected in sensations), is capable of effecting changes in individual concepts or signifieds within the system of *langue*; these changes affect other signifieds, shifting the values of the signs of which they are constituents and thus the ways in which those signs may be used in *parole*. Language can in this way be regarded as slowly but continuously redividing conceptual territory. In Richard Gregg's words, language 'exists as a rich and flexible means of "cutting the edges of experiencing" ' (91).

The above sketch is enormously simplified. I have written pretty much as though all signifieds participated in carving up our sensations of brute reality, whereas many divide up feelings, others (abstractions generally) are only mediately related to our sensations, and others relate to human institutions ('institutional facts') as opposed to sense reports. It is not difficult to picture how quite abstract signifieds arise. Lok, prehistoric joker that he is, points down a trail and utters signifiers that tell Nok that two deer are coming. Nok hides behind a rock, bow and arrow at the ready, only to see two sabre-toothed tigers appear. Assuming that Nok escapes, he will have a clear enough concept of 'untruth' to which he need only attach a sound to have a sign. The trope that assigns the signifier for 'leg' to each of the three poles from which meat is suspended over the fire requires little explanation; neither does the social need for a sign that will convey the expectation that those who don't help defend against cold, wild animals, and hunger will not be defended against the same by others. But the sketch I have given will serve to outline the interdependence of reality, conceptual thought, and language, as, to quote Gregg again, a 'closed feedback loop, with the interaction of all points on the loop being mutually dependent and mutually interactive' (95). It further suggests a sense in which the total system of language represents the culture of a linguistic community. Our knowledge of reality is a communal construction rather than a set of discoveries, and words are humanly purposeful divisions of reality rather than names designating chunks of reality that exist in discrete particularity prior to language.

C.S. Peirce's philosophically motivated analysis of signs, often erroneously regarded as competing with the linguistically grounded system of Saussure, is actually complementary. In fact, it is fascinating that two reclusive, rather eccentric thinkers produced systems that display so much correspondence while drawing on different disciplines. However, Peirce was much more the systematizer, dividing and subdividing his categories of signs and exhibiting a particular fondness for trichotomies. One trusts that he was humorously conscious of exaggeration when he wrote:

On these considerations I base a recognition of ten respects in which Signs may be divided. I do not say that these divisions are enough. But since every one of them turns out to be a trichotomy, it follows that in order to decide what classes of signs result from them, I have 3^{10}, or 59049, difficult questions to carefully consider; and therefore I will not undertake to carry my systematical division of signs any further, but will leave that for future explorers.   (viii. 343)

Peirce's commitment to detailed taxonomy aside, if we compare his basic schema not only with that of Saussure but with the standard 'referential triangle' as presented by Ogden and Richards in *The Meaning of Meaning* (1923), the complementary ways in which Peirce and Saussure supersede the older notion of the referential triangle will be apparent. Starting with Helmholtz's argument that 'The sensations that lie at the basis of all perceptions are subjective signs of reality' (79), Ogden and Richards set out a simple but highly influential diagram (Fig. 1.1). In Saussure this becomes the version shown in Fig. 1.2. For Peirce, the triangle would look like the version shown in Fig. 1.3. At the point of the triangle where Richards confidently placed the 'referent' (real object) and Saussure rather vaguely placed a series of demarcations on the plane of thought, Peirce recognized considerably greater complexity. Specifically he asserted three points. First, that we can never verify the external world of objects in which nevertheless we have good grounds for believing. Second, that our evidence of external objects depends on neural responses or 'percepts' (ii. 141–2). Third, that signs can be assigned to percepts only after they have been interpreted by what

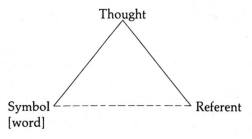

Fig. 1.1

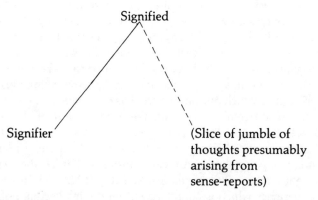

Fig. 1.2

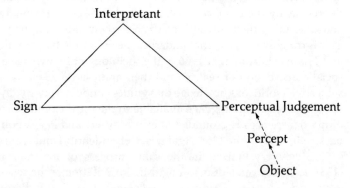

Fig. 1.3

he called 'perceptual judgements' (v. 54–5). He is thus explicit that we are only able to link a percept to a concept through the system of concepts that has been built up out of percepts. On the other hand, he saw less clearly than Saussure that his 'interpretant' or concept cannot in fact exist without the sign nor the sign without the interpretant.

Peirce also recognized that the relation of sign to percept to reality necessitated the admission that there are no certainties to which we can anchor our reasoning. As his commentator T. A. Goudge phrases it, 'We can only validate the judgment in terms of other judgments; and since the series thus involved is infinite, no particular judgment can have more than a degree of cognitive certainty.' (33–4.) However, the conclusion he draws from this is not that all thought must pursue an infinite regress into the abyss, but that we can never be sure we are wholly correct even though the very fact that we are able to predict anything suggests that there is a uniformity in reality that we at least partly grasp. Thus Peirce's 'fallibilism': 'Every proposition which we can be entitled to make about the real world must be an approximate one . . . Approximation must be the fabric out of which our philosophy has to be built.' (i. 404.)

Despite differences in detail, the general view of the relations between language, thought, and reality just described in the thought of Saussure and Peirce is to be found in an intriguing number of contiguous disciplines. An early instance lies at the centre of Susanne Langer's *Philosophy in a New Key* (1942): 'The formulation of experience which is contained within the intellectual horizon of an age and a society is determined . . . not so much by events and desires, as by the *basic concepts* at people's disposal for analyzing and describing their adventures to their own understanding.' (6.) This is roughly the view that underlies the definition by Peter Berger and Thomas Luckman in 1966 of the sociology of knowledge as the social construction of reality, and their analysis of a largely intersubjective world 'of knowledge that guides conduct in everyday life' (19). 'The common language available to me for the objectification of my experiences is grounded in everyday life and keeps pointing back to it,' they write (26). Again, 'society, identity, and reality are subjectively crystallized in the same process of internalization' (133). A closely related socio-linguistic formulation of the schema is expressed by Allen Grimshaw in *Language as Social Resource*: 'social structure is an intervening variable between language . . . and speech . . . [which] defines social structure' (3). The same general schema supports the linguist Roger Fowler, who calls his broadly based analyses of language and literature 'linguistic criticism'. 'Whatever "reality" is, we do not think directly in terms of it,

but in terms supplied by language.' (*LL* 95.) 'Together, the complete
set of objectivations in a culture constitutes the representation of
reality, or world-view, enjoyed by the community and its members.
In a nutshell, we see the world in terms of the categories through
which we and our society have constituted it.' Thus, 'all knowledge,
all objects, are constructs' (*LSD* 25).

The view of human experience outlined is further compatible
with the rhetorician Richard Gregg's study of the way in which the
patterned firing of neurons in the brain underlies rhetoric and
communication. Gregg formulates the process by which Saussure's
'chaos of thought' is carved up in terms of a 'bordering' process: 'The
processes of bordering provide the contents of experiencing by
stabilizing the ecological flux around us, and this is achieved
through detection and creation of structure and form. Of special
importance to our inquiry is the fact that bordering activity is an
activity that is instantly symbolic. It is not a copying experience.
There is no experiencing but formed experiencing.' (41.) Or, considered from a higher level, ' "Reality" is symbolic reality. That is all we
have.' (133.)

3. The Discrimination of Fictions

Having committed itself to the position that the concepts we form
from the reports of the senses do not necessarily carve reality at the
joints (if joints there be), our theory of interpretation must take
account of the frequent and insistent argument that all that we think
of as knowledge is actually fictional.

To take the most intriguing example from the humanities, Frank
Kermode's *The Sense of an Ending* (1967) finds mankind's need to
make sense of the world inexpungeable. The collapse of even the
most central systems of belief in the face of fact is immediately
followed either by the modifications needed to keep as much as
possible of the belief intact or by the erection of a new system. Basic
to the human sense-making activity is the extrapolation of human
mortality, which necessarily falls between a beginning and an ending, to the entire history of the race.

Men . . . make considerable imaginative investments in coherent patterns
which, by the provision of an end, make possible a satisfying consonance
with the origins and with the middle. That is why the image of the end can
never be *permanently* falsified. But they also, when awake and sane, feel the

need to show a marked respect for things as they are, so that there is a recurring need for adjustments in the interest of reality as well as of control. (17.)

We thus make sense of the world by imposing models or patterns, that is, fictions, on the world, continually revising them as the pressure of our experience of reality requires. However, not only do our patterns or paradigms require constant adjustment, but we must in some sense know that they are fictive even while we take comfort from them. Otherwise they become what Kermode calls myths, fictions mistaken for reality. One value of 'literary fictions' for Kermode is that they help explain our experience without becoming myths in which we invest belief. Nevertheless, the distance between 'literary fictions' and all other explanatory fictions, including those of science, appears very small indeed in his account.

Even more dramatic than Kermode's exploration of our constant rationalization of history has been the abandonment by scientists of the claim that they were progressively revealing the nature of external reality. Where it once seemed safe to assert that atoms are made up of electrons, protons, and neutrons, the increasing indirectness of verification in the web of theories supporting the existence of 'elemental' particles like 'quarks' with qualities like 'charm' makes it much more appropriate to say that atoms behave *as if* they were made up of a certain set of particles interacting with each other in certain ways. Thomas Kuhn's celebrated revaluation of the meaning of progress in science, *The Structure of Scientific Revolutions* (1962), has been an influential solvent of the barriers between fact and fiction. Its central thrust is that the goal of science is not the discovery of reality but the development of internally consistent systems of explanation. New theories that solve major problems in a scientific field establish paradigms which are then shared by researchers in the field until sufficient anomalies lead to the emergence of a new paradigm. The 'normal science' that engages most researchers is not aimed at new discoveries, but is rather 'an attempt to force nature into the preformed and relatively inflexible box that the paradigm supplies' (24). True 'discoveries' are really revolutionary explanations formulated to explain anomalies that have gradually become apparent as researchers operated within a reigning paradigm.

But, and this is one of the conclusions that caused Kuhn's book to effect a revolution of its own, the choice between competing paradigms can be referred to no external criterion for resolution: 'As in political revolution, so in paradigm choice—there is no standard higher than the assent of the relevant community.' Therefore the 'issue of paradigm choice can never be unequivocally settled by logic and experiment alone' (94). Science proceeds then not by sure accumulation but revolutions that destroy previous paradigms. Even more revolutionary is Kuhn's argument that paradigms must be regarded as constitutive of nature, as well as of science—new paradigms create different worlds since they do not merely reinterpret the same data, but create new data by constituting a new mode of 'seeing', of experiencing. Progress becomes a solution of ever-new problems through the construction of new models (cf. Kermode's 'fictional patterns'), not movement toward 'some one full, objective, true account of nature' (170). Heretical as this seemed in 1962, and intriguing as it seems to many now, it is recognizable as one more restatement of the scepticism about relationships between sense reports and reality, and one more testimony to the view of the relationship between language, thought, and reality that I have been setting forth.

The sense in which one may wish to speak of all human knowledge and belief as 'fictional' therefore must be understood as a figurative application of the literary sense. There is a clear family resemblance in the uses of 'fiction' as applied to (1) scientists' explanatory models, (2) beliefs and patterns of thought imposed on the world by a society in order to make sense of it, and (3) narratives reporting that which both narrator and audience know not to have actually occurred. In each case from the user's point of view that which is termed a fiction does not correspond to a reality external to it, but the three ought not to be conflated. In the first case, a 'fiction' is an incomplete or provisional account of a brute reality only indirectly accessible. In the second, a 'fiction' is a pattern or model of some portion of reality believed not to be in accordance with certain ascertained facts about reality but nevertheless understood to have value for others as a means of making sense of the world. In the third case, a 'fiction' is a narrative which the author intends to be interpreted within the context of certain generic conventions (see Chapter 4, section 3).

4. *The Complexities of* Parole

So far this chapter has been focused on the relationships between individual words within the system of *langue* and between *langue* and reality. Before turning our attention to *parole*, it will be useful to remind ourselves that *langue* is an abstraction. Though definable as the total system of relationships between words in a given language at a given time, there is no repository to which one can go to find it. No one person possesses it; members of a linguistic community are familiar with very unequal amounts of it; and disagreements about the exact relationship between words in the *langue* must be expected simply because changes spread slowly through the community. The very notion of a synchronic study of *langue* is of course only an abstraction: to what period of time (a day, a month, a decade?) would one restrict the meaning of 'synchronous'? It might seem that a dictionary is a close approximation to a codification of *langue*, but the more complete the dictionary, the more obsolete and uncommon words it will record, and the less therefore will it reflect the average native speaker's competence in the *langue*. Again, though I have discussed *langue* as though it were made up of signs each neatly packaging a signifier and a signified, this is not always the case: for instance in homonyms the same signifier is shared by more than one signified. Finally, as we shall shortly be noting, it is not always easy to draw the line between what knowledge about a word should be assigned to *langue* and what to *parole*.

And so to *parole*. Words are in some sense *known* as part of a mutually defining system, but in use they enter a highly complex context, or, more accurately, set of contexts. The present section outlines some of the sources of this complexity. The most immediate contextual element is the sentence in which the word is used; and of the relationships within the sentence, the one we are most likely to think of first is syntax. Persons with that knowledge of the language regarded as typical of the 'native speaker' are able to understand the general path of the baseball in:

> John hit Bill's pitch over the head of the shortstop but right into the glove of the centre fielder.

They recognize that

> Him and I were playing catch.

is, though understandable, an error; and that

He the ball.

is neither an acceptable sentence nor, in and of itself, interpretable.

We normally greatly underestimate the amount of syntactical knowledge we bring to bear in understanding sentences because we don't explicitly formulate the rules we use. George Dillon has reminded us how cumbersome many of our unconsciously assimilated rules would be if we spelled them out: 'If there is an initial noun phrase preceding the verb and if it is congruent semantically as the Subject of the verb, assign it the function of the Subject.' (4.) And '. . . the first eligible noun phrase to the left of the pronoun should be the antecedent.' (69). Moreover, the implications of which we are made aware by syntactic constructions alone is greater than we are apt to remember. For instance:

Jim believed that Joe was the winner.

Jim said that Bob believed that Joe was the winner.

We know that the first sentence asserts not that Joe was the winner but that Jim believed that he was. In technical terms, '. . . Joe was the winner' is 'intensional' and therefore does not assert that it is true that Joe won. The proposition asserted by the sentence is false if Jim did not believe that Joe was the winner, not if Joe was not the winner. Similarly, the second proposition is false if Jim did not say 'Bob believed that Joe was the winner'; if Jim did say it, it is true no matter what Bob believed or whether Joe won or lost. We keep track of such distinctions almost effortlessly.

Ann Banfield has explored a further distinction that syntactical indicators, often quite subtle ones, allow us to make. The difference in narrative between direct quotation (of thoughts or speech) and indirect reports of thoughts or speech has often been noted, but there is also such a thing as 'represented' speech and thought.

Bill said, 'I doubt that that is true.'

Bill challenged the truth of the statement.

Bill asked whether the statement he had just heard was really true.

The first purports to report Bill's exact words; the second interprets what Bill said (the same statement might be reported as 'Bill mentally questioned the statement', 'Bill doubted the claim'); whereas the third, an example of represented speech, neither gives us the exact

form of Bill's thoughts nor interprets them. Two further examples
from Banfield, taken from *Mrs. Dalloway* and *Lady Chatterley's
Lover*:

And yet Richard couldn't have said that to save his life! Why these people
stood that damned insolence he could not conceive. (72.)

Ah! that in itself was a relief, like being given another life: to be free of the
strange dominion and obsession of *other women*. How awful they were,
women! (73.)

In the first Woolf has not produced the exact sequence of Richard's
thought, but 'couldn't have said that to save *my* life' and 'damned
insolence' are presumably forms of words that were part of his
thought, just as 'relief', 'free', 'other women', and 'awful', in the D.H.
Lawrence quote, seem intended as accurate transcriptions of perhaps isolated phrases in the character's mind.

Stanley Fish's theory of 'affective stylistics', first argued nearly
twenty years ago, describes another facet of *parole*. The mental
process required to understand a sentence or line of poetry,
including wrestling with word order and syntax and resolving tem-
porary ambiguities, becomes itself part of the understanding of the
line. Because our assimilation of the line, 'Nor did they not perceive
the evil plight' receives a momentary check when we encounter the
'not' closely following the 'nor', the line is not understood in the
same way, argues Fish, as 'They perceived the evil plight.' (*ITT* 25.)
Whether readers' corrections of momentary misreadings of sentences are as common as Fish suggests is debatable, but certainly
instances are found more often, even in narrative prose, than we are
consciously aware of. Early in *Vanity Fair* Becky Sharp and Rawdon
Crawley are returning one night to Crawley Hall: '. . . the walk over
the Rectory fields and in at the little park wicket, and through the
dark plantation, and up the checkered avenue to Queen's Crawley,
was charming in the moonlight to two such lovers of the picturesque
as the Captain and Miss Rebecca'. For the instant before 'of the
picturesque' is mentally processed, the reader is very likely to
assume that the word 'lovers' announces a new stage in the relationship of Becky and Rawdon. They *are* on the way, but are not lovers
yet—the momentary misreading proves in fact to point the way.

The New Critics sensitized readers to the many possible ways in
which words within a sentence react on each other in ways not
directly syntactical. Lamb's 'Grace Before Meat' opens:

The custom of saying grace at meals had, probably, its origin in the early times of the world, and the hunter-state of man, when dinners were precarious things, and a full meal was something more than a common blessing! when a belly-full was a wind-fall and looked like a special providence.

'Belly-full', emphasized by the partial repetition of sound in 'wind-fall' and known by the reader to be an informal word with somewhat vulgar overtones, contrasts with 'special providence' (a contrast in register), alerting us to a tension between the writer's attitude towards providence and the one officially authorized in the culture. Stevenson writes in 'Aes Triplex': 'All the world over, and every hour, someone is parting company with all his aches and ecstasies.' Not only do the chiming of the vowels 'over' and 'hour', and the intricately related sound structures of 'aches and ecstasies' emphasize those words, but the phrase 'aches and ecstasies' acquires additional resonance by its departure from the 'joys and sorrows' or 'pains and pleasures' we expect.

> Meanwhile the South, rising with dabbled wings,
> A sable cloud athwart the welkin flings,
> That swilled more liquor than it could contain,
> And like a drunkard gives it up again.

Thus begins the second section of Swift's 'A Description of a City Shower', the effect depending on the discord between the diction of the two couplets. Such contrasts in register or tone need not of course occur in a single sentence, but the greater the contiguity between the two contrasting portions, the more immediate the effect on interpretation.

Beyond the purely syntactical is a kind of knowledge that may be called 'grammatical' in the broad sense: the knowledge of the necessary implications of words. For instance, the following is an acceptable sentence:

I said that I went.

However one that seems to follow the same syntactical form is not:

I promised that I went.

One can acceptably say,

I ordered him to think about it.

but not, under ordinary circumstances,

I ordered him to understand it.

Now it is easy enough to see that the notion of futurity in 'to promise' requires 'I promised that I would go' rather than 'I promised that I went', while in the second case the notion of capability or capacity in 'to understand' requires one to say something like 'I ordered him to try to understand.' However, that we continually exercise much knowledge that is strictly speaking neither part of the definitions of words nor incorporated in syntactical rules has only recently begun to receive adequate notice. The total situation of promising has to be understood in order for us to recognize when 'promise' is used properly. Philosophers of language, building on the pioneering efforts of J. L. Austin, have given considerable attention to developing rules for the correct or felicitous or non-defective use of a word like 'promise'. For instance, one cannot properly make a promise that one is not in a position to fulfil, nor promise something that has already happened, nor promise something that the person to whom it is promised does not want. However, as 'native speakers' we do not have such rules filed away in our minds for application to particular cases. Rather, we become aware of the usual uses of words only through the contexts in which we learn them—that is of course one reason why children with meagre reading experience have so much difficulty in learning conventional constructions.

We have not yet reached the end of the awarenesses that a single word may bring with it. An additional Saussurian distinction is between a word's relations within a sentence, and those external to the sentence. The first Saussure called 'syntagmatic', the second 'associative' (now more frequently 'paradigmatic'), of which syntactical relations are the more important. By 'associative' Saussure meant the relationship between a given word and other words it may suggest to us through similarities of form (painful, frightful, delightful) or meaning (teach, instruct, educate, train). Our interpretation of a word may be coloured by the words of similar sound or those of similar meaning of which it reminds us. Our awareness of near synonymns *not* chosen is often recognized as especially significant. The fact is, in addition to the causes of association discussed by Saussure, we become aware of clusters of words whose associations come from frequent contiguity in use. I. A. Richards was explicitly recognizing as early as 1936 that we interpret the meaning of a word not only through the other words of the sentence in which it appears but through the clusters of unuttered words we associate with that word and indeed with the other words in the sentence. Thus Richards: 'As the movement of my hand uses nearly the whole skeletal system of the muscles and is supported by them, so a phrase may take its powers from an immense system of supporting uses of other words in other contexts.' (*PR* 65.)

Many of what we think of as connotations arise from such associations. 'Damp' in T. S. Eliot's lines,

> I am aware of the damp souls of housemaids
> Sprouting despondently at area gates,

picks up implications of futility from association with 'damp squib', 'damp powder', 'damp kindling'—those housemaids' souls will never explode in rapture or burn brightly. It also picks up implications of hiddenness through the association of dampness with darkness, and with that which is rusted, mouldy, unsalubrious from association with 'damp cellars' and 'damp walls'. William Empson taught a generation of readers to recognize such associative possibilities, the limits of which are of course set by interactions within the *total* context.

For several reasons, then, what we think of as the 'literal' meaning of a word is not simply the 'dictionary meaning', but a dictionary meaning appropriate to the context of a sentence *and* to our awareness of the verbal contexts in which it is generally encountered in the *parole* of the linguistic community. We can speak of two 'linguistic' contexts, one within the sentence itself and the other a general awareness of a word's ordinary uses and implications. The 'literal' meaning of a *sentence* is a matter of more difficulty than the literal meaning of a word. One definition of the literal meaning of a sentence is the meaning we would assign in a 'null context':

> The cat is on the mat.

If we consider the sentence written by itself on a sheet of paper, we interpret it as meaning that a domestic feline is lying on some sort of small, flat cloth or straw material. If, however, the sentence were to occur in a story about zoos or game reserves in Africa, 'cat' might well mean 'lion' and 'mat' the covering hiding a pit-trap. If we were talking about a construction project, we might recognize immediately that the 'cat' is a caterpillar tractor and the mat some sort of metal mesh. John Searle has pointed out that sentences are never without a minimal sort of context or 'background' (*EM* 117). That is, if we encounter the 'contextless' sentence about the cat being on the mat, we understand its meaning in terms of a number of assumed conditions: the earth's gravitational field continuing to be in force, the mat lying flat, the mat's being of a reasonable size (not postage stamp size or football field size). What the notion of 'null context' really implies is rather something like 'in the most usual contexts'. Most people asked to draw their image of 'cat on the mat' would probably draw the cat lying down, perhaps in front of a fire—thus do our normal associations influence us. 'It is impossible even to think of a sentence independently of context,' writes Stanley Fish (who is hardly in the same camp with the speech-act theorists), 'and when we are asked to consider a sentence for which no context has been specified, we will automatically hear it in the context in which it has been most often encountered.' (*ITT* 310.)

The context we assume might be called common, or ordinary, or usual, but as all these terms have many other uses, it will perhaps be better to speak of the 'wonted' context. For example:

John hit Bill.

The 'wonted context' meaning for most readers would be that a human being, John, struck another human being, Bill, probably with a fist. Given other contexts the sentence could mean that John ran into Bill with a car, or that John shot Bill with a gun. In the context of a fencing match John has scored a hit; in the context of a blackjack game John has given Bill an additional card.

Isolated sentences are noticeably ambiguous only when either of two contexts is equally probable. If asked what 'It is funny' means, most of us would immediately note that 'It is amusing' and 'It is peculiar' are equally possible. But 'It is odd' would be unhesitatingly translated as 'It is peculiar' since that is the meaning of 'odd' in most contexts, even though one has no trouble imagining a context in which 'It is odd' would mean 'It is not even.'

Then there are sentences that appear deviant in the wonted context though they would not in certain others:

Golf plays John.

The apparent deviance in this standard example is not a result of purely syntactical classifications. That is, it is not the case that such inanimate words as 'golf' cannot be assigned a verb that implies their action on an object. One can understandably enough say 'Golf refreshes John.' In the appropriate context, which might be intonation, facial expression, or gesture, 'Golf plays John' is understood to mean that the game of golf drives John to play frequently, or absorbs a great part of his energy and interest, or is a game that he just can't seem to master. Moreover, once one has encountered such an example and a probable context is established, it hardly seems deviant. In poetry, of course, apparently syntactically unacceptable sentences are often retrospectively restored to acceptability by the context created by the poem itself, though the process calls on a wide variety of contextual information, to be explored in later chapters:

> Anyone lived in a pretty how town . . .

or

> Márgarét áre you gríeving
> Over Goldengrove unleaving?

Different contexts can change the meaning of certain sentences so that they have implications that seem at quite a distance from the words used to express them:

> I don't like idle chatter.

If uttered following a question like 'Do you want to go to the Smiths' cocktail party?' this is not only an assertion of a personal taste in social situations but also a negative answer to the question. Such indirect meanings are much more common and important in discourse than one at first realizes.

The definition of the 'literal meaning' of a sentence as that which the native speaker of the language would be most likely to assign to it, if assuming it to occur in the most usual context, will help us avoid some confusions about the 'literal meaning' of a metaphor. There is general agreement now that a metaphor can only be recognized in context. As a sentence by itself,

> William is an aardvark

will almost certainly be taken as giving the name of an actual ant-eating mammal; only if the sentence occurred in a context that made us aware that William was, for instance, the speaker's uncle, would we begin to consider what aspects of an aardvark might be applicable to William. However,

> William is a fox

by itself will probably be seen as ambiguous—we have met the trite
metaphor too often not to recognize that William may be a person
and the sentence metaphorical. The point is that wonted contexts
which we bring to the interpretation of certain isolated sentences
may be metaphorical ones.

An additional distinction of major importance is that between the
'sense' and 'reference' of a word. Isolated sentences are on the whole
made up of words that have a general rather than a specific reference:

> The general crossed the river.

Which general? Which river? Here Gottlob Frege's 1892 distinction
between 'sense' and 'reference' is useful. In the cited sentence,
'general' and 'river' both have a quite understandable 'sense' though
no identifiable 'reference'. Contexts confer reference: in a narrative
of the American Revolution, we might understand the sentence as
equivalent to 'Washington crossed the Delaware', just as in hearing a
friend's anecdote about his army experiences we might understand
'general' as 'the-general-who-commanded-our-division' and 'river'
as the Han. When Frege wrote that words have reference only in the
context of a sentence (see Searle, *SA* 25), he had in mind not artifi-
cially isolated examples but sentences in a full context of use. Except
in the case of proper names, even words as used in a sentence generally acquire reference only through the context in which the sentence
occurs. Reichert sums up the distinction between sense and reference
in saying that 'People refer, words don't.' (*MSL* 62.) That is, only
words used by people in context refer. The logician's chestnut,

> The present King of France is bald

causes no difficulty so long as the sentence is isolated from any
external context and each word is understood simply in its dictionary sense; it is only when the context indicates that 'present' refers to
the actual present time that we have trouble: it is only then that we
find there is no referent for 'King', bald or no.

5. *The Errors of Rendering to* Langue *What Belongs to* Parole

My insistence on the obvious role of context is directed against two
primary errors. The first is that of confusing the technique of
deconstructive analysis, introduced by Jacques Derrida, with interpretation. The post-structuralist erosion of easy assumptions about
agreed senses of words, the stability of language, and the relationship

of words to a non-linguistic reality has been healthy, though the very vocabulary of its champions suggests a certain delight in arguing against straw men. If, as Saussure so influentially argued, *langue* is a system of mutually defining signs, so long as one resolutely remains within *langue* the meaning of any given word is indefinitely postponed while one pursues the meaning of word A as implied by word B as implied by word C.

The heart of deconstructionists' strategies, however, lies in conflating that which may be said of a word regarded under the aspect of *langue* which that is true of it under the aspect of *parole*. Thus Geoffrey Hartman, wielding Derrida's concept of 'presence', writes, 'We assume that, by the miracle of art, the "presence of the word" is equivalent to the presence of meaning. But the opposite can be urged, that the word carries with it a certain absence or indeterminacy of meaning.' (viii.) J. Hillis Miller's strategies as a deconstructive critic are especially visible in his well-known 1976 essay 'Stevens' Rock and Criticism as Cure', which scours the dictionary for possible uses of 'cure' preparatory to announcing 'The multiple meanings of the word "cure," like the meanings of all the key words and figures in "The Rock," are incompatible, irreconcilable.' (SRC 10.) The procedure is an infallible recipe for leading oneself into the abyss which Miller then proceeds to discover.

Though the analysis of or creative play with individual *words* ought not to be confused with the interpretation of *parole* or discourse, the vision of the system of *langue* has been so heady that many of those who have been inspired by Saussure have found it more intriguing to think of individual utterances and texts in terms of *langue* than the *parole* of which they are instances. Indeed, even I.A. Richards, who wished to emphasize the nature of *parole*, thought of Saussure only as the formulator of the structure of *langue* and in *The Meaning of Meaning* accused him of failing to see that the relation between the symbol (read 'signifier') and reference (read 'signified') was modified by the purposes of the user. Though formally and ultimately meaning may depend on difference, on the relations between signs themselves, we do not normally respond to texts through a linguistic differential calculus.

> Western Wind, when will thou blow
> The small rain down can rain?
> Christ, if my love were in my arms,
> And I in my bed again!

> (Anon.)

One really cannot say that, *as one reads the poem*, a wind from the west, or rain, or one's love in one's arms, or a bed, require to be understood by systems of differences; we can call up an image of rain without first imagining a dry day, and can understand the love the poet wishes in his arms without first speculating on the differences between that love and a teddy bear. We can call up images of hawks without first considering handsaws and should not confuse what makes language possible with what happens when we employ or respond to language.

Recent theorists have found it necessary to insist on the contrast between the system and the instance. Since lack of a uniform terminology has tended to obscure the extent of their agreement, it will be worth our while to bring together efforts by important theorists to delineate this distinction. For example, Paul Ricœur differentiates *langue* and discourse. The first is made up of signs, virtual objects that belong to the science of semiotics; the second is made up of actual objects that belong to the science of semantics. Ricœur also expressed the contrast as one between the anonymous linguistic code and the intentional message. In *The Conflict of Interpretations*, Ricœur adopts Hjelmslev's definition of *langue* as 'an autonomous entity of internal dependencies' while discourse is an act consisting of choices producing new combinations and in which language has reference and a subject, that is, an audience (*CT* 82, 86-7). 'Discourse in action and in use refers backward and forward, to a speaker and to a world.' (*IT* 22.) In *Symbolism and Interpretation* Tzvetan Todorov translates *langue* as language and *parole* as discourse. 'Discourse is a concrete manifestation of language, and it is produced, necessarily, in a specific context that involves not only linguistic elements but also the circumstances of their production.' (9.) John Reichert pursues a similar distinction in contrasting 'type meaning' with 'actual meaning' (30), while H. P. Grice employs the terms 'timeless meaning' and 'occasion-meaning' (UMSM). Mikhail Bakhtin contrasts the linguistic structure with the non-reiterative and unique utterance because, in Todorov's translation, it includes the situation 'as a necessary constitutive element' (*MB* 26, 41). Barbara Herrnstein Smith employs another set of terms:

I must emphasize that I am speaking here of the meaning not of *words* but of *utterances*, a distinction not always grasped even by those most concerned with these problems. One may ascertain the meanings of those abstract classes called *words* by determining the conventions governing their usage in the relevant linguistic community, usually by consulting one's experience of the language, or, when difficulties arise, either a dictionary—or an analytic philosopher. Dictionaries and philosophers are of only limited help, however, in ascertaining the meaning of particular verbal events. (21.)

Contemporary argumentation theory supports these distinctions through its heavy emphasis on the context in which language is used. When Stephen Toulmin contrasts 'the standards and value of practical reasoning' with 'the abstract and formal criteria relied on in mathematical logic and much twentieth-century epistemology' (viii), the central distinction is between the abstract and supposedly timeless status of logical propositions and the context-dependent nature of ordinary language in ordinary situations of reasoning. This leads to his contrasting the *canons* for the assessment of arguments, which are 'field-dependent', with the *force* of our terms of assessment, which are 'field-invariant'. 'Certainly language as we know it consists, not of timeless propositions, but of utterances dependent in all sorts of ways on the context or occasion on which they are uttered.' (180.) Charles Willard's *Argumentation and the Social Grounds of Knowledge* pursues this argument further into the question of the amount and kinds of knowledge on which depend not only communication but the validity of arguments within different fields. Interestingly enough, Jerrold Katz's study of propositional structure, which sets out the distinction between a theory of grammatical competence (where 'grammar' has the broad definition set out in Chapter 1) and a theory of pragmatics or performance, arrives at a criticism of formal logic similar to that of Toulmin and Willard. Katz's 'inheritance properties' operate to guarantee validity in informally constructed arguments in the same way that entailments guarantee them in formal logic (228 ff.).

A different approach to the powers of context will be found in George Dillon's work in discourse analysis. Rather than beginning with a general distinction between *langue* and *parole*, he analyses levels of contextual processing. His first level, 'perception', consists of identifying propositional structure through such syntactic processes as matching subjects, verbs, and objects. The second level, 'comprehension', 'involves the integration of its propositional content into one's running tally of what is being described or argued in the passage'. 'Interpretation' is the construction of the 'author's constructive intention' through incorporation of the results of the first two levels into 'a general contextual frame' (xvii). The first level corresponds roughly to the linguistic context, though it appears to lean towards purely syntactical information to the exclusion of broad 'grammatical' knowledge of the implications of words; the second describes the reader's consultation of the general context *within* the discourse, the place the sentence (proposition) in question occupies in the sequence of sentences; the third describes something like the process of relating the sentence to contexts outside the discourse as well as within it. I do not know whether Dillon would agree, but I doubt that these processes ought to be thought of as sequential—if they do not occur simultaneously, we switch back and forth between them very quickly indeed. For example, the total context may aid in determining the very syntax of a sentence, while encountering a problem of fit at Dillon's level of interpretation may require us to revise a provisional 'perception'.

I have intended only to suggest a converging recognition of the importance of the total context of language-in-use or discourse by the above very brief citations bearing on the importance of the context. I do not wish to imply that the scholars cited and their colleagues pursuing more or less similar endeavours are not divided on both issues and terminology or that they would not dispute many aspects of the total scheme I am sketching. Ricœur, for instance, draws a much sharper line between literature and other uses of language, and between written and spoken discourse, than most theorists who focus on the essentiality of context for the interpretation of discourse. He also gives much less attention to extralinguistic contexts than, say, Todorov. Todorov uses the word 'interpret' in a special sense (my use of 'interpret' essentially follows E. D. Hirsch, see Chapter 3, section 1) and draws a sharper line between literal and non-literal meanings than speech-act theorists. Dillon assigns the term 'interpretation' to only one component of the process of understanding discourse rather than to the total process. But one does not after all expect to find a peaceable kingdom prior to the millennium, nor is this the place to attempt to adjudicate among rival claims and conflicting definitions. What I wish to emphasize is a general area of agreement on the contextual dependence of all discourse, and that this dependence cancels the free play of signs assumed for the purposes of deconstruction.

Of course, not all critics who employ deconstructive strategies are motivated simply by the seductive deferment of meaning possible if one regards words only as units within *langue*. Since deconstruction

tends to subvert or reverse hierarchies and challenge accepted interpretations, it has appealed to critics seeking to demonstrate political, economic, or social assumptions and prejudices that have been
silently accepted by authors and readers. I will comment in Chapter
7 on the way in which consciousness of the interpretive process can
help one towards the critical analysis of political significances. At
this point I wish only to note that the same deconstructive techniques that one uses to undermine an assumption or argument can be
used to undermine the deconstructive manœuvre one has just
employed. Precisely because deconstruction denies the possibility of
closure, it can only lead down the garden path of an infinite series of
reversals. The more serious one's interest in the political significance
of a text, the more readily will deconstruction prove a betrayer.

It is worth pondering two passages written well before the emergence of deconstructive criticism. The first, from Paul Valéry's
'Poetry and Abstract Thought' (1939), warns against over-indulgence
in that concentration on the isolated word or concept that distinguishes deconstruction.

You must all of you, at some time or another, have noticed this curious
fact—that a given *word*, which may be perfectly obvious when used in the
ordinary course of conversation, has a way of becoming almost magically
embarrassing, strangely resistant and quite unmanageable in definition, as
soon as you withdraw it from circulation with the object of examining it
closely and apart from its neighbors; as soon, that is, as you try to establish its meaning in isolation from its momentary function.

. . . . .

Every word, each one of those words which make it possible for us to
traverse quickly the spatial extent of a thought and to follow in the wake of
an idea which formulates its own mode of expression, appears to me in the
light of a slender plank laid across a ditch or mountain crevasse. It will carry
a man *provided* he does not loiter. But he must not throw his full weight on
it. Above all, he must not start jumping about on the fragile gangway just to
see how strong it is! If he does that it will tip up or break and precipitate him
into the depths. (73-4.)

The second, from Hugo von Hofmannsthal's 'The Letter of Lord
Chandos' (1902), is a yet earlier description of what it would be like
to *live* as a deconstructionist, not simply write for learned journals
as one.

My case, in short, is this: I have lost completely the ability to think or to
speak of anything coherently.

At first I grew by degrees incapable of discussing a loftier or more general subject in terms of which everyone, fluently and without hesitation, is wont to avail himself. I experienced an inexplicable distaste for so much as uttering the words *spirit, soul,* or *body.* I found it impossible to express an opinion on the affairs at Court, the events in Parliament, or whatever you wish. This was not motivated by any form of personal deference (you know that my candour borders on impudence), but because the abstract terms of which the tongue must avail itself as a matter of course in order to voice a judgment—these terms crumbled in my mouth like mouldy fungi.

.   .   .   .

For me everything disintegrated into parts, those parts again into parts; no longer would anything let itself be encompassed by one idea. Single words floated round me; they congealed into eyes which stared at me and into which I was forced to stare back—whirlpools which gave me vertigo and, reeling incessantly, led into the void.   (133–5.)

The second error resulting from a failure to give context its due arose with the New Critical pronouncement of the autonomy of the individual work. In attempting to free the individual poem, short story, novel, or drama from subordination to moral, historical, and biographical framworks, such critics as Robert Penn Warren and Cleanth Brooks insisted that poetry be dealt with 'as a thing in itself'. The emphasis of their profession-challenging textbook *Understanding Poetry* (1938) was thus 'on the poem as poem', avoiding such substitutes 'for the poem as object of study' as biography and history (vi, ix, iv). Those delighted with the freshness of their approach all too often interpreted this as meaning that one must stay narrowly within the words of the text. But one cannot:

> The Rainbow comes and goes,
> And lovely is the Rose,
> The Moon doth with delight
> Look round her when the heavens are bare,
> Waters on a starry night
> Are beautiful and fair;
> The sunshine is a glorious birth;
> But yet I know, where'er I go,
> That there hath passed a glory from the earth.

Strictly to stay within Wordsworth's text would be, presumably, to assign to each word a dictionary sense that seems appropriate given the text as a whole. But the dictionary will not tell us that the rose is regarded as beautiful by most people nor that by convention it has come to seem the epitome of floral attractiveness, though New Critical explication commonly assumes such knowledge. In addition, though a blind reader who had never seen rainbow, sunshine, rose, moon, or waters on a starry night could somewhat understand the poem through knowledge that pleasure was conventionally associated with these things, the poem depends immensely on the images stored up by the average reader's experience. The New Critics smuggled in reality by silently depending on common experience. Beyond that, New Critical readings commonly assume such knowledge as the brevity of rainbows, the convention of personification, and the long tradition of personifying the moon. In explicating 'Soliloquy in a Spanish Cloister', 'Ode on a Grecian Urn', or 'Spring and Fall', many a New Critic simply overlooked the external knowledge of monasticism, Greek pottery, or the doctrine of original sin being applied. Many also forgot that works like Gwendolyn Brooks's 'We Real Cool', or Swift's 'Modest Proposal', or John Galsworthy's 'The Silver Box', or Langston Hughes's story 'On the Road' require a knowledge of contemporary situations that is equally external to the text.

A number of English men of letters writing in the early 1950s were setting forth the essentiality of knowledge external to the poem much more explicitly than their American colleagues. F. W. Bateson's *English Poetry: A Critical Introduction* (1950) opens with an attack on the absence from standard anthologies of contextual information of all sorts, from broad historical context to obsolete uses of individual words. These 'provide the spectacles through which the poems can be read. Without their assistance a poem's central point may be missed, the grammar may be misconstrued, the allusions may be misunderstood, and instead of a clear-cut, sharply focused experience the reader may only register a semantic blur, an emotional haze.' (*EPCI* 4.)

William Empson's *The Structure of Complex Words* (1951) advances a set of symbols by means of which he attempts to indicate all that goes to make up the meaning of a particular word in a particular context of use: primary sense, secondary senses, evaluative force, moods, and tones. Empson's symbols are heavier going than the analysis of word use that they are intended to clarify— speech-act theory now does the job better—but the book is at least a decade ahead of its time in the issues it raises while defending a seemingly old-fashioned view of the need for scholarly knowledge.

Donald Davie's interests in *Purity of Diction in English Verse* (1952) led him quickly to the meanings of words within different historical milieux. Extensive knowledge of classical literature or of the Bible are thus 'fields of force' upon which writers for certain audiences at certain periods could rely. For all three writers—Bateson, Empson, and Davie—true 'literary history' is a history of changes in the language reflecting changes in the culture as a whole. Bateson wrote as early as 1934:

My thesis is that the age's imprint in a poem is not to be traced to the poet but to the language. The real history of poetry is, I believe, the history of the changes in the kind of language in which successive poems have been written. *And it is these changes only that are due to the pressure of social and interllectual tendencies.* (*EPEL* vi.)

More recently, Roger Fowler has written, 'All languages are provided with . . . structures which . . . [link] text and life. To deny these links seems to me to dehumanize the very texts which the critics claim have special significance for humanity' (*LSD* 170). If our understanding and response to 'Western Wind' depend on something more than a system of differences, they also depend on more than the interactions between the dictionary meanings of words within the four lines of the poem. They depend on the reader's own knowledge and experience ultimately induced by brute physical reality. In Elder Olson's words, 'When we are moved by poetry, we are not moved by the words, except in so far as sound and rhythm move us; we are moved by the things that the words stand for.' (564 n.)

We began with a minimal definition of reality and moved through the manner in which what our senses report of brute reality provides the material that is divided up by language to form experience. We then pursued a quick survey of the ways in which our total experience and the awarenesses it generates guide our interpretation of words and sentences. The shared awareness of reality and the shared knowledge of language thus become two of the set of contexts, two of the 'dimensions' of the total context, upon which our understanding of discourse depends. What precisely is meant by the process of interpretation, the basis of our trust in such a process, and the number of 'dimensions' that must be considered awaits an examination of the speech-act, that is, the act either of speaking or writing.

2

Exploring the Speech-act

1. The Foundations of Speech-act Theory

Though it originated in the pursuit of quite other questions, speech-act theory gives us the most fertile approach to the way in which *parole* is interpreted. In the series of William James Lectures (1955) subsequently published as *How to Do Things with Words*, J.L. Austin addressed the apparently quite limited question of whether there are uses of language that do more than refer to things, that actually bring things about: christening, promising, betting, arriving at verdicts, bequeathing. Such uses of language Austin called 'performatives' as distinguished from 'constatives'. The propositions of performative sentences are not such as can usually be called either true or false, though they may be successful or unsuccessful, or in Austin's terminology, felicitous or infelicitous. Thus a bet is neither true nor false, but either follows or violates understood rules: it is infelicitous to bet someone when the outcome is already known, or make a promise that one knows cannot be fulfilled. Further, the felicity of performatives would seem to depend on the existence of institutions (the social institution of marriage, the legal system) or commonly understood rules; they depend on what John Searle calls 'institutional facts'.

The characteristics of performatives as Austin developed them proved fascinating, but by the time he had reached his final lectures, the distinction between performatives and constatives had broken down. To oversimplify a subtle and at times elegant argument, it turns out that performatives also state: if my bequeathing $1000 to someone was not also a stating, the bequeathal would be unknown. And constatives also perform: if I state, as the peaceable Quaker is said to have done in warning a trespasser off his property, 'Friend, I would not harm thee, but thou standest where I am about to shoot', I have made a statement that performs the action of warning. Moreover, it becomes evident in the course of Austin's argument that the full understanding of either performatives or constatives depends on context: 'what we have to study is *not* the sentence but the issuing of an utterance in a speech situation' (139). That, in brief, is why it is the 'speech-act' and not simply 'speech' that Austin and his successors have explored.

In the process of trying to distinguish between performatives and constatives Austin developed the very useful set of terminological distinctions that have become basic to speech-act theory. A sentence regarded in itself is a *locution*. Locutions present propositions, but further, Austin pointed out, they have a certain intentional or *illocutionary* force: that is, a locution may be intended as a statement, or a promise, or a command. Each locution will also have some effect on its audience, which may or may not be that which was intended. This effect is the *perlocution* of the sentence. Let us consider some examples.

(A) The rain has stopped.
(B1) I order you to leave the room.
(B2) Leave the room.
(C1) I promise that I will do it.
(C2) I will do it.
(D1) I'm warning you not to do that again.
(D2) Don't do that again.

Each of these sentences has a particular illocutionary force: (A), for instance, has the force of a statement, (B1) has the force of an order, (C1) has the force of a promise. Illocutionary force does not have to be made explicit in the locution: (B2) and (C2) are also respectively orders and promises. In addition, each locution will cause in the hearer or reader a *perlocutionary* response. Obviously the author of a locution may intend a certain perlocutionary effect, but he or she cannot be certain of achieving it. This leads to a significant distinction: using J.L. Austin's terminology, the felicity of an utterance depends on the proposition having been understood, its propriety under the circumstances having been accepted, and its illocutionary force having been grasped, not on the perlocutionary effect having been achieved. So long as (D2) is understood as a warning not to do 'that' (whatever it is) again, spoken by someone with sufficient reason to give a warning, it is felicitous, even if the warning is ignored.

The tendency to use the term 'locution' to designate both the form and the content of the sentence leads to confusion. 'Locution', the form of words that make up the sentence, is not on all fours with

'illocution' and 'perlocution', which designate the force and effect of
that form. The triumvirate of key terms is actually 'proposition',
'illocution', and 'perlocution', all of which are begotten by a given
locution appearing in a given situation. A locution sets forth a propositional content accompanied by an illocutionary force and producing a perlocutionary effect. (B1) and (B2), (C1) and (C2), (D1) and
(D2) are therefore pairs of different locutions embodying the same
propositional content and carrying the same illocutionary force.

Now literary scholars and critics have tended to dismiss speech-
act theory as irrelevant to their major interests, and it is not hard to
see why. Speech-act theorists have devoted most of their efforts to
questions raised in Austin's original explorations: whether there are
in fact both performatives and constatives, what Austin meant
by calling illocutionary acts 'conventional' (is 'conventional' a
synonym for 'institutional', 'formulaic', or 'culturally accepted'?),
and what is the best way of classifying kinds of illocutionary force.
These questions, which prove both intriguing and complex, have
generally been pursued by the examination of individual sentences
that are regarded as anomalous or unexplainable according to someone else's version of speech-act theory.

Nevertheless, much of speech-act theory does address our central
question: 'How is the communication of intended meaning possible?'
John Searle, Austin's most immediate successor, opens *Speech Acts*
thus:

How do words relate to the world? How is it possible that when a speaker
stands before a hearer and emits an acoustic blast such remarkable things
occur as: the speaker means something; the sounds he emits mean something; the hearer understands what is meant; the speaker makes a statement, asks a question, or gives an order? (*SA* 3.)

In the following section I will be both highlighting the aspects of
speech-act theory that bear most directly on the ways in which
meaning is expressed and understood, and augmenting the theory
where necessary to establish its relevance to students of discourse
generally and of literature in particular.

2. Speech-act Theory and the Interpretation of Meaning

From the point of view of interpretation theory, the notion of the
illocutionary force of a sentence is in special need of refinement.

Philosophically oriented theorists have been much more interested in formulating broad categories of illocutionary force than in recognizing the diversity of nuances that may be intended. J.L. Austin found five categories: verdictives (which deliver a verdict: 'acquit', 'assess'), exercitives (which announce a decision: 'command', 'appoint'), commissives (which commit one: 'promise', 'plan'), behabitives (which express feelings about relations to others; 'apologize', 'welcome'), and expositives (which clarify: 'inform', 'agree to'). Bach and Harnish recognize four kinds of 'communicative' illocutionary acts, each with sub-categories, and two kinds of 'conventional' illocutionary acts, where 'conventional' means related or endemic to a specific social/cultural institution. Jerrold Katz has developed a list of eight categories. John Searle finds five types: assertives ('we tell people how things are'), directives ('we try to get them to do things'), commissives ('we commit ourselves to do things'), expressives ('we express our feelings and attitudes'), and declarations (we bring about changes in the world through our utterances).

Since each of these taxonomies is constructed on a different principle, direct translation from one to another of the four sets of categories is not possible. However, a table of very rough equivalents may be useful. (See Table 2.1: dotted lines represent the splitting away of a portion of a category.)

However, if we are to understand the processes of interpretation we must not confuse speech-act theorists' categorizations of basic kinds of illocutionary force with the number of verbs that express illocutionary force (state, insinuate, order, beg, challenge, ask, bless, denounce, propose, etc.), a list which Austin facetiously estimates to be somewhere between 1,000 and 9,999. For the purposes of literary analysis, specifications of illocutionary type are not fine-grained enough to illuminate the full interpretive situation. 'To order' and 'to suggest' fall within the same 'directive' classification in Searle's terminology, while 'to describe' and 'to evaluate' fall into the same 'assertive' classification, but these represent very different attitudes on the part of the speaker and elicit very different responses from the hearer. Discrimination of such attitudes is essential to the full description of any speech-act. Though in many cases such descriptions can only be approximate, there is obviously a deal of difference between 'grudging assent' and 'enthusiastic endorsement', though both might be assigned to the broad class of 'commissives'.

Table 1

Austin	Searle	Bach and Harnish[2]	Katz[3]
Commissives	Commissives	Commissives	Obligatives
Expositives	Assertives[1] or Representatives	Constatives	Expositives (performative) Assertives (constative)
Verdictives	Declarations	Effectives ◄------► Stipulatives[4] Verdictives	
Exercitives	Directives	Directives	Admissives Requestives Permissives
Behabitives	Expressives	Acknowledgements	Expressives

[1] Searle calls this type 'assertive' in *Expressions and Meaning* (1979) and 'representative' in *Speech Acts* (1969).

[2] The first four types of illocutionary act are classed by Bach and Harnish as 'communicative'; effectives and verdictives make up their 'conventional' class.

[3] Strictly speaking, Katz lists 'propositional types,' not 'illocutionary acts', and explicitly states that his list is not intended to be complete (it lacks, for instance, classifications of many of what are usually called 'verdictives').

[4] 'Stipulatives' include only a sub-class of effectives having to do with naming.

Therefore, though contrary to general practice, I will regard the 'illocutionary force' of an utterance as the tone and attitude associated with the author's intent and refer to broad classifications as 'illocutionary categories'.

Up to this point we have been considering exemplary sentences as isolated entities, but, as noted in Chapter 1, this is an artificial exercise. Searle writes, 'Utterance acts consist simply in uttering strings of words. Illocutionary and propositional acts consist characteristically in uttering words in certain contexts, under certain conditions and with certain intentions.' (*SA* 24–5.) Austin's own examples suggest that the same locutions may function rather differently in different contexts: they may have a different or additional illocutionary force and their propositional content may acquire implications that are in no way present when the locutions are considered in isolation. Thus, let us suppose that a person has been given permission to stand inside a doorway during a rainstorm. 'The rain has stopped', as spoken to that person by the proprietor, remains within the illocutionary category of a statement, but functions in addition within the category of a directive: 'It's time you moved on.' One can easily come up with situations in which 'Don't do that again' becomes a challenge, even an enticement, rather than a warning. When uttered with the proper intonation and look by a lover to his lass after an embrace, it might be intended to be interpreted as 'I dare you to kiss me like that again; if you do I'll immediately carry you off.'

There are also cases in which the context clashes with the propositional content of apparent illocutionary force. For instance, two people look out of the door, obviously hoping to find that it has stopped raining, and discover that it is coming down harder than ever. One says, 'See, the rain has stopped.' That we take immediately as ironical. Or again, I say to a friend with whom I am planning a trip, 'I order you to make the sun shine,' or, more likely, 'Be sure the weather is good.' Since he and I both know that I can't order or request him to do something beyond his power, he will interpret the remark as expressing a hope for good weather or as acknowledging the fact that we won't be able to control the weather (which interpretation is more likely will depend on other elements of the context: what we have said earlier about the weather; what the friend knows about my personality). The two cases—that in which as a result of context a second illocutionary force and perhaps additional propositional implications are present and that in which the context changes what would be the illocutionary force in the wonted context—are distinguished by some theorists as 'indirect' and 'non-literal' respectively. Locutions in which neither the propositional content nor illocutionary force imply contextual elements beyond the expected and immediate may be called 'transparent'.

How is an indirect or non-literal interpretation possible? How indeed is it possible to identify the illocutionary force of a locution that contains no specific evidences of illocutionary intent? How is it that 'Two to one on Penn State' has the illocutionary force of a bet? Or 'I'll take you home again, Kathleen' that of a promise? The answer, first cogently formulated by H. P. Grice in 'Logic and Conversation (1975), is that we share certain expectations of discourse; specifically we expect language to be used to express things in a manner that is truthful or at least grounded in evidence, clear, relevant and neither briefer nor more extended than required. These are of course counsels of perfection; all we can actually expect is reasonable adherence. Expressed as maxims of (1) quality, (2) manner, (3) relation, and (4) quantity, they make up what Grice calls the 'Co-operative Principle'. Unfortunately, different theorists have adopted different terminology. Bach and Harnish speak of the 'Communicative Presumption' (hereafter 'CP'), which they define as the belief in 'recognizable illocutionary intent'; Tzvetan Todorov uses the term 'pertinence'. When the CP, or expectation of pertinence, is violated in a way that appears intentional, the reader or hearer assumes that a different illocution than would appear on the face of the locution is intended. This Grice calls 'illocutionary implicature'. A standard example is 'Can you pass the salt?' Asked at a dinner party, the question appears relevant to nothing and, since it is most likely addressed to someone who obviously *can* reach the salt, wholly unnecessary; it violates the maxim of quantity. We therefore assume that what is asked for is not redundant information but the salt itself.

It is not only in European cultures that implicature is signalled by lack of correlation between the *parole* and the situation of utterance, or usual expectations, or understood conventions. An instance from Korean culture is the operation of forms of address in Korea as described by Dell Hymes:

. . . a mode of address [term, style, speech variety, whatever] has associated with it a usual or 'unmarked,' value—say formality. Social relationships and settings have associated with them usual, or 'unmarked,' values. When the values of the mode of address and the social context match— when both, say, are formal—then that meaning is of course accomplished, together with the meeting of expectations. When the values do not match— when, say, an informal mode of address is used in a formal relationship or conversely—then a special, or 'marked,' meaning is conveyed. The unmarked and marked meanings are each defined by a particular rule or relation, mapping the set of linguistic alternatives onto the set of social relationships and settings. What the particular marked meaning— deference, courtesy, insult, change of status—will be is of course an empirical question . . . (111–12.)

For a literary example we may jump to a well-known scene (I. v) from *Hamlet*:

HORATIO. What news, my lord?
HAMLET. Oh, wonderful!
HORATIO. Good my lord, tell it.

HAMLET. No; you will reveal it.

HORATIO. Not I, my lord, by Heaven!

MARCELLUS. Nor I, my lord.

HAMLET. How say you then; would heart of man once think it?
  But you'll be secret?

BOTH. Ay, by Heaven, my lord!

HAMLET. There's ne'er a villain dwelling in all Denmark
  But he's an arrant knave.

HORATIO. There needs no ghost, my lord, come from the grave,
  To tell us this.

HAMLET. Why, right; you are i' the right;
  And so, without more circumstance at all,
  I hold fit that we shake hands and part—

Even without the suspense Hamlet builds up before he announces his 'news', the statement that villains are knaves violates the CP: it appears patently uncooperative, impertinent, unmotivated, irrelevant. Horatio and Marcellus presumably have no difficulty in interpreting the implicature and recognizing that Hamlet has chosen not to tell them what he has heard from the Ghost. The expected illocutionary force of his reply was that of a report; the actual direct force *is* that of a statement, but of so irrelevant and tautological a proposition that its indirect force is that of an evasion. Of course this is even more obvious to the audience, since it has heard the Ghost's message to Hamlet. (One can go on to ask the illocutionary force of the whole of Hamlet's words to Horatio and Marcellus as quoted above, but consideration of second and third levels of force had better be postponed.)

If illocutionary implicature is a common feature of language, what prevents us seeking such implicature under every locution? The answer is, 'nothing except Ockham's razor'. We can always construct an interpretation through implicature by first fetching in a violation of the co-operative principle, however far we may have to go to fetch it. Indeed, importing an interpretation not required to explain a violation of the CP is a well-recognized form of wit. Hamlet employs the technique to good purpose:

GUILDENSTERN: . . . On Fortune's cap we are not the very button.

HAMLET: Nor the soles of her shoe?

ROSENCRANTZ: Neither, my lord.

HAMLET: Then you live about her waist, or in the middle of her favours?

GUILDENSTERN: Faith, her privates we.

HAMLET: In the secret parts of Fortune? O! most true; she is a strumpet.

Hamlet of course adopts the technique of importing implications precisely to suggest an antic madness.

POLONIUS: . . . What do you read, my lord?
HAMLET: Words, words, words.
POLONIUS: What is the matter, my lord?
HAMLET: Between who?
POLONIUS: I mean, the matter you read, my lord.

We enjoy Hamlet's punning play with Polonius, but his serious purpose is achieved because habitual disregard of obviously direct meaning, even in a punster, suggests intellectual perversity (perhaps not unknown among literary critics), if not mental disorder. Bach and Harnish propose that interpretation operates on the principle of the presumption of literalness, which presumably means that unless some evident violation of the CP makes it impossible or manifestly inadequate for one to interpret illocutionary force directly, one does so. However, in addition to obvious anomalies or violations of the CP, experienced readers are alert for implicature wherever a word receives special emphasis, or is drawn from a different register, or appears in some way anomalous. In addition, the text itself helps set the level of the reader's alertness to implicature: encountering evident implicatures at the beginning of a text, a reader expects more. And of course genre is an especially important indicator: the experienced reader expects a greater degree of implicature in a lyric poem than a narrative poem, and a greater degree in either than in a novel. On the other hand, novels are likely to trade on several levels of implicature: each character interprets in terms of his or her own contextual knowledge, as does the reader. Evidently the process of recognizing and interpreting implicature is governed by no rules. However, in practice our interpretations are less idiosyncratic than one might expect. Michael Riffaterre constructs his 'superreader' by noting the points at which most commentators on a given text think it important to give explicit interpretations. However, where readers disagree, we can only argue probabilities.

How far afield is it reasonable for a reader to go in seeking an implied context that will resolve apparent violations of the CP? Discourse analysts point out that if there were no internal controls on the mind's search for the knowledge relevant to the interpretation of each particular bit of discourse, the sheer quantity of random association would be overwhelming. In describing their model, van Dijk and Kintsch explain that instead of a more or less blind activation of all possible knowledge, in the understanding of a word, a clause, or the construction of a global theme, we assume that the use of knowledge is strategic, depending on the goals of the language user, the amount of available knowledge from text and context, the level of processing or the degree of coherence needed for comprehension. (13.)

Brown and Yule more simply offer what they call *the principle of local interpretation*, which 'instructs the hearer not to construct a context any larger than he needs to arrive at an interpretation'. (59.)

Such an answer again provides us with no rule except the experience-hallowed one that the simplest explanation that will resolve an anomaly or bring order out of confusion is to be preferred over more complex ones. But its application is hardly Delphic. Consider a simple instance, a review of a concert in which we read:

The quartet played Beethoven. Beethoven lost.

Now, unless we assume a reader who has never heard of music played by a quartet, nor of Beethoven, nor of the range of common meanings of 'play', there can't be much doubt about the implication. Any native speaker would be expected to recognize the existence of implicature, locate its basis in the pun on 'play', and then, having recognized it, rest satisfied with the interpretation.

Charles Altieri has pointed out that recognition of illocutionary implicature causes us to seek more than the implied illocutionary force (86). When the Co-operative Principle is violated in a way that causes us to pursue illocutionary implicature, we also recognize that the author expects us to be aware not only that the implicature exists, but that the author must have had a reason for choosing indirection or non-literality. We thus ask ourselves not only *what* illocutionary force is being implied but *why* it is being implied rather than directly stated. This aspect of communicative intent Altieri calls 'expressive implicature' (86 ff). In the case of asking 'Can you pass the salt?' the reason has to do with the conventions of politeness. In simple cases the reason for implicature may be mere economy: 'Are you going to the banquet? 'It costs $100.' The reply is of course a negative: 'The banquet costs $100, which is more than I think I can spend (or than it is worth), and therefore I don't plan to go.' However, the most general use of non-literal and indirect expressions is to indicate the speaker's attitude towards the subject at hand. 'Of course, I have $100 that is just burning a hole in my pocket,' or 'Sure, just like I'm flying to Paris next week,' convey the speaker's sense of the absurdity of the very idea. Hamlet's announcement that all the villains of Denmark are arrant knaves avoids a direct lie ('The ghost said nothing' or 'The ghost only gibbered'), or a directly discourteous reply ('It doesn't concern you'), or a reply that would lead to further questioning ('He told me a terrible thing').

The following locutions are all ways of answering 'yes' to a single question; but whereas the first four are direct or literal, the second four are not. The illocutionary force varies across the whole set, although without knowing more about the context, one could not be sure whether (2), (3), and (4) are approving or disapproving.

Did the President veto the bill?

1. Yes, that's what the newspaper said.
2. Of course.
3. With great pleasure.
4. He did it again!
5. The President's grasp of reality hasn't improved.
6. Any true statesman would.
7. What do you expect of an ideological conservative?
8. Thank heaven he can't be elected for a third term.

Full consideration of authorial intent requires further supplementation of our terminology. When a hearer or reader understands not only the proposition but the illocutionary force of a sentence (and where force is expressed through implicature, the expressive implicature), he or she may be said to understand what the author intended to be understood. In Austin's terms, 'uptake' has occurred, the effect of which uptake Austin called the perlocution. But since an utterance may be understood without having the desired effect, we need a term for the effect the author intended; 'perlocutionary intent' will do.

We are more likely to go astray in interpreting perlocutionary intent than illocutionary force since that is not directly implied by the illocutionary force of a sentence. For example:

Look out for that rattlesnake!

appears to set forth the proposition that the hearer should note that there is a rattlesnake in the vicinity, with the illocutionary force of a warning and the perlocutionary intent of preventing the person addressed from being bitten. But even in this apparently transparent example, our interpretation, which can never be certain, is most open to error at the level of the perlocutionary intent: the speaker may enjoy frightening others and not believe there is a rattlesnake anywhere around; he or she may be issuing the warning hypocritically while hoping in fact that the person will be bitten.

Once we consider perlocutionary intent, a further complication suggests itself. Person *A* may hope to achieve an additional effect that he or she does *not* intend *B* to understand. Such an intended effect might seem to lie outside the realm of discourse, of the communicative use of language, in that *A* does not intend to communicate it to *B* and, if the speech-act is successful, does not. But *A* may well intend that *C*, who also hears the utterance, should understand the intention concealed from *B*. *A* may be making fun of *B* without *B* being aware of it, or *A* may be a parent speaking to child *B* so that parent *C* understands an additional intention. In prose fiction and drama, one form of dramatic irony depends on the audience's awareness that character *A* has knowledge or intentions of which character *B* is ignorant. Thus Montresor, the first-person narrator of Poe's *The Cask of Amontillado*, piques Fortunato's pride as a connoisseur of fine wines in order to ensure that Fortunato will follow him to the family catacombs where his wine is stored.

'As you are engaged, I am on my way to Luchresi. If any one has a critical turn it is he. He will tell me—,
'Luchresi cannot tell Amontillado from Sherry.'
'And yet some fools will have it that his taste is a match for your own.'
'Come, let us go.'

The reader has little doubt that Fortunato is being lured to the catacombs even though Montresor's purpose remains veiled almost to the end of the story. We do not, however, need a special name for this situation; we need only remember that different interpretations are possible because the interpreters are relating the utterance to different contexts.

Finally, we should recognize that speech-act theory suggests how actions and facts as well as discourse are interpreted. Speech-act theory ought probably to be regarded as simply one aspect of a comprehensive theory of interpretation. When Wordsworth tells us that his Michael 'never lifted up a single stone', or Meredith describes the husband and wife of *Modern Love* as lying like carved figures on a tomb, or the Josephine of Kate Chopin's 'The Story of an Hour' dies at the moment she learns of her husband's return, or

Henry James's Isabel Archer returns to Osmond, or Hawthorne's minister adopts his black veil, we interpret these actions, like innumerable less dramatic, or puzzling, or significant ones on the stage or in narrative poems and prose, by trying to relate them to the total context. The more an action or fact violates our expectations, the more directly we engage in the resolution of implicature.

It's time we sought further illustration in a literary text. Section I of Faulkner's 'A Rose for Emily' describes the visit to Emily's house by a deputation of aldermen after she has ignored the town's tax notices. Here is the close of the section:'

She did not ask them to sit. She just stood in the door and listened quietly until the spokesman came to a stumbling halt. Then they could hear the invisible watch ticking at the end of the gold chain.

Her voice was dry and cold. 'I have no taxes in Jefferson. Colonel Sartoris explained it to me. Perhaps one of you can gain access to the city records and satisfy yourselves.'

'But we have. We are the city authorities, Miss Emily. Didn't you get a notice from the sheriff, signed by him?'

'I received a paper, yes,' Miss Emily said. 'Perhaps he considers himself the sheriff . . . I have no taxes in Jefferson.'

'But there is nothing on the books to show that, you see. We must go by the—'

'See Colonel Sartoris.' (Colonel Sartoris had been dead almost ten years.) 'I have no taxes in Jefferson. Tobe!' The Negro appeared. 'Show these gentlemen out.'

Narration increases the complexities of interpretation by causing readers to consider the illocutionary force and perlocutionary intention of both direct narration and the utterances of the characters, and further to consider the dialogue from the point of view of one or more characters within the narration as well as their own. 'I have no taxes in Jefferson' has less the force of a statement than of a decision: that is, given the context (the deputation's attempt to try to get Miss Emily to understand and agree to their authority), it expresses her own decision that the matter is closed. 'Perhaps one of you can gain access to the city records and satisfy yourselves' is a suggestion that has the indirect force of a denial of the authority of the aldermen. As does 'I received a paper, yes' and 'Perhaps he considers himself the sheriff', both of which imply a denial of the relevance of whatever arrangements have been made for carrying on the city government. The brusqueness and imperiousness of 'See Colonel Sartoris' implies that she is responding to the more irritated tone of the spokesman's 'But there is nothing . . .'. An example of a locution that has different illocutionary forces to different audiences is Emily's 'Show these gentlemen out.' It is an order to Tobe and a signal to the deputation that the interview is at an end. 'Show these gentlemen out' can as well be seen as an indirect directive to the deputation, in which case we have the same illocutionary force in a locution that directly expresses that force to one audience and indirectly to another. We hardly need to belabour the perlocutionary intent of any of Miss Emily's locutions. Actions and reported facts are interpreted in much the same way: that Miss Emily did not ask the delegation to sit constitutes an implicature, as does the narrator's later report that upon Miss Emily's death the servant 'walked right through the house and out the back and was not seen again' or the 'long strand of iron-gray hair' that closes the story.

We can also consider the narrator's illocutionary force or perlocutionary intent in constructing the dialogue. For instance 'See Colonel Sartoris', followed by the narrator's parenthetical 'Colonel Sartoris had been dead almost ten years', is understood as a device for reinforcing the reader's recognition of the impenetrability of Emily's mental world. Readers interpret and integrate speech-acts on several different planes at once. Reading a novel requires keeping track of the propositional content, illocutionary force, and perlocutionary intent of the utterances of a narrator, of each character, and of the author who created the narrator. This makes an accurate analysis and adequate discussion of many of the speech-acts that occur in fiction quite complicated. However, the average reader finds it no more difficult to keep track of these interrelated aspects than to sort out a cocktail party conversation through his or her awareness that Bill is making fun of John who does not realize this because Bill's references are to an event which John doesn't know about though both the hearer and Mary understand what is happening, and further that Mary probably does not understand why Bill is being cruel since she doesn't know the reasons Bill doesn't like John though the hearer does, and finally that Bill intends just this distribution of awarenesses.

We can also ask the illocutionary force and perlocutionary intent of the narrative structure. The scene from 'A Rose for Emily' can be described as setting forth the proposition that Miss Emily was able to dominate the aldermen presented with an illocutionary force of admiring description and an perlocutionary intent of making clear how it was that Miss Emily had enforced her will all her life. We can even move to the level of text as a whole, and describe it as presenting the proposition that the gallantries of the old South concealed and abetted internal decay with an illocutionary force of horrifying description and a perlocutionary intent to intrigue the reader by combining narrative surprise and cultural insight.

However, properly speaking, the extension of speech-act analysis beyond the individual sentence can only be figurative. The probability of our being able to make an adequate summation of what might be called macro-illocutionary force and macro-perlocutionary intent decreases in proportion to the complexity of the text. We have good reason to be impatient with statements about the theme or, worse, moral of a text—both are attempts at radical capsulization of the perlocutionary intent of the total work. It can be useful to think of a text, even one as extended and sophisticated in structure as 'A Modest Proposal', *Othello*, or *Modern Love*, as expressing a very complex proposition with a dominant illocutionary force and central perlocutionary intent. 'A Modest Proposal' can be regarded as literally expressing the proposition that the problems of Ireland can be solved by eating Irish children with explanatory illocutionary force, while non-literally expressing the proposition that the English have treated the Irish cruelly with a savagely ironic force and the intent of causing the English to recognize their own cruelty. But summing up extended discourse through speech-act terminology yields very loose summaries. It is generally preferable to confine speech-act analysis to individual sentences or at least to several closely related sentences. We may adopt from Charles Altieri a useful distinction between at least three levels of intent: the 'intention' of the sentence, the 'purpose' of a part or section of the text (a scene, a chapter, a stanza), and the 'project' which constitutes the intent of the whole (41–4). (See also van Dijk and Kintsch, 65–6.) While the first can be very usefully analysed in speech-act terms, 'purpose' and 'project' yield more adequately to discursive description.

Examples (not Altieri's) of these levels, as grasped on the one hand by another character and on the other by a reader or audience, would be almost any of Iago's speeches as he insinuates suspicions of Desdemona and Cassio into Othello's mind. For instance, when Iago says 'For Michael Cassio, / I dare be sworn I think that he is

honest' (III, iii), the surface illocutionary act is evidently the assertion of the proposition that Cassio is honest. However, to say 'dare
be sworn' rather than 'I swear' and then to interpolate 'I think' violates Grice's maxim of manner (which includes avoiding obscurity,
ambiguity, and prolixity). Othello's natural response is to wonder
whether the violation is not caused by an attempt to honour the
maxims of quality ('Do not say what you believe to be false' and 'Do
not say that for which you lack adequate evidence'). That this assertion of Iago's is a somewhat oblique response to Othello's immediately preceding speech also suggests that the maxim of relevance is
being flouted.

Of course Iago's speeches from the 'Ha! I like not that,' at the
moment he and Othello first see Desdemona talking with Cassio,
help create a context in which the implicatures of each innuendo
seem clearer and clearer to Othello. Some of Iago's speeches may
seem individually to be—have the illocutionary force of—questions
that Iago asks in order to resolve his own doubts, or evasions, or
mere statements of the ways of the world, but these particular intentions implicate a purpose of a higher order. Othello thus comes to
understand that he is being warned (illocutionary implicature) and
interprets Iago's halting indirectness as reluctance to give him pain
(expressive implicature). The audience or reader of course interprets
Iago's purpose as a warning indeed, but one intended to make
Othello jealous, and therefore assigns Iago the quality of cunning
malevolence. Othello assimilates Iago's purpose here to the project
of being a true friend; the reader or audience sees the project as the
destruction of Othello.

We thus have a set of levels of intention: 'intentions' interpreted at
the level of the individual sentence or small group of sentences,
'purposes' interpreted at the level of something like a scene in a novel
or a discrete portion of a lyric poem, and the 'project' at the level of
our overall understanding of a character. A change at any level is
likely to entail changes in interpretation at the other two levels. In
this way interpretation of speech-acts at the sentence level ramifies,
cumulates, and continually revises itself to arrive at an interpretation of the text. And of course just as one builds up an interpretation
of the total intention and qualities of each character as one pro-
gresses through the play or novel, one also builds up an interpretation of the total intention and qualities of the author. These are
implied by the narrator or implied author's strategies for presenting

the setting, the events, and the characters' intentions as we understand them through their speech-acts.

The process is more immediate, though not necessarily simpler, in
the case of the lyric poem, where interpretation of the intentions and
qualities of characters is not part of the process. Although Altieri
says little about the complex language use we find in poetry, the
choice of words, the images evoked, the ambiguities introduced, the
emphases given by sentence structure, or line endings, or metrical
variations are all presumably analysable under the Co-operative
Principle. A simple, easily detached example from a well-known
poem is the forty-eighth quatrain from Fitzgerald's *The Rubáiayát*.

> A Moment's Halt—a momentary taste
> Of BEING from the Well amid the Waste—
> And lo!—the phantom Caravan has reached
> The NOTHING it set out from—Oh, make haste!

The illocutionary categories intended are direct enough—description followed by an imperative. The indirection that must be taken
into account here results from the figurative nature of the proposition: the caravan's halt at the oasis is a metaphor for the brief
moment allowed for the enjoyment of life.

Assuming for the present purpose that we have *The Rubáiyát*
before us and find ourselves interpreting the poem pretty much as
most readers have, the three levels of intention, stated in the barest
form, would be something like the following: the immediate intention of the metaphor is the dramatization of the contrast between the
tiny oasis of life and the immense realm of nothingness stretching on
both sides. The purpose of the stanza is to link the poem's various
metaphors for the brevity of life with those for the emptiness that
stretches before and after. That purpose determines the reading of
the closing imperative: 'Oh, make haste!' This, which at first reading
might be taken as an exhortation to the caravan to hurry on, is a
warning to drink as much and as deeply from the Well of Being as
possible. The identification of Being with pleasure, and of everything beyond the brief moment of individual existence as a desert
waste, implicates the 'quality' or attitude of the implied author. The
overall project then is to urge that wisdom lies in crowding as much
pleasure as possible into the brief compass of a life about which the
only certainty is that it flies.

3. Cohesiveness, Coherence, and Discourse Analysis

I have been pursuing the way in which, though its origin lies in a much more limited question, speech-act theory addresses the question of how communication is possible, and how, in the process, it comes to give prominent place both to the total context of the utterance and to the intention of the utterer. Though I personally find that speech-act theory offers an appealing way of describing the processes by which we understand what we hear or read, the pursuit of other questions by means of different methodologies has generated much the same general principles. For instance, the analysis of cohesion in discourse has become a field of study in and of itself. Chapter 1 of Halliday and Hasan's *Cohesion in English* begins: 'If a speaker of English hears or reads a passage of the language which is more than one sentence in length, he can normally decide without difficulty whether it forms a unified whole or is just a collection of unrelated sentences. This book is about the difference between the two.' (1.)

That first sentence hardly needs illustration, but to reinforce the point, here is a paragraph formed by taking the first sentences of sections of the first chapter of Gombrich's *Art and Illusion*:

The illustration in front of the reader should explain much more quickly than I could in words what is here meant by the 'riddle of style.' There was a time when the methods of representation were the proper concern of the art critic. This debate revealed what it was bound to reveal: science is neutral, and the artist will appeal to its findings at his peril. Evolutionism is dead, but the facts which gave rise to its myth are still stubbornly there to be accounted for. To tackle these central problems of our discipline, I believe, it cannot be sufficient to repeat the old opposition between 'seeing' and 'knowing,' or to insist in a general way that all representation is based on conventions.

'Cohesion' is now conventionally discussed in terms of two kinds of relationship, syntactical and lexical, the first consisting of relations like those created by the reference of pronouns or the substitution of equivalent terms, and the second by repetition of the same word or the subsumption of a word within a more general term. Thus the two sentences

Close your books. Put them under your desks.

are related syntactically, while the sentences

Put away that hammer. Tools shouldn't be left lying around.

are related lexically. Simple as is the concept of cohesion, analysis of the kinds of relationship that produce cohesion discloses a surprising number of categories: anaphoric and cataphoric forms of reference for instance cut across generalized, extended, and personal reference. Ellipsis seems a simple enough mode of cohesion:

Have another doughnut. I bought a dozen.

However, Halliday and Hasan distinguish not only nominal, verbal, and clausal ellipsis, but five further sub-categories within the class of nominal ellipsis alone.

Now the artificial 'paragraph' I created from *Art and Illusion* clearly lacks cohesiveness. However, once one asks the question of how we recognize unified discourse, the cohesiveness given by syntactical and lexical relations proves insufficient to produce unity. Michael Hoey has illustrated this point by a game which he describes as follows:

Person *A* is given a sentence to which he or she has to append another sentence which must follow naturally from the first. Person *A* then folds over the original sentence so that it can no longer be seen and passes his or her sentence to person *B* who likewise must add a coherent following sentence to it. *B* folds *A*'s sentence out of sight and passes his or her own to person *C* and thus the game carries on for as long as is wished. (7.)

Here is Hoey's example of an outcome:

(1) It needs scarcely be said, that an Epitaph presupposes a Monument, upon which it is to be engraven. (2) It is very rare to find a monument on which there is no epitaph. (3) Usually there is some hackneyed phrase or other put on by the family of the deceased. (4) In this case though the deceased would have been proud of the epitaph written on the tombstone. (5) He would even have chosen it for himself. (6) Why then didn't she appreciate it? (8.)

As this constructed text reminds us, cohesiveness is not a matter of the mere linking of sentence to sentence: larger patterns of expectation must be satisfied. That is, cohesiveness is violated by sentence (4) because though there the repetition of 'deceased' and substitution of 'epitaph' for 'some hackneyed phrase or other' links the two sentences, there is no reference for the 'this' of 'In this case'. Nor is there any reference for 'she' in sentence (6). But our sense of confusion in these sentences goes beyond such problems, which could after all be solved by substituting 'In the case I have in mind' for 'In this case' and 'he' for 'she' in the last sentence. Rewritten so, we would still find sentence (2) extraneous and sentences (4) and (6) in conflict.

Coherence—the word most generally used to describe the larger unity to which cohesiveness contributes—requires a consistent pattern of thought. Because it depends both on certain conventional patterns *and* on specific knowledge, analysis of what are acceptable and unacceptable collocations of sentences is in fact more complicated than the categorization of modes of cohesiveness. Thus various of the most minimal kinds of knowledge determine the pronoun subject of a main clause we will choose as the most coherent in each of the following sentences.

> When Barbara stepped on the cat's tail, she yowled.
>
> When Barbara stepped on the cat's tail, she screamed.
>
> When Barbara stepped on the cat's tail, she yowled and he ran out of the door.
>
> When Barbara stepped on the cat's tail, they both screamed.
>
> When Barbara stepped on the cat's tail, they both screamed to be careful.

Let us take another example from Hoey:

> I beat off the attack. I opened fire. I saw the enemy approaching. I was on sentry duty. (36.)

Here the sequence is anomalous because the order of events appears to be reversed. Our expectation that in the absence of some indication to the contrary events will be presented in the order in which they occurred joins with our knowledge that a soldier normally fires *after* seeing the enemy and that the firing should occur *before* the attack is beaten off tells us that the sequence is deviant. Hoey discusses two other major patterns, 'problem-solution' and 'general-particular'; there are clearly many others. We not only expect to meet events in a certain order (or in standardized forms of deviation therefrom) but we expect effects to have causes and actions to have goals. Answers presuppose questions; the concept of death presupposes life.

Discourse requires, then, cohesiveness more comprehensive than a mere linking from sentence to sentence, and internal coherence in which the content of the sentences which make up the discourse is related according to patterns of organization and facts of experience that are conventional or at least deducible. But internal coherence is in fact inseparable from intelligible relationships to external patterns of organization and sets of experientially understood relationships.

Obvious as the sources of unity in a discourse seem, one point of importance is how quickly an examination of the sources of cohesiveness leads to larger questions of coherence which demand attention to the meaning of a particular discourse, not simply to the dictionary meanings of the words that make it up. Those in turn soon lead to consideration of the total context of a discourse. The resulting field of investigation, which began to develop only in the 1970s and 80s, is generally called discourse analysis. Malcolm Coulthard comments forcefully that earlier in the century while linguists and grammarians were pursuing a generalized concept of linguistic competence, 'the timebomb of *meaning* was ticking away' and cites the novelty in 1972 of Robin Lakoff's argument that 'in order to predict correctly the applicability of many rules one must be able to refer to the assumptions about the social context of an utterance, as well as to other implicit assumptions made by the participants in a discourse' (3).

Teun van Dijk and Walter Kintsch propose in *Strategies of Discourse Comprehension* 'to sketch the way knowledge is used in discourse comprehension' on the assumption 'that a verbal input is decoded into a list of atomic propositions which are organized into larger units on the basis of some knowledge structure to form a coherent text base' (ix–x). Their model of the way in which the mind 'decodes' language is heavily indebted to computer analogies: the 'buffers', 'searches', and kinds of 'memory' met in their pages differ little from those found in a computer manual. (One does well to remember that such a use of 'memory' represents a double figurative movement: first the word for a very complex mental phenomenon is figuratively applied to electronic storage; that figurative use is then reapplied to those mental processes that can be more or less replicated by electronic means.) But whether or not one accepts the details of their model, van Dijk and Kintsch are persuasive that the understanding of language is dependent on—and here I am condensing and summarizing—presupposed knowledge and a process that is interactional, situational, and strategic. By knowledge presupposed in discourse van Dijk and Kintsch refer to what others call 'background' or 'collective' knowledge—the general knowledge that is necessary to any understanding. 'He wrecked the car' calls up an enormous amount of knowledge of possible situations and consequences. By 'interactional' is meant that interpreters assume intentions and purposes and the use of cultural conventions in the utterers of discourse. By 'situational' is meant that the situation in which the discourse occurs is always taken into consideration by the hearer or reader. By 'strategic' is meant that understanding does not occur through rule-governed algorithms, but by means of tentative interpretations that are matched and rematched against experiential knowledge, the situation itself, and assumptions about the purposiveness and intentions of discourse.

Gillian Brown and George Yule similarly announce in the Preface to their *Discourse Analysis*: 'We have insisted that it is people who communicate and people who interpret. It is speakers/writers who have topics, presuppositions, who assign information structure and who make reference. It is hearers/readers who interpret and draw inferences.' (ix.) Despite terminological differences (Brown and Yule's 'presuppositional pool' includes not only general or collective knowledge assumed in a discourse but knowledge of the situational context and, at any given point, all that has gone before in a conversation or written discourse), they share the view that interpretation consists of processes by which the meaning intended by the speaker/writer is reconstructed. Their discussion of the difficulties of formulating in any explicit model ('frames', 'scenarios', 'scripts', 'schemata') the way in which the mind relates the discourse it is interpreting to stored knowledge suggests again the strategic, trial-and-error, tentative nature of the process.

At this stage in the development of discourse theory, competing models and vocabularies make it difficult to transfer the insights found there to other fields of endeavour. There are, for instance, disagreements about so central a matter as the processing of a reference which is both anaphoric (previously mentioned in a text) and exophoric (to be identified with something existing outside the text). However, the wider principles to which investigators in the field have come to adhere mesh very well with the cardinal principles of speech-act theory: that interpretation requires the assumption of (1) knowledge, both immediate and general, shared between the formulator of the discourse and the interpreter, (2) that the formulator intends a meaning that is to be understood within that shared context, and (3) that the pursuit of coherence (consonance) is essential to the pursuit of meaning. Phrased by van Dijk and Kintsch in their particular terminology:

Hence, the major task for a speaker is the construction of such a macrostructure as a semantic discourse *plan*, composed of elements from general knowledge and, especially, from elements of the situation model (including a model of the hearer—and his or her knowledge, motivations, past actions, and intentions—and of the communicative context). With this macroplan, the next main task is to strategically execute, at the local and linear level, the textbase, choosing between explicit and implicit information, establishing but also signalling local coherence, and finally formulating surface structures with the various semantic, pragmatic, and contextual data as controlling input. (17.)

Let us look at a few simple examples in the light of the two theoretical approaches. Coulthard offers the following as examples of brief dialogue:

A: Can you go to Edinburgh tomorrow?
B: Yes, I can.

and

A: Can you go to Edinburgh tomorrow?
B: B. E. A. pilots are on strike. (10.)

He describes both as coherent, but only the first as cohesive. From the point of view of a speech-act theorist, the first answer is direct, while the second is an example of implicature. But whatever framework we choose, it is obvious that in the second case the interpreter must make use of collective or background knowledge. Discourse analysis does, however, suggest that the line between direct and implicative utterances is a matter of degree. The following example of coherence without formal cohesiveness is taken from Brown and Yule:

It was dark and stormy night the millionaire was murdered. The killer left no clues for the police to trace. (258.)

Here also our knowledge that murders require killers produces coherence without grammatical or true lexical cohesiveness, but no one would be likely to think of the sentences as related by implicature.

Now neither speech-act theory nor analyses of the mechanisms of coherence or cohesiveness directly explain how we recognize functional ambiguity. Our expectations of 'coherence' and 'tellability' (that is, that discourse will be of interest) lead us to recognize puns in jokes:

> ST PETER: 'How did you get here?'
> NEW ARRIVAL IN HEAVEN: 'Flu.'

But how does one recognize double and triple meanings in poetry? For instance, consider the single word 'altered' in stanza 4 of Emily Dickinson's 'These are the days when Birds come back'.

> These are the days when birds come back,
> A very few, a bird or two,
> To take a backward look.
>
> These are the days when skies put on
> The old, old sophistries of June, —
> A blue and gold mistake.
>
> Oh, fraud that cannot cheat the bee.
> Almost thy plausibility
> Induces my belief,
>
> Till ranks of seeds their witness bear,
> And softly through the altered air
> Hurries a timid leaf!
>
> Oh, sacrament of summer days,
> Oh, last communion in the haze,
> Permit a child to join,
>
> Thy sacred emblems to partake
> Thy consecrated bread to break
> Taste thine immortal wine!

Why, in reading a poem about the last fine days of late summer or early autumn, do we recognize that 'altered' carries a sense of 'sanctuary-like' as well as 'changed'? We are guided by our knowledge of the conventions of poetry which counsel us to look for ambiguities that will intertwine the meanings of various words and thoughts and to attempt to link juxtaposed concepts and contexts as fully as possible. Thus reading stanza 4 in the light of the references to 'Sacrament' and 'Communion' in 5 and 6, we retrospectively recognize that 'altered' may work in two ways and thus bridge the external atmosphere and internal mood.

At this point we must consider a quite reasonable objection to the assumption that sentential interests build towards larger purposes related to an overall project. Can one in fact assume that every sentence an author pens, or, even less likely, that a speaker utters, springs from a conscious awareness of its relationship to larger intentions at the level of purpose or project? Intuitively the assumption appears exaggerated. One defence is available in Husserl's formulation of 'intentionality', which holds that consciousness itself is always directed towards an object, is always indeed consciousness of something in relation to something else (see, for instance, the Second Meditation, sects. 19 and 20, pp. 44–9). However, given the philosophical debate over the precise meaning of the very concept of intentionality, for the purposes of literary theory one may well wish a humbler approach. Here another of Altieri's distinctions is useful, that between a *calculated purpose* and the *generally purposive*. We may well hesitate to impute calculated purpose to every sentence a young man utters to his beloved, or a new acquaintance throws out in cocktail-party conversation, or an author includes in a 500-page novel; but in each case we assume every sentence to be 'purposive', to some extent to contribute to, and not clash with, an overall purpose.

Kenneth Burke offers another way of looking at the purposiveness of discourse. Throughout his career Burke has insisted that for an individual to name something is in itself to interpret that something in terms of the individual's total situation. For Burke, all use of language is in essence a strategic orientation to the situation of the speaker (*PLF* 1, 54, 252–62). Thus Burke's term 'motive' is multifaceted: it designates the situation responded to, the response, and the pattern of experience and cultural context that interact with what would be the bare situation if in fact we could perceive a bare situation. The three are so closely intertwined in our minds that they seem identical. The same interdependence is embodied in Burke's 'dramatistic' recognition that act, scene, agent, agency, and purpose are indissoluble (*GM* vii–xxv). We *must* perceive situations in terms of our purposes and act in terms of strategies whether or not we are aware of doing so.

The process of tracing out the complexity of the individual sentence regarded as an act that we are able to interpret because we act on the presumption that it is purposive has led us to consider the purposiveness of larger units of discourse. But to be sure of our

ground, we must circle back and consider the presumption of intentions and purpose more directly.

4. Intention

My continued reference to an author's intention will have put the
teeth of a considerable number of readers on edge. Despite a variety
of recent arguments that all commentary implicitly or explicitly
recognizes the centrality of the author's intention, four large classes
of objection to any consideration of the intention of an author
continue to exercise influence. The first objection is a version of an
argument we have already met, the assertion that since we think and
communicate by means of a pre-existing system of signs, human
beings cannot intend meanings, but only serve as mouthpieces
through which language disseminates its (ultimately self-
contradictory) meanings. 'I . . . claim to show, not how men think
in myths, but how myths operate in men's minds, without their being
aware of the fact.' (*RC* 12.) It has proved to be a short step from that
well-known pronouncement by Lévi-Strauss to a general view that
language speaks rather than is spoken. That such hyperbolical statements result from speaking of discourse as if it were *langue*, and of
reifying the abstraction that is *langue*, has already been pointed out.
A corollary formulation of the same argument regards each text as a
pastiche of other texts. Roland Barthes thus wrote in 'The Death of
the Author': 'We know now that a text is not a line of words
releasing a single "theological" meaning (the "message" of the
Author-God) but a multi-dimensional space in which a variety of
writings, none of them original, blend and clash.' (146.) This
approach has a more sophisticated ring, but the assumption that the
context of discourse is nothing but other discourse again seals language off from all extralinguistic experience.

A second, related objection denies the possibility of intent by
denying the possibility of creativity. The error here is in thinking of
the relationships of signs in the *langue* as fixed rather than recognizing that the infinity of the possible relationships between signs is
precisely what makes possible novel discourse, and therefore new
configurations of concepts. The flexibility required by discourse is
made possible by the indeterminacy of relations within *langue*.
Though what each of us experiences has been divided up in certain
ways by language before our appearance in the world, and the

words of our language have acquired certain constellations of associations and evaluative connotations that we learn as we acquire them, we constantly effect new divisions between concepts and amend the associations gathered around individual words. Arguments against the flexibility and creativity of language ignore the diachronic aspect of both *langue* and discourse. The very fact that words are mutually defining makes it possible for the introduction of words expressing different divisions of reality to effect changes across the whole language.

Parole can be creative because it is purposive. Kenneth Burke explained long ago that the source of the creativity that makes it possible for an individual to see advantages in the readjustment of the boundaries between signifieds or the alternation of the associations surrounding certain concepts is in fact our purposiveness (*PLF* 1, 18). To repeat, since we understand events in terms of our own desires, needs, and orientations, we understand them strategically from the beginning. Our very understanding is immediately purposive. Our strategic use of language is simply a reflection of our strategic mode of assimilating events.

The third objection is essentially the New Critical fear of the intentional fallacy as enunciated by Wimsatt and Beardsley. The argument of that essay, supported by the general New Critical effort to free interpretation from literary-historical and biographical excrescences, led a whole generation of critics who felt they had to tiptoe delicately and apologetically around any suggestion that they were interested in the author's intention. However, the essay itself denies neither that texts have authors, that authors have intentions, nor that we should be interested in those intentions. All it demands is that an author's announced intent, or presumed attitude at the time of the production of the text, or usual practices and attitudes, should not be confused with the intent actually expressed by a given text. Anyone who troubles to read the major New Critics—Brooks, R. P. Warren, Blackmur, Tate, Ransom, Wimsatt himself—will find that they constantly and unselfconsciously speak of authors' intentions as textually embodied. One finds in Brooks's *The Well Wrought Urn* such locutions as 'Shakespeare has pointed up the basic motivation very carefully' (40) and 'I think we shall have to agree there is method in Wordsworth's paradoxes: he is trying to state with some sensitiveness the relation between two modes of perception . . .' (133).

Post-structuralists have their own way of declaring interest in intention to be a fallacy. There is an intriguing cleverness in Derrida's dismissal of the possible 'presence' of the author in a text (as for example in the rhetorical flummery of the attact on John Searle in 'Limited Inc a b c . . .'). But Derrida's dismissal of the author (whose absence from the text is paradoxically said to be guaranteed by his signature at the end of it, in 'Signature Event Context') bears not at all on the possibility of probabilistic inter-pretation of the author's intent. Of course authors are not present in texts, but all sorts of clues as to their intentions are. To anticipate a further objection, let us admit that those clues are not 'present' in the text until interpreted *as* clues; nevertheless, shared strategies of interpretation define what are to be regarded as clues and thus link authors' intents with readers' understanding. To try to regard a text as embodying no authorial intent requires us to regard it as having no author at all—which we can pretend to do in the same way that we can talk about a painting as a natural object if we wish—but we know always that in doing so we are engaged in pretence. Our knowledge that it *is* a pretence is what gives the manœuvre interest.

Post-structuralist attempts to avoid explicit recognition of the existence of the author lead in fact to stylistic peculiarities that are transparent in their circumlocutionary endeavours. Mary Louise Pratt has commented perceptively that the attempt to disguise 'all notions of intention, perception, and value' has produced 'a grammarian's goldmine of agentless passives, statives, reflexives, and attributives' (74). The major argument of the present chapter is that Wimsatt and Beardsley were right though they insufficiently emphasized that the final authority for *interpretation* was the text *as understood in the set of contexts in which the author assumed it would be read*. As Ricœur has commented, the intentional fallacy has as its complement 'the fallacy of the absolute text', that is, the belief that there can be a contextless text (*I T* 30).

Have we not then entered on an infinite regress? How are readers to know what set of contexts will allow them to understand the text as the author intended? *The very possibility of understanding dis-course depends on the user being able to calculate what the audience knows or is aware of and what attitudes it holds, and further to assume that the audience will be aware that such calculations have occurred and such assumptions have been made.* For its part, the audience assumes not only that the author made assumptions about its knowledge, awareness, and attitudes, but attempted to compensate within the text itself for anticipated deficiencies in knowledge, awareness, or attitudes. What an audience does not know it can be told, and it can at least be made aware that others hold attitudes it may not share. Two points must be made here though I repeat them elsewhere. First, such a reconstruction can only be probabilistic: after all, the audience is required to make assumptions about the author's assumptions and reconstruct the strategy on which the discourse was originally constructed. Second, the process in which the audience makes assumptions about the assumptions the author made about the audience, including the author's assumptions about the audience's assumptions, does produce a circularity—this is part of why interpretation can never be more than probable—but it does not necessarily lead to a tautological deadlock, for reasons that I hope will become evident by the final chapter.

The fourth objection to considering authorial intention must be stated in two parts: (a) though authors may think they know what they intend, their thought and language are at the mercy of socio-economic, or psychological, or metaphysical shaping forces that cause them to mean quite other than what they intend, and (b) because of their blindness, what authors intend is of far less interest than the operation of external forces as revealed in their work. I have divided the position into two statements because while (b) in many cases is true, (a) engenders confusion by playing on the word 'means'. 'To mean' can mean in sense$_1$ 'in accordance with dictionary definitions', or sense$_2$ 'to intend', or in sense$_3$ 'to be explained by' ('smoke means fire' or 'shooting down the plane will mean war'). Meaning$_3$ (explanation) is usually achieved by establishing a cause-and-effect relationship—in either direction. These three senses of 'meaning' will be found to correspond reasonably well with those developed by C. S. Peirce: the meaning that makes any communication possible, the meaning intended, and meaning as the consequence or cause of use (viii. 176). They may also be usefully compared with Grice's distinctions between timeless meaning, non-natural occasional meaning, and natural meaning in 'Utterer's Meaning, Sentence-Meaning, and Word-Meaning'.

We can of course mean by 'mean' an understanding of why the author thought what he or she thought and intended what he or she intended. We can, that is, ask the sense$_3$ of the author's meaning. If we ask *that* question, we may discover authorial assumptions that are interesting enough in their own right, but not relevant to sense$_2$. Thus we may find that H. G. Wells meant$_2$ that the world would be better if relations between the sexes were a great deal freer. We may also argue that the meaning$_3$ of Wells's arguments for free love was that he wanted to indulge his own sexual appetite promiscuously. But we ought not to confuse the different questions that produce the two findings. This is not of course a novel distinction. R. S. Crane for instance put it forward clearly in his essay 'History versus Criticism' (1934):

It is important to distinguish clearly between the two meanings of 'understand'—between the meaning in which to understand is equivalent to knowing *why* an author said what he said (in a genetic and historical sense) and that in which it is equivalent to knowing *what* it is that he is saying and his reason for saying it (in the sense of its artistic rationale).   (ii. 16.)

3

The Contexts of Meaning and the Contexts of Significance

1. Intrinsic and Extrinsic Commentary

We have now arrived, by a circuitous route, at a distinction that lies at the heart of our theory of interpretation, that between meaning and significance to which E.D. Hirsch gave currency twenty years ago. 'Meaning' (sense$_2$) is defined by Hirsch as 'whatever someone has willed to convey by a particular sequence of linguistic signs and which can be conveyed (shared) by means of those linguistic signs' (*VI* 3). That is, meaning occurs when someone employs signs that will convey that meaning. That of course is tautological enough; the question is how the user *can* choose signs that will be interpreted by the hearer as intended. The detailed way in which that is possible is the primary burden of Chapters 4 and 5, but I trust I have made evident that expression and interpretation of intended meaning is dependent on shared contexts.

'Significance', on the other hand, denotes the recognition of relationships between the text and external schema. As I have stated it, this begs the question of what schema are external to the text, or, more accurately, to intended meaning. One way of making this distinction is by redrawing the lines between 'extrinsic' and 'intrinsic' commentary as set forth in Wellek and Warren's *Theory of Literature* (1949), the book which consolidated the explicit principles (though misrepresented the actual practice) of the New Critics and exerted major influence on a generation of graduate students.

'Intrinsic criticism' was assumed not to go outside the 'autonomous' text, paying no attention to anything beyond relationships between the author's choices of words, images, figures of speech, and sequence of presentation. Helen Gardner irritatedly gave her opinion of what certain critics were doing:

The work of art has been treated as autonomous and self-explanatory, and the pure critic has tried to concern himself with the poem as it can be explained purely in terms of itself and himself. Loosed from its moorings in place and time, the poem is conceived as floating like a balloon, with the critic caught up to meet it in the clouds.   (18.)

But as we have seen, the very choice of dictionary meanings, the emotional concomitants and clustering of related words that make possible the meaning of a given word in the context of the work, depend on our experiences beyond the given text. The much more useful distinction is between contexts the author could have assumed the anticipated audience would be able to bring to bear and those which he or she could not. Examination of New Critical explications, close readings, or elucidations (whichever term one prefers) will demonstrate that in fact New Critics constantly resorted to extra-textual experience. However, their failure explicitly to recognize what they were doing, and state the grounds on which such activity was legitimate, led to the kinds of excesses of ingenuity and tedious promulgation of minutiae which began increasingly to discredit the New Critical endeavour. It encouraged the sort of activity criticized by T. S. Eliot in *On Poetry and Poets*: 'The method is to take a well-known poem . . . without reference to the author or to his other works, analyse it stanza by stanza and line by line, and extract, squeeze, tease, press every drop of meaning out of it that one can. It might be called the lemon-squeezer school of criticism.' (113.)

'Extrinsic criticism' for Wellek and Warren is the application of all information about the author of the text, the cultural milieu in which it was written, or its relation to literary history, psychology, philosophy, or sociology. Obviously again, their distinction does not cut along the same line as that between what the author could have assumed about his audience's knowledge and what he could not. An author may well assume some biographical knowledge, some knowledge of the surrounding circumstances under which a text was written, certain literary-historical knowledge, and some highly specific cultural knowledge.

I propose then that the 'intrinsic'/'extrinsic' distinction be realigned to make it congruent with E. D. Hirsch's discrimination between meaning and significance. I further propose to follow Hirsch in calling the pursuit of significance 'criticism' and in using 'commentary' as the blanket term for discussion of either meaning or significance. Unfortunately, however, I have found it best to deviate from his terminology in one major respect. Hirsch distinguishes between 'understanding' as the construction of the author's intended meaning and 'interpretation' as the explanation of that meaning to others (*VI* 133 ff.) Though this is a convenient distinction, 'interpretation' is used so generally by other theorists of discourse to designate the process of constructing meaning that I have adopted that use here and rely on the ordinary term 'explanation' to express the explication of interpreted meaning to other people. Thus interpretation = intrinsic commentary = arriving at as full an understanding of an author's meaning as possible. Criticism = extrinsic commentary = relating a text to external schema of explanation or evaluation.

This distinction between meaning and significance can be usefully compared with H.P. Grice's between non-natural and natural meaning. In his terminology non-natural meaning is represented by a situation in which '*A* intended the utterance of x to produce some effect in an audience by means of the recognition of this intention' while natural meaning corresponds to the recognition of cause-and-effect relationships as in 'Those spots mean measles.' (M 377, 385.)

It may be helpful to relate the meaning/significance distinction to the argument of a book I very much admire and nevertheless will have to argue with at several points: Barbara Herrnstein Smith's *On the Margins of Discourse* (1978). Smith has explicitly disagreed with Hirsch. 'All users of language', she writes, 'are ethically governed not by the author's intention but by the conventions of the linguistic community.' (135.) Precisely, but those conventions are largely reducible to the audience's recognition that, in Smith's own words elsewhere in the volume, 'The poet, in composing the poem, will have made certain assumptions regarding his audience, specifically that they are members of a shared linguistic and cultural community, and thus able and willing to abide by relevant linguistic, cultural, and indeed literary conventions.' (37.) By responding to the conventions the author presumed, the audience is interpreting the author's intentions. Smith's view leads to a contrast between meaning and intention as she uses those terms. The essence of that view appears when she criticizes Hirsch for not recognizing that '*although the intentions of all authors are historically determinate, the meanings of all utterances are not*' (137, her italics). By saying that intentions are 'historically determinate', she appears to mean not that the intentions are necessary *determinable*, but rather that they can be interpreted and debated in the light of historical evidence in a way

that 'meanings' (in her sense) cannot. Those utterances whose meanings are historically indeterminate she assigns to the category of
'fictive' as opposed to 'natural', that is, they are *representations* of
natural utterances (examples: poems, novels, proverbs, greetings
card messages) which, she believes, are not acts within the historical
universe. The disabilities of dichotomising discourse in this way will
be a matter for later consideration, but in general her 'intentions'
correspond well enough with 'meaning' as I am using it and her
'meaning' with 'significance'. She however appears to restrict her
'meaning' (my 'significance') to fictive discourse, while I argue that
all discourse offers both intended meaning (propositions, illocutions,
perlocutionary intent—all of which are part of the author's purpose)
and significance (the audience's use of the discourse or its perlocutionary effect in the broadest sense).

A fertile source of misunderstanding must be addressed right
away. In the order of time, interpretation comes first: we can hardly
relate to anything else that which we have not yet grasped as an
object. However, it would be folly not to recognize that our interest
in a text depends primarily on significance, especially when it is
recognized that *all* evaluation falls into the realm of significance.
Though they cannot avoid interpretation, readers have many purposes beyond it. Whether one judges Milton a misogynist, or of the
devil's party, or a mere weaver of verbal tapestries, or a magnificent
spokesman for a Christian understanding of the world; whether one
sees Johnson as an unusually wise and perceptive commentator on
life or a perpetually uneasy soul whistling in the dark; whether one
sees Arnold as a failed poet, a prophet whom we have ignored to our
peril, or a spokesman for an intellectually effete and socio-econom-
ically selfish class, one begins with interpretation of meaning and
proceeds to evaluation by external schema—Christian, Marxist,
Freudian, Nietzschean, prosodical, rhetorical, metaphysical.
Though extrinsic, such judgements are just the ones that give
interest and importance to literature. (This point is developed in
Chapter 6.)

Readers may well have felt a considerable degree of *déjà vu* while
reading the preceding pages in this chapter. The great issue between
the traditional scholars and the new generation of critics between
about 1940 and 1955 was whether the meaning of a text was
restricted to the way in which it would have been understood by the

author and the contemporary audience. (An excellent discussion of this issue appears in Gerald Graff's *Professing Literature, an Institutional History*.) To take celebrated instances, Rosamund Tuve's *Elizabethan and Metaphysical Imagery* (1947) challenged New Critical interpretations of 16th- and 17th-century poetry and J. V. Cunningham's *Woe or Wonder* (1951) took on the confusion between original and modern meaning as for instance in Robert Heilman's reading of *King Lear*. Heilman's discussion, said Cunningham, yields 'a meaning that I can enter into quite as deeply as anyone, but it is not what Shakespeare meant' (8). The conflict died away through a series of compromises rather than any true resolution, partly because the question was conceived in terms of whether 'meanings' could change or not. The distinction between meaning and significance cuts through much confusion here. A second source of confusion was the vague way in which literary scholarship was defined. The question dividing Frederick Bateson and F. R. Leavis in their 1953 debate in *Essays in Criticism* and *Scrutiny* was, one can now see, the manner and degree to which literature-related scholarship—the recovery of biographical, historical, cultural, bibliographical, and linguistic facts—was relevant to understanding a literary work.

As I trust will become clear in Chapters 3 and 4, the answer follows easily enough from our basic distinction: insofar as one is interested in the author's intended meaning, some of it is, some of it is not. A third confusion arising from the inclusion of very different activities under the rubric 'meaning' is reflected in such essays as W. R. Keast's 'Imagery and Meaning in the Interpretation of *King Lear*' (1949) and R. S. Crane's fine 'Critical Inquiry: or, the Perils of the "High Priori" Road' (1967) which deplore the critics' tendency to impose their own schemes of analysis and evaluation. Keast comments on Heilman's *This Great Stage: Image and Structure in King Lear*, 'the primary source and guaranty of the symbolic values that he attaches to elements of the play are not in Professor Heilman's inductions from the evidence of the text, but in the necessities of his own theories of tragedy and morality' (48). Keast found these—and indeed Heilman's central assumption that the play is meant to be read symbolically—arbitrary. Our terms allow us to say rather that much of what Heilman does in *This Great Stage* belongs to the realm of significance, not meaning.

2. *The Principles of Consonance*

By what criteria then does the reader select which elements of what possible contexts the author assumed to be operational? What knowledge, awareness, and attitudes did a particular author presume the reader could draw upon in resolving apparent anomalies and pursuing locutionary implicatures in a specific text? The fact is that readers can never be sure that they have not ignored an element of context that the author assumed they would take into consideration, or that they are not importing an element of context that the author had not taken into calculation. The only criteria for determining probably applicable contexts are that currently much-derided quality of consistency and the even more suspicious quality of unity. Both can be subsumed under *consonance*. At the level of the sentence we have already met this criterion in the form of Grice's Co-operative Principle. As we move from sentence to sentence, the incorporation of each sentence into the discourse of which it is a part, the process that Dillon and most analysts of discourse describe simply as 'comprehension', proceeds on the same presumption of co-operation, pertinence, or consonance. The process includes constant revision and accommodation; previous acts of comprehension must be continually revised so that they become consistent with new information while assigning a meaning to the newest sentence that will be consistent with the discourse to that point.

There are other ways of describing the process. On the level of the work as a whole Hirsch sees interpretation as a process of narrowing down the class to which a work belongs. 'Anything we can do to narrow the class, such as determining authorship, date, tradition, and so on, will decrease the doubtfulness of our probability judgement—that is, increase its likelihood of being true.' (*VI* 179.) In more philosophical terms, we can also regard each sentence, and each unit of ascending size in the structure of the work, as a class that we wish to narrow to a 'type' that fits the individual 'token' as closely as possible.

Recent years have seen a variety of attacks on the assumption of the consonance of literary works. These have been useful insofar as they have reminded the critical fraternity generally that (1) it is difficult indeed to show that the unity we expect in a literary work is the reflection of a deep structure or a metaphysical principle of reality, (2) that the more complex a work, the more likely it is that the reader will find arguments, or actions, or statements that cannot without exorbitant ingenuity be assimilated into a unified, wholly consistent pattern, and (3) that it is always possible for one who chooses to search for inconsistency, contradiction, and aporia to demonstrate its existence. We are thus efficaciously reminded that the assumption of the consonance of any utterance, from a single sentence to *Paradise Lost*, is in fact an *assumption* or *expectation*. Authors expect readers to interpret their works by searching for consonance and readers expect authors to expect them to do so. That consonance is never perfect is no more an argument against its use as a principle of interpretation than would be the contention that maps are pernicious because they can never be totally accurate or include all the possible landmarks. That one can find examples of literary works that exploit the expectation of consonance by constantly undercutting it is no more an argument against the existence of the assumption than the fact that many sentences violate the Co-operative Principle (thereby achieving implicature) is an argument against the existence of the CP.

Critics of a wide variety of critical persuasions have recognized that readers will always seek some explanation for the total pattern of a work, or indeed of any set of words that they believe to be intended as a connected utterance. In the *Philosophy of Rhetoric* (1936), Richards enunciates the principle that 'The mind will always try to find connections and will be guided in its search by the rest of the utterance and its occasion' (126). Michael Stubbs writes in *Discourse Analysis* (1983), 'however odd the utterance, hearers will do their utmost to make sense of the language they hear, by bringing to bear on it all possible knowledge and interpretation' (5). Jonathan Culler, who devotes four chapters of *Structuralist Poetics* (1975) to the conventions through which literary texts are 'recuperated' or 'naturalized', that is, understood as communicating something, points out that if all else fails, anything anomalous in a novel will be referred to the narrator's 'cast of mind'. Thus, 'The most incoherent text could be explained by assuming it is the speech of a delirious narrator' (200). As Frank Kermode's *The Sense of an Ending* (1967) insists throughout, if nothing else will do, a work found to be impenetrably chaotic will be regarded as intended to convey impenetrable chaos.

This is not to say that a reader will necessarily find total consistency or unity in literary or any other discourse. In the process of employing consonance as a criterion for interpretation, readers may well conclude that a discourse is flawed through incompetence, carelessness, or the intellectual disorder of the author. One ought to remain open to persuasion that a unified interpretation is possible, but one will not necessarily be so persuaded. The author's intentions may have been muddled or the intended meaning may not have been adequately conveyed. Nor is consonance an overriding *evaluative* criterion as well as an interpretive one. A wholly self-consistent and unified discourse may be trivial, trite, or just simple-minded, while one which does not fully cohere may have qualities that give great aesthetic delight or intellectual stimulation. The frequent view that the more disparate the concepts or attitudes somehow brought into harmony in a work, the more important the work is likely to be (to which I, within limits, also subscribe) is an evaluative criterion, not an interpretive principle.

It may be well to repeat here that our search for an essential consistency in texts as utterances can claim no metaphysical validation nor ultimate compelling sanction. One can always consciously choose *not* to see it, just as one can consciously choose to construct an utterance in such a way as to create maximum frustration in the interpreter who seeks a consistent intention (leading generally to the attribution of that most minimal of meanings, a demonstration of the meaninglessness of life). We seek a consistent interpretation because we assume that we and the author share certain assumptions about the communication of meaning, the kind of assumptions that Grice sums up in the concept of the Co-operative Principle. John Reichert has written, 'Who among us . . . whatever the object of interpretation, would choose one hypothesis over another on the ground of its greater inconsistency, or on the grounds of its accounting for fewer of the facts that we want to explain, or on the grounds of its being unnecessarily complicated?' (MSI 748.) To choose one's hypothesis on those bases would be to engage in something other than interpretation.

In challenging E. D. Hirsch's statement of such an imperative, Barbara Herrnstein Smith wittily observes that '. . . it is just as well for all of us that the vitality and effectiveness of language do not depend on anything so vagrant as the moral rectitude of any of us'. (135.) But the first portion of the same sentence reads, 'We graciously serve others as instruments because, in doing so, we contribute to, and preserve, the network of social assumptions that permits us to use *them* as instruments . . .' Earlier she has argued that at least in natural discourse the violation of the conventions of language by lying or perversely misinterpreting what others say is condemned because it undercuts the usefulness of language (100–1). All language is purposive, all has a perlocutionary intent. Announcing 'I'm hungry' may have a more immediate purpose than writing a sonnet, but in each case the author has an effect in view. One may think of the importance of language as providing the rationale for an ethical principle that is utilitarian rather than categorical in its origin, but there is of course a sense in which respecting intended meaning *is* an ethical consideration.

That all interpretation of the author's intention is probabilistic has been freely admitted. As already noted, we can never be sure that we have not failed to recognize a crucial instance of implicature because we do not possess certain elements of knowledge or awareness that the author expected. Neither can we be sure that we have not been led astray by the hermeneutical circle, our interpretation of one portion of the text producing a construction of the meaning of the whole that then warps our interpretation of other portions. However, this danger can easily be exaggerated. We soon learn that our interpretations must remain tentative at least until we have finished reading a text; we constantly revise our interpretations of earlier portions in the light of later ones. Moreover, few texts fail to exhibit considerable communicative redundancy. Thus the direction in which implicatures are to be resolved is often indicated by *several* elements of the surrounding context, and the proper interpretation of the whole is often implied in several ways so that a misinterpretation at one point in the text will cause later incongruencies that suggest the need for a revision of the provisional interpretation.

A typical instance of localized redundancy is in the opening of Chapter 48 of *Vanity Fair*, 'In Which the Reader is Introduced to the Very Best of Company'. The irony that being received at court improves a woman's reputation is reinforced by and in turn reinforces the satirical commentary on the worthiness of George IV. 'And as dubious goods or letters are passed through an oven at quarantine, sprinkled with vinegar, and pronounced clean, many a lady whose reputation would be doubtful otherwise and liable to give infection, passes through the wholesome ordeal of the Royal Presence, and issues from it free from all taint' intertwines with 'But when we consider that it was the First Gentleman in Europe in whose high presence Mrs. Rawdon took her examination', and 'be it our remarkable boast to our children, that we saw George the Good, the Magnificent, the Great'. A typical instance of cumulative reinforcement in the same novel is found in Thackeray's care that readers not take Amelia's marriage to Dobbin as the conventional happy ending. There are early implicatures as in the chapter 'Am Rhein' in which we hear of their life in Pumpernickel, 'Perhaps it was the happiest time of their lives indeed, if they did but know it—and who does?' The novel's penultimate paragraph carries the same implication: 'Fonder than he is of me,' Emmy thinks, with a sigh. But he never said a word to Amelia that was not kind and gentle. . .'. But as if not certain that that paragraph has done the trick, the narrator adds: 'Which of us has his desire, or, having it, is satisfied?'

3. Literary and Non-literary Discourse

It will have been noted that the schema of interpretation here presented makes no differentiation between literature and other uses of language. Many a theorist over the more than 100 years since Matthew Arnold first confronted the English-speaking world with new questions about the purpose of literature and criticism has felt obliged to begin with a definition of literature that would distinguish it from 'ordinary' or 'scientific' language, or both. From the point of view here presented, such attempts are not only erroneous but set the discussions they introduce on a wrong track. *The cardinal fact is that all uses of language require interpretation, and interpretation is possible only within shared contexts.* Indeed, differences between the interpretation of acts of speech and the interpretation of acts of writing are less than the differences between the interpretation of drama and the essay, or between living-room conversation and political speeches. There are several kinds of somewhat special competencies required for the interpretation of literature, but most can be understood in terms of generic expectations. Even the status of the language used in fiction, a question that has received much recent attention, is explicable in terms of sets of conventions that are acquired, like all other conventions, in the use of language (how conversations are begun and ended, how ingredients are listed in cookbook recipes, how sermons utilize biblical texts). Moreover, the basic conventions appear to be assimilated in parallel fashion with the learning of the language itself; certainly children acquire the concept of 'make-believe' necessary to interpret fiction soon and easily enough.

I. A. Richards's famous distinction between the use of words 'for the sake of the references they promote' and their use 'for the emotions and attitudes which ensue' (*PLC* 267) is the proximate source of the principle that 'scientific' and 'emotive' language belong to disparate realms. However, in attempting to defend the realms of religion and literature against logical positivists like Rudolf Carnap, Richards was in fact only catching at and trying to transvalue what had been a condescending distinction articulated by Carnap: 'Lyrical poets . . . do not try to refute in their poems the statements in a poem by some other lyrical poet; for they know they are in the domain of art and not in the domain of theory.' (79–80.) The situation was in fact very much that which had been played between Arnold and Huxley some forty years earlier. Huxley had written in 1880, 'all our mental furniture—may be classified under one of two heads—as either within the province of the intellect, something that can be put into propositions and affirmed or denied; or as within the province of feeling, or that which, before the name was defiled, was called the aesthetic side of our nature' (174–5). Arnold quarrelled with Huxley's essay, but compare the opening of his 'Literature and Science' (1882), which contrasts science, lying 'in the sphere of intellect and knowledge', with knowledge put into relation 'with our sense of conduct, our sense for beauty, and touched with emotion by being so put' (x. 64–5).

Richards's unfortunate distinction between the statements of science, which are to be evaluated as true or false, and the 'pseudo-statements' of literature, which are neither but somehow part of an autonomous realm inaccessible to processes of validation, gave occupation to critics for a third of a century. The difficulties which closed round the attempt to give literature an autonomous existence outside scientific uses of language were recognized only slowly but finally became decisive. Only by sleight of hand could statements to which judgements of truth were inapplicable be shown to give more insight into human life than those whose claims to truth were presumably open to empirical investigation. Moreover, it was soon recognized that neither the subject matter, nor the literality, nor the degree of seriousness with which an author appears to invest a discourse is a useful criterion for determining whether it is 'literary'. Plato's vision of the truths beyond empirical experience, Coleridge's attempts to grasp the principles by which the human mind works, Newman's defence of his moral and intellectual integrity, Arnold's attempt to save all that he felt was still salient in Christianity, and indeed the Bible itself, arguably belong to literature. More recently we have become aware that our ordinary conversation is filled with anecdotes, narratives, and brief essay-like reflections on our experience, each of which is ruled by conventions very much like those we associate with literary works. As Mary Louise Pratt has used the work of William Labov to remind us, relatively uneducated youths shape narratives of their own experiences to respond to understood expectations; here again structure is determined by genre.

Richards himself appears to have become rather quickly convinced of the untenability of the ground he had occupied; unfortunately his fellow-soldiers failed to notice when he quietly abandoned the position. In essence *The Philosophy of Rhetoric* (1936) marks a new beginning in his thought about language; from that point he avoids dichotomizing referential and emotive language. Meaning, he found, is dependent on the context created within the discourse itself, the contexts with which we habitually associate the words chosen, and the context in which the language is used. Meanings of words in short become 'resultants which we arrive at only through the interplay of the interpretative possibilities of the whole utterance'. (*PR* 55.) Similarly, though the Russian Formalists of the 1920s directed a major part of their attention to the question of what made literature 'literary', Tynianov himself subsequently found it necessary to abandon the absolute distinction.

I have already referred to Barbara Herrnstein Smith's contrasting of 'natural' and 'fictive' utterances. 'A natural utterance', she writes, 'not only occurs *in* a particular set of circumstances—what is often referred to as its *context*—but is also understood as being a response *to* those circumstances.' (16.) On the other hand 'fictive utterances' can only be *representations* of natural utterances because they are not 'historically unique verbal acts or events' (24). In short, for her, 'A fictive utterance consists entirely of a linguistic structure, unlike a natural occurrence, which consists of a linguistic event occurring in a historical context.' (30.) But, as I will urge in the succeeding chapters, *all* discourse occurs in a cluster of historical contexts. The degree to which the various constituents of that cluster are relevant to interpretation depends on the genre of the discourse.

Nevertheless, to deny differences between the reading of literature and the reading of other forms of discourse seems more an exercise in paradox than a useful simplification. As Walter Pater wrote when considering the distinction between prose and poetry (which he went on to minimize): 'Since all progress of mind consists for the most part in differentiation . . . it is surely the stupidest of losses to confuse things which right reason has put asunder, to lose the sense of achieved distinctions . . .' (*A* 5.)

The key to the problem, it has turned out, is not through the elucidation of an unchanging essence that distinguishes literature from non-literature, but in the recognition of our capacity to read texts as either literary or not and the capacity of texts to suggest the appropriate reading. Louise Rosenblatt's *The Reader, The Text, The Poem* (1978) cogently develops this distinction between modes of reading rather than kinds of discourse. The mode of reading she calls 'efferent' is focused on the acquisition of information to be carried away from the text; 'aesthetic' reading has as its primary concern 'what happens *during* the actual reading'. Rosenblatt goes on to say that 'In aesthetic reading, the reader's attention is centered directly on what he is living through during his relation with that particular text.' (25.) That may sound as though the reader somehow becomes the thrall of the text, but Rosenblatt in fact stresses the *activity* of the reader's mind. Words she quotes from Coleridge will clarify what she means: 'The reader should be carried forward, not merely or chiefly by the mechanical impulse of curiosity, or by a restless desire to arrive at the final solution; but by the pleasurable activity of the mind excited by the attractions of the journey itself.' (28.) What then are those attractions? Our own experience in reading testifies to their variety and independence one from another. We may respond to intriguing relations between words, or between the sounds of words and the concepts they convey, or between concepts, or between events. (Roman Jakobson's 'Linguistics and Poetics' is especially impressive with regard to responses to the sounds of language.) While an attempt to delineate the sources of the pleasure we take in the propositional stratum of discourse can be no part of the present outline, they are very likely pretty much those by which Dr. Johnson defined 'wit': that 'which is at once natural and new, that which, though not obvious, is, upon its first production, acknowledged to be just' and that 'which he that never found it, wonders how he missed.' In other words a degree of freshness must be conjoined with a degree of congruence with our experience. Barbara

Herrnstein Smith stated the principle in a somewhat more sweeping manner: 'It would seem, then, that the optimal conditions for engaging in gratifying cognitive activity are characterized by, among other things, a combination—either a balance or a particular ratio—of novelty and familiarity, repetition and variation, conformity and disparity, redundancy and information.' (118.)

Rosenblatt's thesis that what distinguishes literature from all other discourse is that the first is read aesthetically and the second efferently must not be understood simplistically. Though in theory any text can be read either way, obviously some texts will be much more rewarding read in one way and some in the other. Most indeed are to some extent read both ways at once. Thus while I am happy to recognize the support to be found in Genette's statement that 'any text may or may not be literature, according to whether it is received (either) as spectacle or (else) as message' (*FLD* 4), it cannot be correct to say that a text must be received as one or the other, and there is some danger in reducing what Genette calls the 'literary function' to 'spectacle'.

The interactional nature of the relationship between reader and text that emerges is called 'transactional' by Rosenblatt: as we read a poem the text is the stimulus and guide that allows us to construct a poem—though it is always possible to read even a poem efferently. One presumes that having observed that 'Prose is when all the lines except the last go to the end. Poetry is where some fall short of it,' Jeremy Bentham would have recognized a poem when he saw one, but he seems never to have read one other than efferently, that is, as a non-poem.

And what about a text entitled 'An Ode' that has the look of a poem but has never sustained a reader's interest long enough to be read aesthetically? Or a discursive prose argument—let's say Carlyle on the 'Condition of England' question of 1843—now read almost exclusively aesthetically though intended efferently? Readers try to read works that appear to them to belong to 'literary' genres aesthetically, that is, to find pleasure in the journey through them though in the limiting case they may find none at all—in which case unless such texts offer rewards to efferent reading (which is highly unlikely) they will rarely be read by anyone. Texts that readily fall into the genres regarded as literary and that draw us into aesthetic reading pose no problem. Texts that do not appear to belong to the literary genres but which nevertheless entice us into aesthetic reading may enter the ranks of literature even when they have strong claims to efferent reading as well. These texts will be found for the most part in genres that are in effect amphibious: the argumentative essay, the sermon, essays in history or philosophy. All of these seek to be persuasive; all are most so when the freshness of diction, and/or images, and/or conceptual structure combine with validation in our experience to make the journey pleasurable.

Two caveats: first, it is essential to discriminate between the position I have outlined and an argument that sounds very much like it. After rightly rejecting a number of alternative ways of defining literature through its opposition to non-literary discourse, Terry Eagleton concludes in *Literary Theory: An Introduction* (1983) that what is meant by 'literature' is simply 'highly valued writing' (*L T* 10). This formulation has the virtue of highlighting the honorific sense that literature usually carries (even though we can speak of 'bad literature') and reminding us that evaluations rise and fall over time. However, it has a special value for a Marxist like Eagleton: it allows him to argue that if literature is writing we value highly and if our values are determined by capitalist ideology, then what we call literature is writing that is valuable to capitalism. Such a summary does no justice to the wit and urbanity with which Eagleton makes this argument, but it does not, I think, misstate what that argument finally comes down to. However, Eagleton's belief that in a capitalist society all values are determined by capitalism is as extrinsic a judgement as his negative evaluation of ideology itself. Moreover, literature is *not* an eulogistic term—unless one *chooses* to make the fact that a work can be or has been read aesthetically a criterion of value. The most derivative, trite, and pedestrian of wish-fulfilling love stories is literature so long as there are readers who find the experience of reading it rewarding for other than the information that can be gleaned from it.

Second, the aesthetic appeal may arise as much from personal associations, or appreciation of diction and structure, or interest in external significances as from the author's interpreted meaning. Just as we can read aesthetically and efferently at the same time, so we are able to read for meaning and significance at the same time. One can simultaneously read Gibbon for information about the Roman Empire, be absorbed by the structure of the presentation, understand

Gibbon's anti-Christian meaning, relate that meaning to a particular current in 18th-century intellectual history, and reject his evaluation of Christianity.

In summary, without attempting to enumerate all the qualities that readers have regarded as sources of aesthetic pleasure, we can say (1) that all discourse can theoretically be read either aesthetically or efferently, (2) that much is read both ways at once, (3) that the basic processes of interpretation apply however a discourse is read, and (4) that the distinction between meaning and significance applies equally to all discourse. My subsequent use of the term 'literature' is, accordingly, to be understood as a loose but convenient designation for texts that appear to invite an aesthetic reading, or to reward it, or to have rewarded it in past times.

4. *The Several Dimensions of Context*

A major difficulty in the application of speech-act theory, as in theories of discourse generally, arises from failure to recognize the variety of aspects, or sub-divisions, or sources, or—the term I prefer—'dimensions' of the total interpretive context. This is a major weakness of a book to which discourse theory owes a great deal (and which has not received the recognition it deserves), Mary Louise Pratt's *Toward A Speech Act Theory of Discourse* (1977). A comprehensive synonym for 'total context' is 'experience'—only that which has entered our experience is available to aid us in interpretation. Our experience is a constantly reordered whole in which each source of experience is understood in terms of other sources. Thus the reports of our own senses react with vicarious sense reports and concepts derived from intercourse with others. However, though it is misleading to think of experience or total context as made up of independent forces, it is equally misleading to think of the context of an utterance as a unitary, invariable scene.

We have already considered the first two contextual dimensions: knowledge of reality and of language. We especially forget how much we depend on the former, which is indeed the most pervasive dimension of context. When Pope writes 'To fifty chosen Sylphs, of special note, / We trust the important charge, the petticoat; / Oft have we known that sevenfold fence to fail,' he assumes a knowledge of anatomy as well as of social customs and morality. When the Captain of Conrad's 'The Secret Sharer' describes his course close to the shoreline, understanding of the physical result of a ship striking rocks is expected. When Milton's narrator reports of Samson

> He tugged, he shook, till down they came, and drew
> The whole roof after them with burst of thunder
> Upon the heads of all who sat beneath

the reader is assumed to know from experience of brute reality the incredible strength required of Samson and the necessary fate of all those in the temple. The difference in the appearance, knowledge, and expectations of Yeats's speaker with 'sixty or more winters' on his head and that of the children in the schoolroom emerges from our experience. To take a more trivial example, experience suggests that Thackeray's General Tufto has resorted to artifice when we are told 'When he was about seventy years of age (he is now nearly eighty), his hair, which was very scarce and quite white, suddenly grew thick, and brown, and curly, and his whiskers and eyebrows took their present colour.' (Chap. 28.)

As for the many-faceted linguistic knowledge that readers apply with equal spontaneity, consider the way a reader interprets Thackeray's description of Becky Sharp as having the 'dismal precocity of poverty', through the initially clashing connotations of 'dismal' and 'precocity', or reacts to the description of Rawdon Crawley in the presence of Becky as a 'heavy young dragoon'. Difficulties of both sense and reference, the repetition of words and sounds, and abnormal word order all caution the reader to consider unusual complexities of meaning as well as of diction and syntax in Hopkins's 'terrible sonnets'.

What besides our awareness of brute reality and knowledge of the language do we attend to? Just before Hamlet's fencing match with Laertes we read (or hear from the stage):

HORATIO: If your mind dislike anything, obey it. I will forestall their repair hither, and say you are not fit.

HAMLET: Not a whit, we defy augury; there's special providence in the fall of a sparrow. If it be now, 'tis not to come; if it be not to come, it will be now; if it be not now, yet it will come. The readiness is all. Since no man has aught of what he leaves, what is't to leave betimes? Let be.

To interpret this, or any passage or dialogue, is to understand not simply locutions or propositions but the illocutionary force and per-locutionary intent first of their immediate author (speaker) and then of the author of the text.

Leaving aside for the moment any relationships to Shakespeare as
the ultimate author of the total text, at least the following kinds of
knowledge here bear on interpretation. We consider the character
and personality of the speaker as thus far delineated, contrasting the
Hamlet who had dallied, plotted, and sought fit opportunity to act
with the resolution and resignation conveyed by the present speech.
We are aware of the conventions of the genre, recognizing that
dialogue as well as soliloquy articulates mental states that would
probably be presented through a narrator in a novel. We also recognize the dense texture of even the prose in Elizabethan drama and so
are prepared to note the way the vague generality of the reference to
future events conveyed by the 'If it be not now . . .' comes increasingly to seem a reference to the fall of the sparrow and thence to the
death awaiting each man. Our cultural knowledge of the pagan
tradition of seeking omens and the Christian tradition of faith gives
additional emphasis to the contrast between belief in augury and
trust in providence. The specific situation in which the speech
occurs—in confidential conversation with Horatio, the one person
he trusts—suggests that it is Hamlet's considered attitude towards
life. Finally, our awareness of the importance of textual patterns
alerts us to the way in which the passage echoes 'There's a divinity
that shapes our ends, / Rough-hew them how we will' at the beginning of the scene. That Hamlet returns to this mood after the Osric
scene emphasizes his new attitude and reminds us that Hamlet is not
the same youth Claudius had sent to England with Rosencrantz and
Guildenstern. These then are five additional dimensions likely to
prove useful in interpreting discourse: the authorial, the generic, the
collective, the specific, and the textual. The context of discourse is
like the flow of sense reports: any division is arbitrary. My purpose
is but to provide a comprehensive map of a territory which has been
surveyed in partially equivalent ways by others for somewhat different purposes. Steven Mailloux writes of the 'convention-based
responses that the author, as he is writing, understands he will
achieve as a result (at least in part) of his projected reader's recognition of his intention (99). In addition to the linguistic, the four conventions that he lists are 'authorial', 'literary', 'social', and 'within
literary works' (130). Hans Robert Jauss's 'horizon of expectations'
seems to me to include what I call the authorial, generic, collective,
and specific dimensions, though his interest is not at all restricted to
the horizon the author presumably shares with his original readers.

Roland Barthes's 'proairetic', 'semic', and 'hermeneutic' codes (relating respectively to actions, characteristics, and text-engendered enigmas) fit fairly well under my conception of the textual dimension while his 'symbolic' and 'cultural' or 'referential' codes fall within my collective dimension (17–20). Mikhail Bakhtin's concept of heteroglossia (multiplicity of voices, especially in the novel) would appear to include the contributions of social dialects and professional argots, the individual attitudes of the author and of each character, and the conflicting views of the world that interact within the total (collective) society.

4

The Authorial and Generic Dimensions

I have urged that language in use is always strategic in that the author assumes that the reader will attempt to achieve a coherent interpretation, calculates what the reader can be expected to bring to bear in interpreting the text, provides clues as to which contextual dimensions are relevant, and makes available whatever the reader is not expected to have to hand by way of information or awareness necessary to interpretation. I further suggest that the reader's assumption that the author has made these strategic assumptions and carried out these strategic actions is the basis of the reconstruction of authorial intention. Though we can never be sure of the author's assumptions, we set boundaries and assess probabilities. *Pace* phenomenological critics like Georges Poulet, what the reader must enter is not the mind of the author, but the world in which that author has strategically arranged knowledge and beliefs that the reader is presumed to share. The very possibility of expression of intended meaning is dependent on shared knowledge of contextual dimensions and mutual assumptions about coherence.

Authorship and genre are normally the first two dimensions of context we assess in interpreting any kind of discourse, the pedestrian and routine as much as the sophisticated and literary. We want to know who is saying what kind of thing. Moreover, authorship at times implies genre and genre authorship. We open a book of poetry with different expectations from those of a novel, and a novel by Thackeray with different expectations from those of one by a contemporary novelist of whom we have never heard. We also open the envelope from the bank or electricity company with different expectations from those of one that bears a friend's return address. We open a letter from a wife or husband with rather different expectations from those of one from a friend: letter-from-spouse could indeed be regarded as one genre, letter-from-friend another, letter-from-children as perhaps another. On the other hand the same author may address us in different genres. As we open a piece of mail from a friend, our expectations will differ depending on whether it appears to be, for instance, a Christmas card containing a hand-written note (we will expect the author to have taken what we know of each other into consideration in writing the note), a mimeographed Christmas letter (we expect an impersonally phrased report, a good bit of which we may already know or not really be interested in knowing), and a printed invitation to a Christmas party (which we expect to be impersonal and contain nothing not relevant to an invitation). The same interaction between knowledge of the author and awareness of differing genres occurs in the case of a poem, short story, and novel by, say, Thomas Hardy. While the authorial dimension remains the same, the generic one changes.

1. The Authorial Dimension

To what extent can knowledge about the author be said to constitute one of the contextual dimensions? On the principle that the only elements of any contextual dimension relevant to interpretation are those the reader can be assumed to share, we are obviously required to distinguish between the innumerable facts that arise from the author's day-to-day life and the body of information about that author of which a reader could reasonably be presumed to be aware and use in reconstructing the text. Let us consider a homely example. Bill Smith writes Ray Jones the following letter:

> Dear Ray,
>
> I'm sorry I won't be able to attend this year's meeting. The fact is that I'm having to spend most of my time on some personal problems right now.
>
> > Sincerely,
> >
> > Bill

Two weeks later, Smith's friends find out that he had made unwise investments, gone heavily into debt, and filed for bankruptcy. Now, did Smith's letter to Jones *mean* that he was in financial difficulties? The question itself suggests the ambiguity. In one sense, yes: the financial difficulty was presumably the cause of Smith's inability to attend the meeting. But in another sense, no: Smith does not appear to have intended to tell Jones the nature of his difficulties. Is the matter altered if Jones already knows that Smith has financial problems? That is, if Jones has such antecedent knowledge, is the meaning of the letter changed? Again we must distinguish two cases. If Smith does not know that Jones knows anything about his debt, even though the letter will signify to Jones that Smith's problems are financial, Smith will not have intended it to convey that. But if Smith knows that Jones knows of his debts, he knows also that his letter will imply worsening, or at least serious, financial difficulties to Jones. The letter will therefore carry such an implicature, one that is intended or at least anticipated by its author. Finally, in knowing whether Smith is aware of his (Jones's) knowledge, Jones will almost certainly know whether Smith intended him to understand the nature of the problem.

In this way interpretation, as the reconstruction of intended meaning, depends not simply on what the audience knows of the author, nor even what the author believes the audience knows, but what the audience believes the author believes the audience knows.

·It is no more true in the case of literary texts than of other uses of language that no information about the author as a person bears on interpretation. The cardinal principle is not to confuse the author's intended meaning (sense$_2$) with meaning in the sense of casual explanation (sense$_3$). Authors may be quite justified in assuming that the anticipated audience will be aware of particular pieces of information about them and in expecting that information to be used in interpretation. To take clear-cut examples, the first volume of *Modern Painters* had to make its way without support for its authority or clues to its interpretation derivable from readers' knowledge of its author. Indeed, it was because he was both young and unknown that Ruskin judged it best to publish the volume as by 'A Graduate of Oxford'. But eight years later Ruskin could expect *Stones of Venice* to be read against the background of his known opinions and reputation. Again, the very strategy of Ruskin's letter to *The Times* that helped change the critical climate of opinion toward the Pre-Raphaelites depended on the reputation he had achieved by that time. By way of contrast, we are all familiar with letters to the editor that wholly fail because their authors write as though their credit has already been established. What rhetoricians call the 'ethos' of an argument—the audience's sense of the author's authority or reliability—thus depends on a dimension external to the text as well as the author's strategies within the text. The latter will in fact be partly a result of the former.

Not only does what authors reasonably expect readers to know about them vary (from author to author and from period to period in a given author's career), but the degree to which authors depend on the knowledge they can expect varies as well. We know that George Gissing could not have expected readers to be aware of the grimness of his speculative thought as worked out in his essay 'The Hope of Pessimism' (written in 1882 but not published until 1970). He could assume some degree of public awareness of the view of life expressed in his novels by the time he published *New Grub Street* and *Born in Exile* a decade after his first novel, *Workers in the Dawn* (1880), but unlike the case of Ruskin's prose, Gissing's novels give no evidence that the reader is expected to approach them with a general knowledge of that world-view. The argument of Kant's *Critique of Judgement* presupposes an understanding of the *Critique of Pure Reason*; the argument of Mill's *On Liberty* does not presuppose an understanding of Mill's *Logic*. To take an interesting example from the field of art, unless it is part of an explicit series, we assume that a painting is interpretable by itself, but as E. H. Gombrich has pointed out, Mondrian's *Broadway Boogie-Woogie* can be regarded as representing 'gay abandon' only when contrasted with Mondrian's usual style (369).

I should like to take one further example, this one drawn from Barbara Herrnstein Smith's *On the Margins of Discourse*. Here, as at many other points, Smith comes to essentially the same conclusion as I do, though she starts from what I believe are somewhat erroneous premises. Urging the shallowness likely to result from regarding a poem as a historical utterance, she writes:

For example a recent editor of Shakespeare's *Sonnets* prefixes the following note to Sonnet 107 as part of his running commentary on what was happening in Shakespeare's personal life at the very moment he was writing the poems: 'Shakespeare had just escaped from the danger of his Company's involvement in the Essex rebellion and . . . the Queen, furious with Pembroke for fathering Mary Fitton's child and refusing to marry her, had sent Pembroke to jail. . . .' Then comes the sonnet:

> Not mine own fears, nor the prophetic soul
> Of the wide world dreaming on things to come,
> Can yet the lease of my true love control,
> Supposed as forfeit to a confined doom. . . .

Forfeit, indeed, to a confined doom, if interpreted as this editor suggests. (35)

Yes, but there are historical/biographical details that are relevant to interpretation and historical/biographical details that are, as here, egregiously not.

The evident problem is how to steer between an unrealistic denial that knowledge about the author can constitute part of the total context of interpretation and the temptation to draw on information that could not have been part of that shared context. Evidently anything known only by the circle of family and friends, or expressed only in private letters, as even more obviously anything not yet written or any event in the author's life that has not taken place *at the time of writing of the given version of the text*, is excluded. Whether what the author has published to that point or the semi-public events in his or her life (age, marital status, published interviews) are to be included in the authorial dimension depends on the likelihood of readers being aware of them. (Of course there are various ways in which an author may call attention to already published texts or personal information—in which case readers know that the author is presuming familiarity with these.) As F.W. Bateson wrote more than thirty years ago, 'Since poetry exists only in the poet–reader relationship, and the ideal reader approximates as closely as possible to one of the more intelligent of the poet's original readers, all that is necessary for us to know about the poet is the personal information he could take for granted in his contemporaries.' (*EPCI* 73.)

What then of information that subsequently becomes available, as in the course of time further works are published, the author perhaps becomes familiar to a reasonably wide public, biographies are written, and the author's letters are published? All such information may be valuable, perhaps very valuable, for purposes extrinsic to interpretation, that is, for the consideration of significance. The discovery, for instance, that Wordsworth fathered an illegitimate daughter in France may be of great interest for the critic seeking to understand more fully Wordsworth's attitude towards love, or France, or human relationships, but not for the interpretation of his poetry, not even for the interpretation of the story of the young lovers Vaudracour and Julia as told in the 1805 version of *The Prelude*. Nor would the discovery of the precise identity of the subject of the Lucy poems help us interpret their meaning. Nor indeed does our latter-day knowledge of Wordsworth's total *œuvre* directly and necessarily bear on interpretation. If the authorial dimension is not limited appropriately, the interpretation of particular poems becomes locked into assumptions about what the poet must have meant in order to be wholly consistent with what earlier poems are interpreted to have meant. There is a good deal of confusion on this point. For instance, 'A Slumber Did My Spirit Seal' appeared in the 1800 edition of *Lyrical Ballads*. It would be hard to argue that readers of that volume would have brought to it an awareness of Wordsworth's belief in the essential benevolence of nature beyond what the volume itself would have conveyed. For them, and for the intrinsic interpreter, as that activity is here defined, the problem of reconciling the speaker's despair that the dead Lucy is now

> Rolled round in earth's diurnal course,
> With rocks and stones and trees.

did not, and does not, exist.

'A Slumber Did My Spirit Seal' is one of those texts that have become special challenges as each successive commentary begets further commentaries. But the crux originated in a conflict between the apparent *meaning* of the poem and what our general understanding of Wordsworth's thought leads us to think his meaning should be. Thus Hillis Miller's celebrated discussion of the poem plays back and forth between the two activities to create its stunning critical web. Wordsworth's youthful sense of immortality, two quotations from Heidegger, several passages from *The Prelude*, the early death of Wordsworth's parents, and an entry in Dorothy Wordsworth's journals are called upon as evidence for an argument leading to such conclusions as that

Lucy is both the virgin child and the missing mother, that mother earth who gave birth to the speaker and has abandoned him. Male and female, however, come together in the earth, and so Lucy and the speaker are 'the same,' though the poet is also the perpetually excluded difference from Lucy, an unneeded increment, like an abandoned child. (OE 28.)

These are some of the irresolvable oppositions Miller pursues to demonstrate that 'Whatever track the reader follows through the poem he arrives at blank contradiction.' Miller calls his commentary a 'reading' of the poem; the terms is a useful one if understood in its most usual contemporary sense as an exercise of the critic's personal powers of association in the service of an externally derived theory of the significance of literature. 'A Slumber Did My Spirit Seal' *is* difficult to reconcile with all we now know about Wordsworth's attitude towards nature at the time he wrote the poem and this difficulty *is* worth careful critical consideration. But our *interpretation* of the poem ought not to give way to our desire to fit it into our external construction of a consistent history of Wordsworthian thought.

But, an objector might ask, are we indeed correct in assuming that Wordsworth was writing for readers who knew nothing about him as a person? Might we not assume that, even though published and thus available to a larger public, certain of his poems were regarded by Wordsworth as addressed to his intimates, perhaps to Coleridge (or Dorothy) alone? We could, but to do so leads towards swampy ground indeed. We can always assume that a text was written for a special group of readers (perhaps consisting of one person) whose members knew just what we think they should have known in order for us to interpret the text on the basis of information that has now come to light. There undoubtedly are situations in which an author constructs a text all or portions of which are to be interpreted in a special way by a privileged group of readers. Where a case can be made for the author's having assumed distinct audiences, the interpretations appropriate to each audience deserve recognition. There is no a priori reason that a discourse cannot have been intended to express an esoteric meaning to a group of initiates and an exoteric one to the general reader. However, we can hardly make it a general practice to assume that poems, essays, and stories are written to be interpreted primarily by those with special relationships to the author. Rossetti's father is said to have regarded the *Divine Comedy* as an attack on the Catholic religion, its true meaning accessible only to those initiated into the Masonic Brotherhood. But one must assume that a text published with every sign of being a poem addressed to the world at large indeed belongs to the genre of the poem, not to that of private communication or cryptogram. Put another way, though the genre of a work may be implied by the audience to whom it is addressed, the anticipated audience is partly implied by the apparent genre of the work.

There are cases of special difficulty: what use, for instance, is an interpreter of Yeats's poems to make of his comprehensive if eccentric explanation of human history, personality, and life as developed in *A Vision*? We might consider two words, 'pern' and 'gyre',

which appear in some of Yeats's best-known poems and are therefore commonly glossed in classroom texts. (That many editors
simply provide synonyms for the two words might suggest that
knowledge of *A Vision* is inessential, but it will be useful here to go
into the matter a bit further.) The Parrish and Painter concordance
tells us that 'gyre' or a grammatical variant thereof is found twelve
times and 'pern' four times in Yeats's poems. 'Pern' first appears in
'Shepherd and Goatherd' published in the Macmillan edition of *The
Wild Swans at Coole* in 1919. 'Gyre' first appears, coupled with
'pern', in 'Demon and Beast', published in *Michael Robartes and the
Dancer* in 1921. Yeats tells us that his wife's automatic writing, the
basis for the system set forth in *A Vision*, began shortly after their
marriage in 1917. The first version of *A Vision*, privately printed in
an edition of 600, appeared in 1925 and the final revised edition in
1937.

That first use of 'pern' occurs in the Goatherd's song for the dead
youth:

> Jaunting, journeying
> To his own dayspring,
> He unpacks the loaded pern
> Of all 'twas pain and joy to learn,
> Of all that he had made.

What is a 'pern'? A 1919 reader of 'Shepherd and Goatherd' might
have had real difficulty with the word; it does not appear in standard dictionaries, nor in the *OED* (the relevant fascicle of which had
come out in 1907). That is, the reader might have had difficulty if
Yeats had not provided a note explaining that 'When I was a child at
Sligo I could see above my grandfather's trees a little column of
smoke from "the pern mill", and was told that "pern" was another
name for the spool, as I was accustomed to call it, on which thread
was wound.' (594.) Armed with that information, a reader has a
chance of recognizing that the word in question is normally spelled
'pirn', under which spelling it will be found in most dictionaries; the
OED defines it as 'a small cylinder on which thread or yarn is
wound'. That a man's accumulated experience is like yarn wound on
a bobbin then becomes an easily interpreted metaphor. However,
without that note, 'pern' could cause major problems, not because of
any esoteric meaning that Yeats attaches to it, but simply because
the word 'pirn', which has an available, if not immediately familiar,

dictionary meaning, has been oddly spelt. A reader who encountered it for the first time in 'Demon and Beast' could only guess by its association there with 'gyre' that it had to do with turning or winding. And had Yeats not glossed that early use, heaven knows what scholars might have made of it.

And what of 'gyre'? 'A turning round, revolution, whirl; also a vortex.' An uncommon word, it is most often used poetically. The *OED* cites nineteenth-century uses by Southey, Mrs. Browning, Rossetti, and Henley. 'Gyre' appears twice in 'Demon and Beast.' Here is the first stanza of the poem:

> For certain minutes at the least
> That crafty demon and that loud beast
> That plague me day and night
> Ran out of my sight;
> Though I had long perned in the gyre,
> Between my hatred and desire,
> I saw my freedom won
> And all laugh in the sun.

'Gyre' appears again the third stanza, where the poet stops

> Beside the little lake
> To watch a white gull take
> A bit of bread up into the air;
> Now gyring down and perning there
> He splashed . . .

Yeats provides no note to 'gyre' as used in this poem, but none is needed—to circle or spiral between 'hatred and desire' is fully intelligible, as is 'gyring down' for spiralling. Yeats did append to 'The Second Coming' a note taken from what was to be published as the argument of *A Vision*, describing the spiralling movement of the concentric gyres of history. However, the reference to the falcon turning in the 'widening gyre' is perfectly clear without such a gloss, as is the sense of a new cycle of history very different from that conventionally thought of as the Second Coming—neither the allusion to a cyclic structure of history nor to a Second Coming depend on *A Vision*.

Let me summarize cardinal points about the relation of knowledge of the author and his/her work and thought, that is, the authorial dimension as illustrated by Yeats's use of 'pern' and 'gyre'. First, the purpose of interpretation is to reconstruct the meaning the author intended when constructing the text while recognizing that such reconstruction is unlikely to be complete and can never be certain. That then is the overriding goal, not the pedantic one of drawing a hard line between what evidence is admissible in interpretation and what is not. That one simply must always be on one's guard against importing extraneous meaning does not mean that nothing the author tells us, or that scholarship discovers, outside the text can be relevant to the author's meaning. When we discover through Yeats's note that pern = pirn, we discover the meaning Yeats assumed that the reader would (or could through the dictionary) share. That for Yeats pern = pirn would be equally pertinent to the interpretation of his poems if it had been first discovered by a scholar after Yeats's death. On the other hand, that in *A Vision* 'gyre' refers to ineluctable structures of the human mind and of history is not something one needs to know to interpret 'Demon and Beast'. Yeats did not think so, or he would probably have added a note to that poem as he did to 'The Second Coming'. Before we give 'gyre' its 'visionary' meaning in 'Demon and Beast', we must be very sure the poem gains in coherence if we do so. And to transfer the visionary or world-historical meaning of 'gyre' to 'pern' as used in 'Shepherd and Goatherd' on the grounds of their later association seems to me to obfuscate rather than give greater consonance to that poem (though any practised reader could, as an exercise in ingenuity, produce an explication in which the dead youth's pern was a conical and spirally-wound spool).

Whether Yeats assumed a shared knowledge of his special meaning of 'gyre' *after* publication of *A Vision* is problematical. The subscribers to the privately printed edition of 600 were presumably interested in Yeats as man and/or poet, and though he does not explicitly link *A Vision* and his poetry until the edition of 1937, he could have assumed a band of *cognoscenti* who perceived an additional level of intended meaning. On the other hand, one must always be wary of that fallacy of the private audience already mentioned, and I am aware of none of Yeats's poems that are uninterpretable without a knowledge of *A Vision*. The safest formulation of the relationship of the author to his own *œuvre* and to the facts of his life is that if these are neither referred to nor implied by the existence of a textual puzzle that can be resolved only by bringing such information into consideration, they ought to be ignored. Since illocutionary implicature works by violating the apparent context in order to cause the reader to consider less immediate contexts, we ought to be suspicious of interpretations that use information the apparently anticipated audience could not be expected to have in order to *create* an inconsistency.

What clearly has no place in interpretation is the use of implications drawn from patterns in authors' total canons to construct psychological or intellectual portraits. Explanations in terms of Harold Bloom's assumption that every author struggles against belatedness, Freudian or neo-Freudian theory, Marxist analysis of the relation of the author to the economic sub-structure, or old-fashioned biographical criticism can well prove more interesting than interpretation, but they are investigations of *significance*, not meaning. One may accept the argument that Matthew Arnold's struggle against his father's dominance was the force driving him far beyond his father's Liberal Anglicanism. Or that Gissing's belief that he was unworthy of the love of a good woman shaped his fictional worlds. Or that a suppressed homosexuality is the source of the strong emotional overtones in Pater's special aestheticism. But even if established irrefutably these causal explanations are not part of the total context of interpretation.

2. *The Generic Dimension*

By 'genre' is here meant any kind or class of discourse about which we learn to have certain expectations, from capacious classes like 'instructions' or 'poetry' to narrow ones like 'introductions to word-processing software' or 'Petrarchan love sonnets'. Our experience from the time we begin to learn the language develops expectations about different kinds of both spoken and written discourse. How finely and on what principles we choose to discriminate between these kinds of discourse are largely matters of convenience. In the realm of verbal utterance we may, if we wish, speak of the genre of bus-stop conversation with a stranger, or of that of asking for information, or of that of the after-dinner speech. All have their conventions. For instance, one does not introduce oneself—'I'm Bill Jones'—when asking for information from a stranger, and the after-dinner speaker who does not begin with light-hearted informality is almost obliged to justify the departure. Ignorant or thoughtless violation of these conventions results at the least in social awkwardness, at the worst in total failure of communication. On the other hand, clever and obviously intentional departures from them may increase the effectiveness of the communication.

An attempt to classify all genres of communication would soon become exceedingly tedious, but we may begin an illustrative list simply by reflecting on our expectations about the varieties of discourse encountered in a single week. We expect that recipes will list the ingredients required, that clerks in stores will answer our questions about merchandise rather than give us their opinions about things in general, that sermons will be built around a brief text (most likely taken from the Bible), that newspaper stories will avoid editorializing and will provide the background necessary to the most uninformed reader (reminding readers for instance that the Mrs. Thatcher whose speech is being reported is Prime Minister of England). Recognition of the genre of a discourse and the degree to which it fulfils or violates the conventions expected to accompany it often goes a long way towards disclosing the author's intentions. If a recipe published in the cooking section of the local newspaper begins the listing of ingredients for a dessert with

> One hogshead claret
> A hundredweight fine sugar
> Twenty-five gallons cream

we know that it has been published more for the interest and humour to be derived from the recipes with which the cooks of a great, landed estate would have been familiar than for instruction. If under the front page headline 'City Faces Bankruptcy' we were to find a story without a byline beginning with the unattributed statement, 'This city has tolerated the incompetence of the mayor long enough,' we would assume that the paper's editor had been driven beyond the bounds of reason or that the paper's compositors had somehow printed an editorial where the lead story was to go. When one reads 'iff the statement is true' in a newspaper, 'iff' is assumed to be a misprint; when one reads the same phrase in a philosophical journal, 'iff' is assumed to mean 'if and only if'.

Despite the importance of genre in all discourse, literary genres have generally been regarded as special cases. The arguments against setting literature in some special realm to which ordinary rules of language do not apply have been presented in the previous chapter. I have also there explained that by calling a genre 'literary', I denote simply that its recognition leads one to expect that aesthetic as well as or instead of efferent reading is likely to be rewarded. The relationship works in both directions: we tend to assimilate prose which calls attention to itself into poetry and speak of prose poems, just as we tend to assimilate highly persuasive prose arguments into the genre of the personal essay, and well-told anecdotes into that of the short story.

However, I have not yet touched on the questions of the mode of existence, or number, or mutability of specifically 'literary' genres. In his impressive *Kinds of Literature: An Introduction to the Theory of Genres and Modes*, Alastair Fowler builds upon a simple but essential foundation: 'Every work of literature belongs to at least one genre.' (20.) From the ecological view this is a necessary conclusion from the strategic nature of language use, though 'belongs to' ought to be understood here as 'may be assigned to'. In the process of constructing an interpretable text, the author regards what he is doing as belonging to at least one genre recognizable by the reader; in the process of interpreting that text the reader assigns it to at least one genre seemingly intended by the author.

It is important to be clear about what is *not* being said here. It is not being asserted that genres are either legislative or immutable or mutually exclusive—the assumption that a theory of genres entails one or more of these assertions is the major reason for the decline of explicit critical discussion of genres. The fact is that the way in which an author modifies a genre, or fulfils our expectations about it in a novel form, or mixes genres is of at least as much importance as his/her fulfilment of generic expectations. As Fowler says, the relation of literary works to genres 'is not one of passive membership but of active modulation' (20). Nor is it being asserted that an author is always fully and consciously aware of the conventions or characteristics of the genre in which a critic might classify his or her text. An author might well write a novel describing the process of growing up without ever having heard of the *Bildungsroman*, or a poem urging a woman to heed the fleetingness of life and not delay in responding to his passion without ever having heard of the *carpe diem* tradition. However, that readers in each case referred the texts to these genres would cause no difficulties of interpretation (though the texts might disappoint us in failing to exploit our expectations in interesting ways). Moreover, our expectations become specific in proportion to our certainty about the genre of a discourse, which in turn depends on the number of generic characteristics we note. We would not necessarily think of a poem written in celebration of a wedding as an epithalamion unless it exhibited some of the conventions we associate with that genre, and therefore we would not be concerned with what epithalamic characteristics had been added to, omitted from, or modified in the given poem if we found no such characteristics to begin with.

We assume then that an author's intent to write will include some sense of genre, perhaps broad and rudimentary (poem, novel, letter), perhaps detailed and sophisticated (blank verse, domestic tragedy, comic drama parodying the conventions of the detective story). We assume further that the author is very likely to exploit the generic conventions of which he or she is aware as one of the means of guiding readers to the proper interpretation. Of course a writer may parody or violate certain generic expectations for the humour of it, but if so the humour is part of the author's intent and the humorous intention is achieved only if we recognize parody as the implicature of the violation that is occurring.

From the reader's point of view the assignment of genre is an essential part of the process of interpretation, but this does not mean that an exact reproduction of the author's awareness of the genre of a text is necessary for a reasonably accurate interpretation of the illocutionary force and perlocutionary intent of a text. We may understand that a poet is praising his lady without recognizing that the poem before us is a blazon-type sonnet, or even that it is a sonnet. Experienced readers will undoubtedly feel a difference in the tone of the opening lines of *An Essay on Man* and *The Prelude* that will affect their expectations as they proceed through their reading of each without feeling the need to *name* the generic differences. After all, genre is only one of the dimensions, and its importance for interpretation will vary with the work. But the rougher our approximation, the more inexact our interpretation is likely to be. The importance of genre for anyone but the literary historian is in its contribution to interpretation. Let us hear Alastair Fowler again:
. . . genres have to do with identifying and communicating rather than defining and classifying. We identify the genre in order to interpret the exemplar.' (38.)

Genres are best regarded as loosely related clusters of characteristics, or better, conventions, not all of which need be present in any given example. Identifying a genre therefore involves the tentative following of clues as much as any other part of interpretation. Title, opening, typographical format, length, diction, and propositional

content are among the characteristics that suggest a genre; and as we
read we look for further associated conventions. A standard definition of a sonnet tells us that it is 'A lyric poem written in a single
stanza, which consists of fourteen iambic pentameter lines linked by
an intricate rhyme scheme. The rhyme, in English, usually follows
one of two main patterns . . .' We further know sonnets tend to be
divided into sections by their rhyme schemes, and that sonnets very
often treat of love or praise. To ask how many of these conventions
are required if we are to regard a particular poem as a sonnet is
wrong-headed, since the purpose of genre classification is wholly
heuristic. It is useless to argue over whether a given example is *really*
a sonnet—the useful questions are simply what genre or genres a text
most closely approximates, what features that heuristic classification alerts us to look for, and what might be implied by departures
from the cluster of expectations. To avoid misunderstanding, I must
add that such expectations are historically derived in two senses:
from the commentary of literary historians on the one hand and
personal reading experience on the other.

To call the characteristics we associate with a genre 'conventions'
implies participation by the reader. Presuming that which has the
appearance of a poem on the page to be a poem, we know that
poems conventionally ask us to perform certain activities as we
read. Once one has recognized that literature is what results when
we choose to read a text in a certain way (generally through the text's
invitation), the relationship between literary conventions and
generic expectations is easier to see. What we give our attention to
varies largely with the genre: recognition that we are reading a poem
leads us to attend more carefully to the sounds of words, the relations
between them, the associations that accompany them, and the precision of their choice. From the point of view of discourse analysts
like van Dijk and Kintsch, genres are one form of those 'super-
structures' the degree of whose 'cognitive relevance' varies widely
from discourse to discourse (235–7).

The reader of any but the original periodical version of *Vanity
Fair* is confronted first by a brief section titled 'Before the Curtain'.
The immediate question is the relation of the section to the novel,
which is a question of genre. 'As the Manager of the Performance
sits before the curtain on the boards, and looks into the Fair, a
feeling of profound melancholy comes over him in his survey of the
bustling place. There is a great quantity of eating and drinking,

making love and jilting . . .'. At some point the reader will recognize that he or she is reading a kind of preface commenting on the narrative to come, not the opening of the first chapter. Something like this preface could have been included in the novel proper, the narrator of *Vanity Fair* being perfectly comfortable in commenting on his own skills and techniques. Yet the speaker who describes the manager is not quite the narrator of the novel itself even though the 'Manager of the Performance' seems to be commenting in the third person on his own management of the story. The genre remains that of preface or introduction in which the narrator (or author, if one prefers) comments on both that which is narrated and himself as narrator. The difference is there, and the various clues to its genre (capitalization, reference to previous readers, reference to characters as puppets) are precisely what would cause someone who began to read 'Before the Curtain' as the opening of the fictional narrative to be uneasy until the proper genre was recognized.

The opening sentences of the personal essay tend to launch the reader directly into the unfolding of a set of observations which, the experienced reader of the genre knows, is to be judged less by the canons of logic than by freshness, aptness of illustration, cunning diction, and ingenuity of construction. For instance the opening sentences of many of Lamb's and Stevenson's essays plunge the reader directly into the ambience:

The human species, according to the best theory I can form of it, is composed of two distinct races, *the men who borrow, and the men who lend.* To these two original diversities may be reduced all those impertinent classifications of Gothic and Celtic tribes, white men, black men, red men.

('The Two Races of Men')

Every man hath two birthdays: two days at least, in every year, which set him upon revolving the lapse of time, as it affects his mortal duration.

('New Year's Eve')

With the single exception of Falstaff, all Shakespeare's characters are what we call marrying men.

('Virginibus Puerisque,i')

There is a strong feeling in favour of cowardly and prudential proverbs.

('Crabbed Age and Youth')

Leaping into the thick of their arguments, they choose their words with careful audacity (how nicely that 'impertinent' in the first Lamb quotation mingles its associated meanings—irrelevant and impudent—and how easily Stevenson's yoking of 'cowardly' and 'prudential' hangs a pejorative placard on 'prudential').

One of the best-known modern considerations of the nature of literary conventions is to be found in Jonathan Culler's *Structuralist Poetics*, particularly as summed up in the frequently reprinted chapter 'Literary Competence'. 'Any one wholly unacquainted with literature and unfamiliar with the conventions by which fictions are read,' Culler writes early in his key chapter, 'would, for example, be quite baffled if presented with a poem.' (*SP* 114.) He then enumerates operational conventions. 'The primary convention is what might be called the rule of significance: read the poem as expressing a significant attitude to some problem concerning man and/or his relation to the universe.' Further conventions are those of metaphorical coherence ('one should attempt through semantic transformations to produce coherence on the levels of both tenor and vehicle'), inscription in a poetic tradition (for instance the identification of the sunset with death), and thematic unity.

Culler reminds us that it is misleading to think of poems as 'harmonious totalities, autonomous natural organisms, complete in themselves and bearing a rich immanent meaning'. Rather, the poem is an 'utterance that has meaning only with respect to a system of conventions which the reader has assimilated' (*SP* 116). That way of putting it, however, makes conventions sound rather too much like arbitrary importations. Generic conventions are arbitrary in that nothing in the nature of language requires their adoption, but they are not arbitrary as interpretive clues because knowledge of them is shared between reader and author. The obvious corollary is that so far as intepretation goes, only genres of which the author could have been aware—clusters of conventions that had come to be associated by the time the author wrote—have relevance.

Opposed to Culler's emphasis on literary convention that combines so readily with a view of genres as unstable clusters of conventions is a much more typical kind of structuralist thought. Most structuralists have searched either for a primal structure of mind, thought, or language that necessarily produces a particular set of literary genres or for a particular structural form within various more or less stable genres.

Northrop Frye's *Anatomy of Criticism* (1957), which impressively pre-dates Anglo-American interest in the linguistically derived

European structuralist movement, is the most ambitious form of the first. Though it announces itself as an investigation of 'the possibility of a synoptic view of the scope, principles, and techniques of literary criticism', it is much more an attempt to develop a comprehensive matrix of the possible kinds of literature. The further one follows Frye, however, the clearer it becomes that what he offers is a set of suggestively useful taxonomies. None of these is necessary in the sense of being grounded in an inherent structure of the mind or universe (though at times Frye's argument appears to imply one or the other); each is based rather on an external schema (the seasons, traditional genres, modes of allegorical criticism). Frye's kinds thus turn out to be heuristic rather than constitutive—which denies them any privileged status but in no way decreases their value in providing a comprehensive way of organizing one's thinking about the mani-fold varieties of literature.

Much more common have been structuralist attempts to define the universal components of literary structures. Examples are Greimas's *actantial* structure of six categories, Barthes's five narra-tive codes, Todorov's 'grammatical' analysis of plots into 'proper names', 'adjectives', and three levels of 'verbs'. These offer vocabularies through which plots, themes, and functions within a text, and especially within narrative, can be redescribed, the process of redescription bringing out relationships not previously noticed. However, all are essentially arbitrary models (why precisely *five* codes in Barthes?) or externally derived schemas (what is the link between grammar and human action?). In contrast, the conception of genres as continually modified clusters of conventions recognized through their association in our experience of discourse allows for both continuity and change, for pleasures afforded both by the tradition and by creativity.

3. Fiction

In recent years several confusions have centred on the broadest of generic classifications, fiction, many of them engendered by attempts to define literature as essentially fictional. Though much of what we have tended to think of as 'literature', as opposed to other uses of language, *is* fictional in the usual literary sense of the term (the third sense discussed in Chapter 1, section 3), not all of it is. An essay, whether by Bacon, Lamb, Stevenson, or Pater, or a story of a sequence of physical and/or mental events which actually took place, can be read, to use Rosenblatt's terms, as aesthetically as a novel or sonnet. To take the sort of example that most easily leads to confusion, Ruskin's *Stones of Venice* can be read largely efferently or largely aesthetically. One who believed it an absolutely accurate picture of Venetian architecture and culture could read it primarily efferently; so also could one who believed that Ruskin was in error at almost every point (perhaps to discover the cause or extent of Ruskin's wrong-headedness). On the other hand, readers with or without interest in Venice, architecture, or the relation of art to morality can read it primarily aesthetically if Ruskin's diction, imagery, and/or structure of thought draw them into such a reading.

A second confusion results from the attempt to over-simplify the difference between fiction and non-fiction by saying that fiction does not refer to the real world. A moment's thought reveals the difficulty: a novel set in New York refers to New York, making available all kinds of knowledge the reader has about the real New York as part of the total context of interpretation. Authors of (1) a 1985 novel set in the New York of 1885, (2) an article on New York meant to be read by New Yorkers, and (3) a story set in contemporary New York intended to be easily interpretable by readers who had never seen the city would obviously make different kinds of calculations. A more general principle I would urge is that words in fictional discourse retain the senses (denotative and connotative) they have acquired in our experience. When we read 'Shall I compare thee to a summer's day?' all sorts of knowledge and awareness, including our common experience of real summer days, become potentially relevant. At the same time of course fiction presents that which is understood to exist only within the fictional narrative. As Searle comments in *Speech Acts*, 'in real world talk one can refer only to what exists; in fictional talk one can refer to what exists in fiction (plus such real world things and events as the fictional incorporates)' (*SA* 79).

A third misconception has arisen through attempts to define fiction as an 'imitation' of an illocutionary act. However, if we recall that the definition of an illocutionary act is the uttering of a locution incorporating a proposition and an illocutionary force, it is hard to know in what sense either the locutions or illocutions which make up a fictional narrative are imitations. Here is the opening of Dorothy Parker's 'You Were Perfectly Fine'.

The pale young man eased himself carefully into the low chair, and rolled his head to the side, so that the cool chintz comforted his cheek and temple.

'Oh, dear,' he said. 'Oh, dear, oh, dear, oh dear. Oh.'

The clear-eyed girl, sitting light and erect on the couch, smiled brightly at him.

'Not feeling so well today?' she said.

'Oh, I'm great,' he said. 'Corking, I am. Know what time I got up? Four o'clock this afternoon, sharp. I kept trying to make it, and every time I took my head off the pillow, it would roll under the bed. This isn't my head I've got on now. I think this is something that used to belong to Walt Whitman. Oh, dear, oh, dear, oh, dear.'

The narrator's sentences are as much propositions as if they were sentences in a newspaper story: 'The Oakglen bank was robbed this morning' or 'The fire was discovered about 2 a.m. by a passing motorist.' They belong to the illocutionary class of assertives. The first calls on our general stock of experiential knowledge to suggest that the young man is experiencing considerable discomfort; the second, by the contrast in its description of the girl, suggests that the difference in the way they are feeling is going to be of importance (Grice's maxim of relevance). The girl's question is a request for information that, given the context, carries the implicature that she knows not only the answer to her question, but the reason her companion is in that state. The irony of his reply is similarly recognized through all sorts of violations of the CP.

What is lacking is specific reference to an identifiable reality outside the narrative. The cancellation of the expectation that all indexicals in the narrative will have reference to a set of events that took place at a particular time and in a particular place is the primary convention of fiction. There are clearly many others. It is presumed that the story has a point or is interesting; that the fictional narrative tells the reader all that is needed to understand the story (or, more accurately, to understand the author's intention in telling the story); that details can be filled in from the reader's knowledge of how things are (in science fiction and fantasy for instance, it is presumed that whatever physical or psychological facts are not specifically stated to be different in the fictional world are the same as in the reader's experience), etc. Violations of such conventions are handled in such a way as to make them visible and purposeful; thus a pointless (shaggy dog) story is told for the purpose of the surprise occasioned by the violation of expectations.

The same sort of objection must be made to Barbara Herrnstein Smith's distinction between 'natural' and 'fictive' discourse. Natural discourse, for her, is constituted by the 'verbal acts of real persons on particular occasions' (15) in which the 'context occasions the utterance'. 'Fictive' discourse, which includes, but is not limited to, the central literary genres—poems, plays, novels—is a 'representation' of natural discourse. It 'consists entirely of linguistic structure, unlike a natural utterance, which consists of a linguistic event occurring in a historical context' (30). Further, it seems, natural utterances are always straightforward (they have, in my terms, direct illocutionary force) so that to speak figuratively is to speak fictively (see 104). But the 'marketplace' and 'playground' of language that Smith describes as contiguous (132) are in fact partly coextensive: purposes are achieved through indirect, ambiguous, tropic employment of language as well as direct uses. 'Dinner is served' and 'Ask for me tomorrow and you will find me a grave man' both are indirect (have indirect illocutionary force) and both are purposive.

Though one sees what is meant by singling out certain discourses as *not* occurring in a historical context, the description appears forced. How can a discourse *avoid* occurring in a historical context? Whether a person tells an experience to a friend, writes a letter about current issues to the local newspaper, or produces a novel, the process has occurred in history and the resulting discourse communicates only through dependence on shared knowledge (linguistic, cultural, experiential) which is historical in that it exists at the moment and the author presumes it will in some way exist for the audience. One of Smith's formulations that I like very much explains that the writer of a poem or novel 'has constructed a fictive member of an identifiable class of natural ("real") objects' (25). However, the more accurate, if considerably less elegant, statement would be that the generic conventions of poems and novels inform us that some of the persons, objects, or events named or described in the text are almost certainly fictive in that they have sense without reference. The hedge 'almost certain' is necessary because, for instance, Wordsworth might have indeed written the sonnet 'Composed upon Westminster Bridge, September 3, 1802' without stirring from a particular spot on the bridge, but whether or not this is the case is irrelevant.

As noted in Chapter 2, the real complications in interpreting fiction arise from the fact that discourses are likely to be embedded in each other. One character may report another character's speech which may in turn be reported by the narrator. Since the narrator and characters, *A*, *B*, and *C* may all be calculating their utterances, and the reader, narrator, and each character interpreting utterances on the basis of different total contexts, the resulting illocutionary force, perlocutionary intent, and pelocutionary effect may differ at each level of embedding.

Thus at the crisis in Tennyson's handling of the Becket story, King Henry cries out:

> Sluggards and fools, why do you stand and stare?
> You are no king's men—you—you—you are Becket's men.
> Down with King Henry! up with the Archbishop!
> Will no man free me from this pestilent priest?

(v. i)

In Anouilh's version, the King's words are:

I'm as limp and useless as a girl! So long as he's alive, I'll never be able to do a thing. I tremble before him astonished. And I am the King! (*With a sudden cry*) Will no one rid me of him? A priest who jeers at me and does me injury! Are there none but cowards like myself around me? Are there no men left in England?

(iv)

In both cases the four Norman knights who hear the King understand him to be calling for Becket's murder. But in Tennyson's version the audience or reader, knowing both that on the one hand the King has been manipulated by the Queen and that the relationship between the King and Becket has frayed, will judge the King actually to desire Becket's death at this moment. In Anouilh's play, where there is less immediate reason for blind anger at Becket and where a much more complex relationship between the two men has been portrayed, the King will likely be judged not to have actually wished for Becket's murder, even though his immediately subsequent actions suggest that he accepts the murder when he realizes he has set it in motion. At the end of Tom Stoppard's *Jumpers*, George includes both his agonist Archie and an Archbishop of Canterbury in his dream of the long-awaited symposium. Within the dream Archie irritatedly calls out 'Will no one rid me of this turbulent priest!' Though a throw-away allusion, the audience or reader has no doubt, from knowledge of the 'real' Archie and George, that the dreamed Archie means murder.

We must also remember that actions described in any narrative or presented on the stage are also signs that we interpret in relationship to discourse in the same way we interpret discourse itself. Hamlet's treatment of Ophelia, Rawdon Crawley's rage when he discovers Becky with the Marquis de Steyne, Belinda's anguish at the loss of her locks, are interpreted by the same process as is the speech of these characters. Much significant implicature would indeed be lost if we were not able to interpret speeches in the context of actions and actions in the context of speeches.

Let us look again at one of Miss Emily's replies to the delegation of aldermen: 'I have no taxes in Jefferson. Colonel Sartoris explained it to me. Perhaps one of you can gain access to the city records and satisfy yourselves.' The illocutionary force and perlocutionary intent will be interpreted by the aldermen and the reader in the same way. But the perlocutionary effects on the aldermen and the reader almost certainly differ. The reader interprets the effect on the alderman as the production of frustration and bafflement—the propositions stated in Miss Emily's sentences are each in its own way in error, but how would one begin to explain? The perlocutionary effect on the reader is likely to be amusement mixed with a bit of admiration for Miss Emily's bearing. In addition the reader also assumes a perlocutionary intent on the narrator's part in including the episode and speech, a perlocutionary intent made clearer by the narrator's succeeding 'So she vanquished them, horse and foot . . .' Stepping back to the author, in the absence of implicatures that allow us to distinguish between the knowledge and intentions of the author and narrator, we assume the same perlocutionary intent in the creation of the speech as ascribed to the narrator.

I have been putting the case for (1) recognizing that all utterances, verbal or written, are interpreted partly by assigning them to particular categories about which we have expectations, that is, to genres; (2) that all utterances *may* be read primarily aesthetically or primarily efferently; and (3) that theories that try to divide off literary from other texts by making the distinguishing quality of the former either a fictionality that does not refer to reality or an imitation of illocutionary force are not defensible.

It will have been noticed that I have been using the term 'genre' very loosely, speaking for instance of the poem and the blazon equally as genres. The instability of generic distinctions makes a comprehensive terminology impossible, but one can do much worse than take Alastair Fowler's general scheme. Fowler divides the umbrella term 'genre' into 'kinds', 'sub-genres', and 'modes'. Kinds are more or less what have historically been called genres, having both substantive (contentual) and formal (structural) elements (as, for instance, in the short story). Sub-genres specify more exactly the content of the text (the academic novel as opposed to the factory novel). Modes are general features, often derived from genres, that modify kinds (comic, satiric); such terms can modify the genres like that of the novel or the ode equally. There are also 'constructional types', that is, formal structures that appear in more than one genre. Thus *Amoretti* 64 'is amatory in mode, Elizabethan sonnet in kind, of the blazon sub-genre', and it includes a collection as constructional type (56).

The sophistication of the terminology one requires depends on one's purpose. The average reader may need only an awareness that certain conventions or characteristics tend to belong to certain genres. The reader who is able only to say that a certain novel seems closer to *Tristram Shandy* than to *Waverley* or *Middlemarch* or that a poem is closer to *The Prelude* than to *Don Juan* will find interpretation easier than one who cannot make such distinctions, while the reader who knows at least that there is such a thing as a 'pastoral' in which the poet in some sense speaks in the person of a shepherd will be much less baffled by *Lycidas* than one who does not. Since genres are continuously modified and come into and go out of fashion, full knowledge of the differences between genres in different periods is hardly to be expected of anyone but the literary historian. On the other hand, the wider the readers' acquaintance with literature and the fuller their acquaintance with the more or less standard terminology used in discriminating between genres, the more fully they can respond to the genre of a discourse.

5

The Collective, Specific, and Textual Dimensions

Mark Antony's speech over the dead Caesar has become a classic schoolroom exercise: the ironies by which it works on the crowd of Roman citizens are simultaneously clever and apparent. Even the inexperienced reader enters easily into the interpretation of Antony's implicatures as the proposition that Brutus and Cassius were honourable men clashes with the proposition that Caesar had demonstrated before all Rome that he was not the ambitious man Brutus had alleged. One of these propositions then must have a non-literal force. However, interpretation—that is, determination of that non-literal force—proceeds so smoothly only because of the amount of textual information that guides it.

The linguistic dimension of Antony's speech has been impressively analysed by Roman Jakobson (375–6); here I should like to concentrate on two other dimensions. The reader is aware of certain pieces of knowledge shaping the crowd's point of view: (1) that Caesar had counted both Brutus and Antony as his friends, that Caesar's reputation had steadily increased as he had benefited Rome over the years, that generosity and charity are not often qualities of the ambitious, that a speech of praise is appropriate at the funeral of a great man. The crowd also knows (2) that Brutus had been one of those who killed Caesar while Antony had not; that Antony had been given permission to speak at the funeral by Brutus. The reader knows in addition (3) that Brutus had been warned not to let Antony live and later not to let him speak; that Antony's soliloquy at the end of the earlier scene in Act III expressed the intention of inciting the crowd. The reader also notes that the opening of Antony's speech adheres to the letter of his agreement not to blame the conspirators but that he does nothing to check the crowd's interpretation of his speech as a denunciation of Brutus.

Now all this is so obvious that no mention of it seems necessary, but that is precisely the point: the general background knowledge on which interpretation draws (1 above) and the specific and immediate details of the situation, (2) and (3), are so constant a part of the interpretive context as to be almost invisible. The line between general background knowledge (which I call 'collective') and the knowledge or awareness 'specific' to a situation of discourse is necessarily vague, but since the distinctions between all our dimensions are for the purpose of conveniently indicating the range of contexts that influence interpretation, this causes no practical difficulties.

1. The Collective Dimension

As Berger and Luckman make abundantly clear in their introduction to the sociology of knowledge, part of what we know is what others know and what others know we know. That arrestingly simple statement is the basic principle of the ecological approach to interpretation as a whole, but it is especially applicable to the knowledge that makes up the 'collective' dimension. We do not in fact know exactly what others know, but we assume that ordinary adults in our own culture have a general understanding of social institutions (government, marriage, jurisprudence), customs (when to shake hands), societal norms (courtesy to old people, kindness to children), topical events (whatever and whoever is in the news), cultural and historical fact (recognition that Plato was an ancient Greek philosopher, that India was once under British rule, that slavery was the major issue in the American Civil War, and all sorts of miscellaneous facts (water freezes at 32°F, petrol is explosive, the News on the television is at a fixed time each evening, it is expected that men will wear ties in certain situations). Such collective knowledge is the subject of investigation from a variety of disciplines: socio-linguistics, ethnomethodology, the sociology of knowledge. John Searle calls such knowledge and awareness 'factual background information' (*EM* 80, 134); Charles Altieri calls it the 'cultural grammar'; Bach and Harnish speak of 'mutual contextual beliefs'; socio-linguists like Dell Hymes speak of the 'ethnography of communication'. Since we also know that we don't all share the same knowledge, we constantly make judgements about how much and what sort of background information or cultural grammar persons to whom we are speaking or writing are likely to possess. We shape our expectations to take account of age, vocation, known interests, assumed educational background.

An obvious but nevertheless important point is that authors constantly take shortcuts and imply judgements by dependence on the collective dimension. Unless there are special circumstances, to say 'Luke lit a match to check the level of the petrol' is to say that Luke is a fool (and perhaps to explain why Luke is no longer with us). Interpretation in such a case responds not to the violation of the CP, but to the violation of what collective knowledge tells us is prudent. A guest who turns up at a formal wedding without a tie is violating social expectations; to consider possible reasons for the violation is to consider possible implications. Difficulties arise only when the situation (as encountered in ordinary experience or in a text) is being interpreted by someone who does not share the expected collective knowledge. The example of a lack of cultural grammar that leaps to the mind of the college professor is the undergraduate who requires a footnote explaining the Cumaean Sibyl, or Bolingbroke, or the four humours, or the ontological argument. But obvious allusions and unfamiliar words, or words used in unfamiliar ways, flag themselves; the reader who wishes can pursue their literal meaning and the implications possibly dependent on them. The real difficulty arises when we are unaware of the implications in locutions we think we understand.

So readily do we apply general knowledge and common cultural attitudes that we are hardly aware of them. Donne's 'The Flea' would lose most of its ironies and surprises if fleas were regarded as lucky, or sacred, or romantic in our culture, or if choices of sexual partners were regarded as lightly as choices of bridge or tennis partners. 'The Indifferent' would lose the interest engendered by paradox if constancy in love were not explicitly accounted a virtue. The narrator of *Vanity Fair* describes the snobbish baiting of young Dobbin at Dr Swishtails' academy:

'If a pound of mutton-candles cost sevenpence-halfpenny, how much must Dobbin cost?' and a roar would follow from all the circle of young knaves, usher and all, who rightly considered that the selling of goods by retail is a shameful and infamous practice, meriting the contempt and scorn of all real gentlemen.

That the illocutionary force here is that of an ironic protest rather than an approving description is conveyed by a combination of linguistic and collective knowledge. Whatever English attitudes toward the shopkeeping class, then or now (and the reader is likely to feel that Thackeray himself is snobbish enough in these matters), 'shameful', 'infamous', 'scorn', and 'contempt' are too strong to be taken as expressing a transparent meaning.

When Stevenson in 'Aes Triplex' describes the inhabitants of cities built next to volcanoes and comments 'It seems not credible that respectable married people, with umbrellas, should find appetite for a bit of supper within quite a long distance of a fiery mountain,' the effectiveness of the interpolated phrase 'with umbrellas' arises not from the dictionary definition of 'umbrella', but from the readers' knowledge that umbrellas are prudential appliances more associated with middle-aged respectability than nonchalance or daring (not to mention the physical knowledge of the inadequacy of umbrellas in a shower of lava).

She was the daughter of Sonoo, a Hill-man of the Himalayas, and Jadéh his wife. One year their maize failed, and two bears spent the night in their only opium poppy-field just above the Sutlej Valley on the Kotgarh side; so, next season, they turned Christian, and brought their baby to the Mission to be baptized.

Thus begins Kipling's 'Lispeth', and the reader's knowledge that natural disasters are possible but not adequate causes for changing religions sets up the background for the irony and scepticism with which Kipling treats missionary Christianity through the remainder of the story.

The fact is that allusions which appeal to specific knowledge are generally of less final importance for interpretation than the most general cultural awareness. Undoubtedly the reader of 'Aes Triplex' gains by knowing precisely what is meant by 'the blue-peter might fly at the truck', or that the 'Permanent Possibility of Sensation' is a phrase from J.S. Mill's *An Examination of Sir William Hamilton's Philosophy*, or that 'Death may be knocking at the door, like the Commander's statue' alludes to the Don Juan story. However, such allusions and references, which call attention to themselves and can readily be looked up by a reader or glossed by an editor, can in fact be skipped over without great loss to the meaning of the essay. But what editor could or would gloss the complex and contradictory cultural attitudes towards death against which the essay plays? Either the reader brings these to the essay, or the force of the essay is lost. This mass of knowledge is essentially what is fashionably called 'intertextuality' these days. That all texts must be understood in terms of other texts is indeed true if we follow the equally fashionable usage that makes every form of communication a 'text'. However, we must continue to remember that while any extant text may inspire criticism of any other text, only a rather rigorously defined group of texts is relevant to its interpretation.

The most pedestrian of situations carries with it a congeries of presuppositions and related bits of knowledge. Discursive mention of cashing a cheque presupposes knowledge of banks, current accounts, and the simple mechanics of exchanging a cheque for cash. Casual mention of a filling station evokes (in the United States) images of pumps and hoses, restrooms, grease racks, the smell of petrol, etc. The usual aspects and concomitants of situations and locales can be thought of as 'default' elements: normally a reader or hearer need not be told that there are counters in a shop, waiters or waitresses in a restaurant, bottles behind a bar, stoves and sinks in a kitchen. Only if the expected concomitants are absent do they merit comment.

Unless we are told otherwise, we interpret discourse on the assumption that the world is the world we know. This assumption of the normality of the world to which discourse refers leads us, as Brown and Yule remark, to 'assume that our muscles will continue to move normally, that doors which normally open will continue to open, that hair grows on heads, that dogs bark, that towns retain their geographical locations, that the sun will shine, and so on' (62).

Unfortunately, when reading a text from an earlier age or different culture, or even from a different contemporary sub-culture, there is no formula that will ensure that we have not missed an implication through ignorance of the appropriate cultural grammar (or, if one prefers, existing intertextual matrix). That is another reason why texts, literary or otherwise, cannot be interpreted 'in themselves'. The more we share the author's cultural grammar, the easier it is to forget how much we are bringing to bear on the text. The New Critics often forgot it, but fortunately the leaders of the movement at least were able to call up a broad knowledge of English and American culture of the past and present. Among English critics one finds that F.R. Leavis, whose emphasis on close reading paralleled the American, was much clearer about the importance of the collective dimension of context. He grumbled in his usual acerbic way, 'The truth is that even the most acclaimed and critical work on English authors—Jane Austen, the Brontës, Dickens, George Eliot,

D. H. Lawrence—betrays a disqualifying ignorance of the civiliza-
tion out of which those authors wrote, and thus an inability to read
them.' (*ELOT* 34.) The further the interpreter is distanced from the
culture the author assumes, the more exertion is required to know
what the author assumed to be shared.

To take examples of ethnic differences cited by Dell Hymes, a
reader of a Wasco narrative in which a newcomer joining a group is
ignored or in which one person pays a visit to another by simply
entering the house, sitting for a while and then leaving would very
likely draw the wrong conclusions without the knowledge that in
that culture to greet a newcomer immediately is impolite and that
silent visits are routine (108). Other such examples of culturally
specific patterns of behaviour given by Hymes are 'that among
Araucanians it is an insult to be asked to repeat an answer, that a
prompt answer from a Toba means he has no time to answer questions, that a Wasco prefers not to answer a question on the day of
asking, that Aritama prefer intermediaries for requests' (110).

Authors may assume an audience with as extensive or as specialized a knowledge as they wish. The *broader* the knowledge of history, literature, philosophy, and science the author expects the
audience to share, the smaller and more privileged or select the
group assumed as readers. On the other hand, there are any number
of narrowly specialized fields of knowledge that an author can
expect a reader to share—from sports to physics to card games to
philosophy to law. What differs from field to field is not only
vocabulary and range of allusion, but modes of argument that in
turn vary with the canons of proof accepted in each field (see
Willard, 12–14). Thus the kinds of evidence collected and cited, and,
to use Stephen Toulmin's terms, the warrants employed and backing cited, will vary from field to field. The author's assumptions
about the audience's knowledge generate in turn a text that helps
imply the anticipated audience and intended genre.

Now of course the customs, attitudes, and institutional structures
of society, what John Searle calls 'institutional facts', influence how
a thing may be said. At the same time, language can communicate
differences in how we think about things and thus serve as the
instrument of change in institutional facts. One can mystify oneself
by arguing that if language depends on the collective context and the
collective context on experience as expressed in language, we are
locked into a circle that makes change impossible. But the great

number of institutions that remain relatively stable at any one time provide a sharable context in which a particular change can be considered. That is in fact the way change occurs in Stanley Fish's model of 'interpretive communities': however radical the change may seem, at any one time the majority of critical tenets is shared, and those in question are argued by appeal to these still-shared tenets.

We must not forget that all dimensions mutually influence each other. Not only does the collective context influence how we use language, and the use we make of language influence the collective context, but these changes influence the dictionary meanings of individual words that cause shifts in the meanings of still other words. Saussure fully recognized the importance of the constant interchange between *langue* and the contexts of its use, describing its study, which he himself did not propose to pursue, as 'external linguistics'. 'First and foremost', he wrote, 'come all the points where linguistics borders on ethnology . . . The culture of a nation exerts an influence on its language, and the language, on the other hand, is largely responsible for the nation.' Then follow 'the relations between language and political history', 'the relations between language and all sorts of institutions (the Church, the school, etc.)' and then 'everything that relates to the geographical spreading of languages and dialectical splitting' (20–1).

2. The Specific Dimension

If the collective dimension includes knowledge presumed general to an entire class of anticipated interpreters, what I call the 'specific' dimension includes only those elements that are peculiar to the situation in which a discourse occurs. There appear to be five major, not wholly separable, elements to the specific dimension:

1. The physical situation: a conversation in a comfortable room in front of a crackling fire; a speech given to a large group after a banquet; the dialogue between two people changing a tyre in the driving rain.

2. The psychological condition of the speaker and hearer(s), which may be pretty much the same or quite different: both may be angry; one angry and the other fearful; one pleased and the other annoyed.

3. The socio-cultural relationship: politician/constituent; parent/child; employer/employee; customer/clerk.

4. Interpersonal awareness: by this I mean rather specific personal knowledge of shared experiences, or of important attitudes, or past events in the life of an intended interpreter. Such knowledge is closely related to that which I have discussed as the authorial, and in many cases may be included in it, but there is a great deal of difference between the knowledge an ordinary reader possesses about the author of a novel and that which intimate friends draw upon as they write letters to one another.

5. For any sentence, the immediately preceding ones:

LORD WINDERMERE. Mrs. Erlynne is coming here to-night.
LORD AUGUSTUS. Your wife has sent an invitation?
LORD WINDERMERE. Mrs. Erlynne has received a card.

Lord Augustus appears to miss at least part of the implication of the peculiar form of the reply, but the audience does not.

Though none of these elements is wholly independent of the others, each plays its own role. One can have an argument, declare love, or boredly pass time in the most comfortable room; a constituent who distrusts a politician is likely to speak differently to or about the politican than if he or she is a boss who distrusts an employee. The permutations are of course manifold: consider simply the differences that are likely to follow from each single pair of alternatives in the following: (A husband and wife/Two strangers) are (angrily/laughingly/one angrily, one laughingly) standing (in the lobby of a theatre/at a windy bus stop) as one says ('I don't want to talk about this'/'We've got to make the best of it').

As with the other dimensions, the importance of various elements making up the specific dimension—and of that dimension itself—depends on the genre. In the case of two friends who meet on the street, the physical situation will be obvious (so that, for instance, what would be an abrupt exchange on a sunny afternoon would seem normal in the driving rain). The psychological situation will either be understood by both (they are embarrassed by a previous argument, or the enjoyable evening they had together the last time they met will still be fresh); or if one is in a mood unaccountable to the other an explanation is expected ('I'm in a great rush, talk to you later,' or 'If I seem confused, it's because . . .'). The social situation will be understood by both (one may be much older or have greater social status). Both will be aware of what experiences they have shared and what things they have said to each other (however, this last interpersonal dimension is not necessarily wholly bidirectional: for instance, *A* may know something about *B* that *B* does not know that *A* knows).

In contrast, in the case of lyric poems or essays, the reader does not normally directly share a physical, psychological, social, or interpersonal situation with the author. While the reader may be aware of the physical situation in which the text was written, or the attitude of the author, so far as there is reason for believing that the author intended these to be taken into account in the process of interpretation, they fall under our authorial or collective dimensions. The specific dimension might then seem relevant only to verbal utterances, letters, and routine communications, not to the usual literary genres. However, as already noted, the structure of fictional narrative, whether conveyed in the form of prose, verse, or drama, demands that we both interpret each character's speeches, and that we consider how each character responds to the speeches of the other characters. This in turn requires that we keep in mind the particular specific dimension that obtains in the case of each dialogue situation.

A simple example will do: Chapter 12 of *Bleak House* is titled 'On the Watch'. Towards the end of the chapter, Lady Dedlock reminds the lawyer Tulkinghorn, 'You sent me a message respecting the person whose writing I happened to inquire about. It was like you to remember the circumstances; I had quite forgotten it again. I can't imagine what association I had with a hand like that; but I surely had some.' From the point of view of the reader, the specific dimension in terms of which this and the ensuing dialogue is to be interpreted includes the following knowledge: that Tulkinghorn had been surprised by Lady Dedlock's interest and that Lady Dedlock had all but fainted in his presence following her question about the handwriting, that Tulkinghorn had later taken considerable pains to discover the identity of the writer, that Lady Dedlock had apparently again felt ill when she learned that Tulkinghorn had information for her about the writer, and that Sir Leicester had attached no importance to her question. The reader further knows that Tulkinghorn may have known more than he has said (or the narrator has told us), possibly as a result of his interest in the law-writer's portmanteau at the time he and Krook discovered the writer's death, and that, alternatively, a clue to the writer's identity may be in Krook's possession, since he had been able 'to steal to the old portmanteau, and steal back again'.

All this the reader bears in mind as the lawyer finishes his report:

'What did they call the wretched being?'
'They called him what he had called himself, but no one knew his name.'
'Not even any one who had attended on him?'
'No one had attended on him. He was found dead. In fact I found him.'
'Without any clue to anything more?'
'Without any; there was', says the lawyer meditatively, 'an old portmanteau; but—No, there were no papers.'

Which reply, with all its possible implications, is added not only to the reader's guesses about Tulkinghorn's knowledge but to guesses about Lady Dedlock's assumptions about Tulkinghorn.

3. *The Textual Dimension*

By the textual dimension I refer to the totality of explicit arguments, events, scenes, or actions in the order and form in which these are presented in the text. I. A. Richards found it necessary to be specific in correcting a possible confusion between the external context of a word (the associations that, having attached themselves to a word prior to its use in a given sentence, have become candidates for interpretive relevance) and the internal context provided by the sentence in which it appears (*IT* viii). It is similarly necessary to distinguish between external interpretive dimensions (linguistic, authorial, generic, collective, specific) and what may be called the secondary equivalents of certain of these within the text itself. By 'secondary equivalents' I designate the way that the use of a given word within a text builds associational significances within that text; the way a certain character's speech or action creates an element of the specific dimension in which another speech or action is interpreted; or the way a particular argument buttresses another argument within that text. We can say then that the elements of the collective and specific dimensions cited at the beginning of this chapter as relevant to the interpretation of Antony's speech are 'secondary'. They are created by the structure of the text. In contrast, an example of external collective knowledge would be a general awareness of the possibility of violence in crowd psychology.

In an essay, the order in which arguments, analogies, illustrations, and images occur creates the secondary equivalents. For instance in Charles Lamb's 'New Year's Eve', 'I am not content to pass away "like a weaver's shuttle." Those metaphors solace me not, nor sweeten the unpalatable draught of mortality.' And 'Can a ghost laugh, or shake his gaunt sides, when you are pleasant with him?' prepare the way for the turn toward jollity in the conclusion:

> More than all, I conceive disgust at those impertinent and misbecoming familiarities, inscribed upon your ordinary tombstones. Every dead man must take upon himself to be lecturing me with his odious truism, that 'Such as he now is I must shortly be.' Not so shortly, friend, as thou imaginest. In the meantime I am alive. I move about. I am worth twenty of thee. Know thy betters!

To return to *Bleak House*, the scenes suggesting Lady Dedlock's interest in the handwriting upon which her eye had by chance fallen serve as a set of internal specific dimensions for the later scene which I quoted. They point the way to Lady Dedlock's interpretation of Tulkinghorn's speeches and actions, to Tulkinghorn's interpretation of Lady Dedlock's speeches and actions, and to the reader's interpretation of the whole of the unfolding narrative. Inasmuch as Esther is the author of her narrative, her description of herself creates the internal authorial dimension we apply in interpreting her narrative. The history and nature of the Jarndyce and Jarndyce lawsuit becomes an element in an internal collective dimension: it is one of the facts with which almost everyone in the novel is acquainted.

These secondary or internal relationships are what the New Criticism has been especially successful in analysing. The New Critics saw that what each word, each sentence, each scene, brings into a text is a set of potentialities that is actualized by relationships within the total text. To choose between potentialities is to interpret. We interpret individual words, speeches, scenes, events, arguments, very much as we interpret sentences, by seeking consistent constructions. The difference is that while in the case of a single sentence interpretation involves discovering the consistency of that sentence with the external contextual dimensions, in the case of extended discourse we must seek interpretations that will be consistent as well with the secondary (internal) equivalents of these to which the text or utterance gives rise. The assumption that a consistent or unified meaning can be found remains paramount as we look in two directions at once. This situation is pretty much what I take E. D. Hirsch to be describing when he writes:

> My purpose is to show that we use 'context' to signify two necessary but distinct functions in interpretation. By 'context' we mean a construed notion of

the whole meaning narrow enough to determine the meaning of a part, and, at the same time, we use the word to signify those givens in the milieu [external context] that will help us to conceive the right notion of the whole. (*VI* 87.)

Though I would prefer the admittedly more awkward statement that the 'givens in the milieu' guide us towards the right interpretation by causing us to seek the necessary implicatures to achieve an external as well as internal consistency, I believe Hirsch is looking in the same direction to which I have been pointing.

It will be helpful here to recognize explicitly the distinction between that which is told and the manner of telling. There is, on the one hand, the story of the events of Oedipus's life from the prophecy before his birth to his discovery of his parentage and anguished self-blinding and, on the other, the order and manner in which these are related in Sophocles' play. The first has variously been designated as *histoire*, fable, or story and the second as *récit*, discourse, or *sujet*. The most obvious difference between the two is in the order of the telling, but, as analysts of narrative have recently made us much more aware, there are many kinds of important variation in the way a story may be told. In *Narrative Discourse*, Gérard Genette, the most prominent of the 'narratologists', devotes a chapter each to the order of telling, variations in the speed or narration ('duration'), repetitions in the presentation of the story ('frequency'), perspectives from which the events of the story are viewed ('mood'), and the choice of narrators ('voice'). There are also 'styles' of narration to be taken into consideration: the degree of reliability of the narrator, dialect, register, degree of figurativeness, and eccentricities unique to a given narrator.

The structure of Stevenson's 'Markheim' may be said to rest on two paragraphs just prior to the conclusion. Urged by the apparition to kill the returning servant girl in order to escape from the scene of the murder he has just committed, Markheim responds, 'But I have still my hatred of evil; and from that, to your galling disappointment, you shall see that I can draw both energy and courage.' The reader may or may not be surprised by Markheim's resolution, but he or she is very likely to be surprised by what follows:

The features of the visitor began to undergo a wonderful and lovely change; they heightened and softened with a touch of tender triumph; and even as they brightened, faded and dislimned. But Markheim did not pause to watch or understand the transformation.

Then the conclusion:

> He confronted the maid upon the threshold with something like a smile. 'You had better go for the police,' said he: 'I have killed your master.'

Essential to the effective *pattern* of this short story is of course the delayed, and implicative, revelation that the apparition is not an emissary of the devil but of heaven. The manner in which the revelation is handled, and the earlier actions and speeches of the apparition that are retrospectively illuminated by the revelation, are as much a part of the pattern as the order of events usually thought of as 'the plot'.

Shifts between narrators (Esther versus third person in *Bleak House* or Benjy, Quentin, Jason, and third person in Faulkner's *The Sound and the Fury*), or anomalies in the narrative style or flow of narrative are also facets of the structure of discourse. Anomalies are often simply deviations from what the text has already taught us to expect: the third-person narration of the 'Dilsey' section of *The Sound and the Fury* calls attention to itself by contrast with the first-person narration of the first three sections.

Each bit of dialogue or event in a novel will be interpreted in terms of the total internal (secondary) set of dimensions created to that point in the text. That interpretation determines the reader's anticipation of the future course of the plot. When the (selectively) omniscient narrator in *Bleak House* presents the scene of Tulkinghorn's murder without naming the murderer—evidently in order to heighten mystery and suspense—that also is an aspect of manner.

Though 'story' is perfectly adequate as the term for the temporal sequence of events incorporated into narrative, it is incongruous as applied to other genres. And 'discourse' serves only awkwardly to describe the form in which the story is told; it is better reserved for its larger meaning of language-in-use. The best alternative for 'story' of which I am aware is simply 'material', and for 'discourse' the best may be 'pattern', which can include order, narrative point of view, and such features as the withholding of information, or skipping over events, or intertwining of sub-plots. Both terms have the advantage of being directly applicable to other genres as well as to narrative fiction. Evidently the argument of an essay, as well as the events of a story, can be patterned in a variety of ways.

Again there is a parallel with the interpretation of the single sentence; as Fish argued when advocating his theory of 'affective stylistics', the order of a locution, including the revisions in our interpretation occasioned by that order, affects our total response. Wolfgang Iser, more than anyone else, has taught us to see that the process of reading consists of forming anticipations, some of which are validated while some are falsified; in the latter case we revise our anticipations, probably revising the provisional interpretations on which we had based those anticipations. I especially like John Holloway's suggestion of 'propone' as the proper word to describe the relation between a narrative event and the possibilities it brings before the reader. To propone is to propose for consideration, acceptance, or adoption (OED). Narrative events do not 'entail' each other as Todorov has described them in his analysis of stories from the *Decameron*, says Holloway, rather, 'To say that a monk has violated a law *brings up the matter* of his abbot's punishing him. This does not mean that it is not possible for the abbot not to do so, nor that he will do so, nor anything of the kind.' (3–4.) Our expectations and therefore our interpretations of characters, events, and purposes remain necessarily tentative until we reach the final sentence of the text. We cannot help constantly forming and revising our interpretations as we read; as analysts of discourse like van Dijk and Kintsch insist, we cannot wait to interpret (in their terminology, 'to construct a textbase') until 'all the evidence is available at the end of a paragraph (chapter, book), but must do so in real time and with a limited short-term memory capacity' (44). This constant revision of our tentative interpretations is what Louise Rosenblatt has termed the 'backward flow': 'As the text unrolls, there is not only the cumulative build-up of effect through the linking of remembered earlier elements to the new one. There is sometimes a backward flow, a revison of earlier understandings, emphases, or attitudes; there may even be the emergence of a completely altered framework or principle of organization.' (60–6.)

So far, I have discussed texts as though they were easily definable entities, though we know that they frequently are not: they exist in various versions and may have explicit or implied relations to other works. However, holding tight to the difference between interpretation and criticism will again help untangle unnecessary confusions. To begin with, the *choice* between, for instance, three author-produced versions of a text is *not* an interpretive question. Let us suppose an author of a novel is responsible for an original version *A* for serial publication, a version *B* for publication as a single volume, and a version *C* for a collected edition. To the extent that the textual differences lead a reader to different interpretations, each version will have its unique meaning. It would be absurd to say that the author really meant in version *A* what he or she means in version *C*. The author meant in each version what that version conveys. If we choose *C* because it represents the author's final revision, or *A* because it conveys what the author intended before having second thoughts, or *B* because biographical evidence tells us that *A* reflects the prejudices of the periodical's editor and the changes in *C* occurred after the onset of senility, we are in each case choosing on the basis of extrinsic criteria—we are making critical, not interpretive, judgements. Such judgements have to be made: one must decide which version one wishes to publish, or interpret, or evaluate, or analyse for whatever purpose. But the question lies outside the process of interpretation.

The question of the relationship to other works by the same author is more difficult because here we *must* at times ask a question that can only be answered by extrinsic evidence. Since interpretation assumes a conscious attempt to achieve consonance, the question becomes the determination of the boundaries within which the author sought unity. An essay in which I. A. Richards sports with the question 'How Does a Poem Know When It Is Finished?' bears on the problem: Richards's point in putting the question in this way is that unity depends on the 'opposition and collaboration' of words. A writer's choice of a word or image here affects what may be said later and how what may be said may be said—though choices made later may require revision of earlier choices. The whole process depends on adjustments between the writer's intended meaning and the implication of the ways the meaning is expressed—adjustments needed to achieve consonance within a defined text:

The completion of a poem may be no matter of addition or exclusion, or of change in phrasing—though the change of one word may make very extensive changes in the opposition and collaboration of other words. The completion may depend upon questions of sequence among parts otherwise invariant. Similarly, heightened attention to one word may lead to great changes in the mutual enablements of other words. (120.)

We need to know the boundaries within which the author assumed the 'opposition and collaboration' to be occurring.

Under uncomplicated circumstances, to insist on interpreting a single sonnet without reference to the larger sequence in which it first appeared seems as arbitrary as to insist on interpreting the middle stanzas of an ode in isolation. But there are a host of complicated cases. Rossetti, for instance, wrote the sonnets that make up 'The House of Life' over many years. Fifty sonnets and eleven songs appeared in the *Poems* of 1870 under the title 'Towards a work to be called "The House of Life" '. Forty-nine of these sonnets plus six that had appeared in the 1870 volume under the title 'Sonnets for Pictures, and Other Sonnets' were included in Rosseti's 1881 volume—some with revisions, most not—where they were interspersed with forty-seven new sonnets. Thus, the second sonnet in the 1870 edition, there titled 'Love's Redemption', is printed in 1881, with important changes to two lines, as the third sonnet with the title 'Love's Testament'.

The interpreter's main care in a case like this is to avoid conflating what are essentially different texts. It would be absurd to argue that none of these sonnets can be interpreted by itself. Rossetti's note in the 1870 edition calls attention to the fact that 'The House of Life' is a work in progress, and careful readers have doubted that the final version is ordered into a true unity. Nevertheless, the following would transgress the principles of interpretation: arguing for a meaning in the 1870 'Love's Redemption' not consonant with interpretation of the fifty sonnets of 1870 as a whole; arguing for a meaning in the 1881 'Love's Testament' not consonant with the meaning of the final version of 'The House of Life'; substituting the 1881 version in interpreting the 1870 sequence; substituting the 1870 version in interpreting the 1881 sequence; arguing for an interpretation of either version on the grounds that its meaning had to fit with one or more of Rossetti's sonnets or poems not part of 'The House of Life'. In short, one must at times ask the extrinsic question, what evidence is there that an author regarded a group of novels, poems, or plays as a unified whole to be interpreted as a single text; and if there is such an evidence, which versions are to be so regarded?

Looked at ecologically or koinonoetically, to think of a text—whether that of an essay, lyric poem, or narrative—as a series of propositions is like thinking of a sentence simply as a locution. A text is in fact a system of propositions that generate implicatures, the interpretation of each of which adds to an internal (secondary) context that guides the interpretation of subsequent implicatures.

As that context unrolls it also not infrequently makes possible the retrospective interpretation of earlier implicatures that may have been noted as puzzling, or as probably of yet undetermined significance (many of the details in the description of the coming ceremony in Shirley Jacksons's 'The Lottery') or may be recognized as significant only afterwards (many of the earlier details of the story being told by Browning's speaker in 'Porphyria's Lover'). John Holloway thus speaks of narratives 'depositing' bits of knowledge that will later be 'called in' (47). That sense of the interweaving of details of setting, action, and dialogue, of understanding achieved through the forward thrust of anticipation and backward flow of recognition is generated by the shared assumption of consonance. It produces, to enlarge a term artfully chosen by Halliday and Hasan (2), the 'texture' of a text.

6

Clarifications, Parallels, Distinctions

We are now in a position to clarify a number of possible confusions that could only be glanced at earlier. First we need to recognize that interpretive probabilities vary not only with the discourse in question but also with the component of the speech-act we are considering. Second, we must examine more fully the relationship between ecological interpretation and other theoretical approaches to discourse in general and literature in particular. The vagueness of the term 'approaches' suggests the difficulty here: the number of kinds of commentary that might be listed depends solely on how finely one wishes to categorize. There are many structuralisms, many types of New Critic, many varieties even of so comparatively recent an endeavour as feminist criticism. Further, the crucial distinction that I have made between interpretation of meaning and criticism of significance cuts across some of the larger categories of commentary. I will therefore enumerate (in section 2) three categories of commentary that I believe are subsumed in ecological interpretation. Then in section 3, after unreservedly affirming the necessity of extrinsic criticism, I will briefly consider some of the major extrinsic approaches.

1. What We Question, What We Don't, and How Sure We Can Be

Interpretations of a sentence, paragraph, stanza, scene, chapter, or total work can never be more than probable. In theory all interpretations are open to question; in practice, given sufficient ingenuity, all can be. Yet we are certain enough of the meaning of most of what we read and hear in carrying out the day-to-day business of life to act on it without qualms. Nor do readers question literary texts at all points. No one, so far as I know, has yet questioned that Conrad's Marlowe tells us that he journeyed up a (probably African) river, and that, within the partially non-referential world of the

narrative, he in fact did so, or that Crane's Henry Fleming participa-
tes in a Civil War battle, or that Hamlet fights a fatal duel with
Laertes, or that the speaker in Wordsworth's 'Three Years She Grew
in Sun and Shower' is describing feelings about a girl who has died.

Now, though every sentence we read and every event we observe
must be interpreted, the interpretations that prove debatable are
least often of events, occasionally of characters' motivations, more
frequently of the values against which an author intends a text to be
seen (all propositional or illocutionary questions), and most often
how the author intended the reader to respond (questions of
perlocutionary intent, purpose, and project). The reasons for the
differences are obvious enough. Even though, indeed because, language divides into discrete objects what would otherwise be, in
Saussure's terms, the 'shapeless and indistinct mass' gleaned from
our senses, we have little difficulty interpreting either direct sense
reports or statements about sense-reported reality. We know
approximately what we would have to see and hear before we would
think 'the tea table was spread' or 'the car sped away'. We can easily
enough imagine the sort of sense reports that would lead us to agree
that:

Miss Brooke had the kind of beauty which seems to be thrown into relief by
poor dress. (Eliot, *Middlemarch*.)

or

> All in a hot and copper sky,
> The bloody Sun, at noon,
> Right up above the mast did stand,
> No bigger than the Moon.
>
> (Coleridge, 'The Ancient Mariner'.)

or

It was nearly the time of the full moon, and on this account, though the sky
was lined with a uniform sheet of dripping cloud, ordinary objects out of
doors were readily visible. (Hardy, 'The Three Strangers'.)

However, motivation, attitudes, and evaluations must be understood in terms of all the sorts of awareness and knowledge that make
up the several contextual dimensions. Moreover, attitudes and
evaluations are frequently expressed indirectly even in everyday
speech and writing, through implicature that depends on knowledge

drawn from specific contexts. 'Jackson Pollock should have worked for a wallpaper company.' 'The 1984 Gary Hart campaign reminded me of the advertising for the Edsel.' 'Liverpool may prove to be the Labour Party's Waterloo.'

We accept reports of our senses, our interpretations of these reports, our routinized interpretations of language, and the intentions of the users of language until we encounter anomalies, contradictions, or incongruities. We interpret everything that enters the mind, asking the significance of events in general, the meaning of the language we hear or read (roughly we ask what is being referred to outside the *parole* itself) and the intent of the user. But generally we are conscious of our interpretive activity only when puzzlement, or unusual complexity, or discrepancy calls our attention to what we are doing. Though the genre of a work suggests how carefully the reader is to proceed, we no more question the apparent interpretation of every sentence in any text than of every report of our senses or every sentence we hear uttered.

For simplicity, let's confine ourselves to a commonplace reading of brief narrative fiction and consider what in general is accepted and what is moot. Consider, for example, how we respond to representative passages in Hemingway's 'The Short Happy Life of Francis Macomber'. Although it is just possible that by the end of the story we may have reason to reinterpret them (the whole story may turn out to be a dream, for instance), we are unlikely to question what I will call the narrative facts presented in the opening sentences. Lacking implicature-triggering anomalies, the reader accepts the locutions as transparent.

> It was now lunch time and they were all sitting under the double green fly of the dining tent pretending that nothing had happened.
> 'Will you have lime juice or lemon squash?' Macomber asked.

We very quickly, however, begin to examine the narrator's intent in presenting the story as he does; we question what is being implied about additional, as yet unstated, facts, and about the characters' attitudes and thus the motivations behind what they say. By the end of the first page we know that Francis Macomber had been carried in triumph by certain of the natives, though not by the gunbearers, and the fact that the narrator thinks it significant to mention that the gunbearers did not take part suggests immediately that we should look for implicatures. We are already prepared to question whether

Wilson's 'You've got your lion . . . and a damned fine one too' is altogether sincere. We make provisional conjectures and wait for corroborating or disconfirming evidence.

Some thirty pages later, we are sure enough that Wilson's actions, speeches, and thoughts all point in the same direction to question what seems a direct statement of fact by a narrator we have so far seen no reason to distrust.

Wilson had ducked to one side to get in a shoulder shot. Macomber had stood solid and shot for the nose, shooting a touch high each time . . . and Mrs. Macomber, in the car, had shot at the buffalo with the .5 Mannlicher as it seemed about to gore Macomber and had hit her husband about two inches up and a little to one side of the base of his skull.

Doubting that Margot Macomber would have tried to save her husband, recognizing that she had just acquired a reason to fear him, and noting that the quoted sentences have the sound of a newspaper article rather than of the narrator's voice (for instance the reference is to 'Mrs. Macomber', not to 'Margot'), we draw our own conclusions and are prepared to credit the implicature of Wilson's 'That was a pretty thing to do . . . He *would* have left you too.'

Now what is arguable? One can hardly imagine serious questioning that Macomber ran from his first lion, gained courage on the buffalo hunt the next day to the extent of seeming a changed man, and was shot by his wife while trying to finish off a wounded buffalo. It is hardly arguable that Margot Macomber is contemptuous of her husband. It would be difficult indeed to argue that Wilson does not hunt according to a particular code or that the author disapproved of that code. It is hardly possible to contend that the author did not regard Macomber's transformation as a victory. A reader feels sure of such interpretations wherever no anomalies, violations, or incongruencies suggest implicature rather than transparency. The reader feels equally certain of many another 'fact' that is either stated or implied by the report of physical surroundings and events: for instance, that the hunt takes place in Africa, though that is never stated.

On the other hand, it is just possible to argue that Margot did not intentionally shoot her husband or that the author intended the ending to be ambiguous. The conclusion we draw from all we know of the relationships in the story is that Margot intended to kill

Francis, but that large-scale implication is opposed by her denial and the almost transparent account of the actual accident. Whether the narrator expects the reader to approve of all Wilson's actions is also debatable. Our interpretation of the author's attitude toward the three characters depends heavily on social values outside the story: since courage is almost always regarded as a virtue, we will take the narrator's attitude toward Macomber's actions to accord with this evaluation unless something in the story explicitly contradicts them. The same thing is true of Margot's relation to Macomber; unless the narrative suggests an alternative assessment, we apply the usual social condemnation to the rubbing of salt in psychological wounds. As for Wilson's sexual encounter with Margot, society generally disapproves of that sort of thing as well, and Wilson's thoughts on the matter reveal an uneasy conscience. On the other hand, social values, even by the 1920s, had shifted rather markedly from what they were in, say, the 1870s. Where public values made adultery far more heinous than cowardice or psychological cruelty fifty years earlier, by the 1920s the word one would have tended to apply would have been 'infidelity', and its ranking relative to intentional cruelty was becoming moot. Experienced readers will correct for the further change in sexual standards between the 1920s and 1980s.

We find then (1) narrative facts we accept, whether presented transparently or through implicature, because they clash with no other narrative facts; (2) narrative facts presented in such a way that we question them; (3) perlocutionary intentions and authorial evaluations about which we may be anything from almost certain to wholly uncertain, depending on the evidence of the text. *However, the propositions expressed by locutions that make up the text will be preponderantly of the first kind.*

The same processes of interpretation apply, *mutatis mutandis*, to all other genres. For an example of a lyric poem, I should like to glance at Hardy's 'The Oxen'.

> Christmas Eve, and twelve of the clock.
>   'Now they are all on their knees,'
> An elder said as we sat in a flock
>   By the embers in hearthside ease.
>
> We pictured the meek mild creatures where
>   They dwelt in their strawy pen,
> Nor did it occur to one of us there
>   To doubt they were kneeling then.

> So fair a fancy few would weave
>   In these years! Yet, I feel,
> If someone said on Christmas Eve,
>   'Come; see the oxen kneel,
>
> 'In the lonely barton by yonder coomb
>   Our childhood used to know,'
> I should go with him in the gloom,
>   Hoping it might be so.

Any New Critical commentator could quickly provide a textbook explication. The speaker is expressing a wry, nostalgic wish that he could believe in such old legends as that oxen the world over kneel at midnight on Christmas Eve in honour of Christ's birth. By extension he wishes that he retained some form of a Christian, or at least generally religious, view of the world, though the larger belief seems to him quite as impossible as the belief that the oxen kneel. The speaker's doubt is expressed quietly but repeated variously, playing linguistic, generic, and collective knowledge against each other. The 'hearthside ease' of the first stanza suggests the comfort of the home on Christmas Eve, especially in the speaker's memory, but it also reminds us that the elders do not choose to verify that the oxen are kneeling. The oxen are pictured as 'meek mild creatures' dwelling 'in their strawy pen'—an appropriate enough image for animals who annually participate in an act of adoration but one that also suggests the sentimentalization of the image the child had formed. The belief is not now seen as absurd but simply too 'fair . . . In these years' (the latter phrase is functionally ambiguous in suggesting both the changed culture and the change in the speaker). The invitation that the speaker imagines, 'Come; see the oxen kneel . . .' continues 'In the lonely barton by yonder coomb/Our childhood used to know.' The implications here are both that he is imagining the invitation taking place on the farm where he was a child and the simultaneous recognition that his hope is nurtured essentially by emotions associated with his childhood. And then there is the effective ambiguity (really a triple reference) in the use of the word 'gloom' in the penultimate line: 'I should go with him in the gloom/Hoping it might be so.' 'Gloom' is at once physical darkness, the speaker's despondency or sadness, and the threatening or mournful atmosphere of the world at large.

Already what at first might seem an analysis that has stayed within the internal structure of the text has tapped various dimensions of discourse. As an obvious instance, the word 'elder', the allusion to passing time in 'in these years', and the reference to childhood in the last stanza combine to determine for us that the poem recalls a memory from childhood. But, authorized by the genre, we seek to bring as much as possible of our linguistic knowledge into play. Our knowledge of uses of the word 'elder' outside the poem suggests other possibilities (one does not have to be a child to regard someone as an elder; the word may refer to status in a church congregation for instance) that remain in solution until a particular meaning is precipitated out. The co-operation of the other indicators of the passing of time since childhood also determines one meaning of 'in these years', but we suspect a doubleness because of our knowledge of the phrase's conventional use to refer to something like 'the current state of things'. The likelihood of this second meaning is of course increased by our knowledge of elements of the collective dimension of the poem, the gradual loss of faith and weakening of religious affirmation that became so visible and debated an issue in the latter half of the nineteenth century. The susceptibility of the word 'gloom' to the same intentional ambiguity increases our comfort with this interpretation (a good example of the way an ambiguity, the meanings of which are compatible, may reinforce the determinability of a particular interpretation).

Acquaintance with depictions of the nativity scene in popular art reinforces our sense of the sentimentalization implied by the mental picture of the oxen as 'meek mild creatures'. Our knowledge of how words are used outside the poem, partly a matter of cultural convention, partly a matter of simply knowing what dialects are, tells us that the words 'barton' and 'coomb' are not only appropriate means of evoking the simpler rural context of the speaker's childhood, but that such words have something of the same quaintness about them that the speaker now finds in the legend of the oxen. Our knowledge of literary conventions alerts us to the probability that alliterative phrases are to be regarded as bearers of particular significance: 'So fair a fancy few' emphasizes the words fair and fancy equally—the belief can be called a fancy because it is so fair or appealing, or we can say that the belief can be regarded as fair because it is a fancy (as opposed to a dogma). At the same time, though the genre suggests careful consideration of multiple meanings, possible meanings that do not contribute to consonance are fenced out. 'Flock', for instance—it may be there only for the rhyme with 'clock' , but there is a possible reference to the Christian 'flock' to which all in the room presumably were gathered on that Christmas Eve. The theme makes it possible; the lack of any strongly confirming use of words makes it no more than possible. On the other hand, to insist that 'flock', for instance, carries a suggestion of birds or the texture of certain kinds of materials would be to substitute attenuated associations for interlocked intensity.

Our knowledge of the cultural environment is necessary for us to recognize why the speaker would hope that 'it might be so', that is , that evidence for Christian belief might force itself upon him; if the greater part of society did not conventionally acknowledge the importance and value of religious belief (whatever the beliefs of individual members of society may be) we would find nothing deeper than nostalgia in the poem. At the same time, the speaker appeals to the collectively accepted value of intellectual honesty: honest doubt or agnosticism held with integrity is generally accepted in the twentieth century as worthy of respect though there have of course been times and places where such an intellectual position would have been judged worthy of an *auto-da-fé*. In short, we have only to think how less exact would be the meaning arrived at by one who knew nothing of English intellectual and cultural history, or was unfamiliar with the nativity scene. Alternatively, to look simply at the contribution of our knowledge of the immediate cultural context in which the poem was written, it is easy to imagine the shifts in interpretation if we thought 'The Oxen' either a modernized version of a fourteenth-century poem or a contemporary poem.

Finally, what is likely to remain most uncertain in a lyric poem like 'The Oxen' is the author's perlocutionary intent. Does Hardy expect us to feel a similar nostalgia? Or does he expect the reader to say 'fair as the fancy may be, it is well that the speaker knows it a fancy; one must get on with living in the real world after all'? Or does he wish us to say, in an Arnoldian echo, that 'the strongest part of religion is after all its unconscious poetry'? Are we to deduce that some fundamental religious sense is impossible to eradicate and therefore must be important, or that one ought honestly to substitute poetry for such unconscious poetry, or that once one recognizes that religion is only poetry one can free oneself from any of its claims? Or, to recognize that though we can't go back, the world was a better place when folk believed in the Christian world-view, kneeling oxen and all? Or, if the truth were known, few except children have ever really believed in Christianity, any more than they really believe in the oxen? A greater uncertainty in reconstructing perlocutionary intentions than illocutionary intentions arises because we cannot assume that the author assumed—or desired—that the contexts necessary for accurate interpretation of the former would be shared.

2. Approaches Subsumed in a Koinonoetic Theory of Interpretation

Our theory of interpretation recognizes validity in a wide variety of critical approaches—to all of which it is indebted for insights it seeks to preserve. Much of New Critical practice, several of the cluster of theories that currently fall under the reader-response rubric, and portions of the results of traditional biographical and historical scholarship are directly incorporated. Glances at these collocations will be helpful prior to consideration of some major forms of extrinsic criticism.

The New Criticism. The New Critical movement in the United States, together with the influence of Richards, Empson, and Leavis in England, revolutionized the whole of Anglo-American criticism of literature in a way that can hardly be exaggerated. It is hardly an overstatement to say that for the first time the *meaning* of a text became the focus of the critic's interest rather than its historical, ethical, or aesthetic value. A quick course of reading in well-known English and American critics of the late nineteenth and early twentieth centuries will bring home the extent of this revolution. Informative and intriguing as is much of the writing of Gosse, Saintsbury, W. H. Hutton, Stopford Brooke, Paul Elmer More, or Irving Babbitt, to turn from these commentators to the brief notes of *The Explicator*, not to mention major New Critical essays, is to enter a fresh new world. That the meaning sought is in fact *the author's intended meaning as communicated by the text* can hardly be doubted by anyone who has read Brooks, Warren, Tate, Blackmur, Empson, or Leavis with attention; it is therefore an especially unhappy confusion that the critical principle announced as the 'intentional fallacy' has been so widely understood to exile from serious literary commentary any interest in an author's intentions.

Koinonoetic or ecological interpretation wholly concurs in the importance of the careful attention to imagery, word choice, figures, and order characteristic of the New Critical movement. However, as already noted, the New Critical movement failed to recognize not only that our response to words depends on much more than their dictionary senses, but that the senses and relationships of a word to others in a given use depend upon the text's external contexts as well as the internal one.

Historical and Biographical Scholarship. Although over the last fifty years allegations of the irrelevance and distorting (even deadening) effect of research into the lives of authors and the historical situations in which texts were written have been considerably more common than theoretical defences of their value, the results of historical and biographical scholarship have in fact been welcomed and used by critics of almost all persuasions. The ecological distinction between the beliefs and knowledge an author could assume to be shared by his anticipated readers and that which it would be impossible or unreasonable to assume (even though in practice such a distinction must always be moot and imperfect) recognizes the great importance of such knowledge while sharpening the distinction between biographical and historical materials of use in *interpretation* and those legitimate only for discussions of the *significance* of works.

This distinction cuts equally across what is now being called the 'New Historicism' in literary studies, a movement especially powerful among scholars of Renaissance literature. As an example we may take Laura C. Stevenson's *Praise and Paradox: Merchants and Craftsmen in Elizabethan Popular Literature*. Considering 296 works, Stevenson reconstructs the way Elizabethans thought of what we would regard as 'the middle class'. Now to move inductively from many examples to the reconstruction of a general view is to make use of literature, not to interpret it. However, if we are convinced by the probable accuracy of the reconstructed view, we may call upon it in the interpretation of individual texts so long as we employ it to explain what would otherwise seem anomalous, not as something that must be present in every text of the period.

The 'New Historicism' recognizes the mutual influence between texts and culture, and recognizes it diachronically. Louis Montrose comments

'The Historicity of Texts and Textuality of History': if chiastic formulations such as this are now in fashion, it may be because they help to figure a current emphasis on the dynamic, unstable, and reciprocal relationship between the discursive and material domains. This emphasis involves a rethinking or wholesale rejection of some prevalent conceptions of litera- ture: as an autonomous aesthetic order that transcends the shifting pressure and particularity of material needs and interests; as a collection of inert discursive reflections of 'real events'; as a superstructural manifestation of an economic base. Current practice emphasizes both the *relative* autonomy of specific discourses and their capacity to impact on social formation, to make things happen by shaping the consciousness of social beings.' (8.)

In other words, neither literary works nor other texts directly reflect the cultural order, though they depend on the cultural background or 'grammar' for their interpretation. They may indeed cause changes to occur in the culture. Moreover, they may have different effects, that is significances, for readers in different historical periods. All these are matters of major interest, though only one has to do with the interpretation of meaning: the probabilistic recon- struction of the cultural grammar which the author assumed his readers would share—which must include the recognition that our present cultural biases and preoccupations may be warping that reconstruction. 'Knowledge' of the past is always partial, always inaccurate, but we cannot do without its approximations.

Literary history is a special case. R.S. Crane's influential essay, 'History Versus Criticism in the Study of Literature' (1935), strongly argued the secondary importance of literary history *per se*. The propositions of literary history, he found, are 'not about literature at all. Their subjects, when the propositions are stated in primary form, are not works or the properties of works but persons—writers or readers as the case may be.' (73.) However, Crane defined the 'literary criticism' he opposed to literary history as 'any reasoned discourse concerning works of imaginative literature the statements in which are primarily statements about the works themselves and appropriate to their character as productions of art' (11.) The phrase 'as productions of art' was intended to exclude the use of literary works for psychoanalysis of their authors, or investigations of cul- tural history, or the inculcation of morals. But while Crane defined criticism as 'the recovery of the words and sense of a literary work when these have been lost by reason of the lapse of time' (16), the kinds of knowledge needed to achieve such understanding are left vague. The fact is that the literary history Crane distinguishes from his 'literary criticism', even when strictly defined as the study of the succession of texts, authors, and genres, is valuable to the interpreter in so far as it establishes readers' expectations in the period in which the text in question was written.

Reader-Response Criticism. At least eight disparate theoretical arguments have been lumped under the name 'reader-response criticism'. Some of these can readily be assimilated to ecological interpretation, some are partially assimilable, some manifestly belong to the realm of extrinsic criticism.

1. The argument that interpretation depends on 'literary competence', that is, the knowledge of genre and other conventions of the sort Jonathan Culler analyses in the central chapters of *Structuralist Poetics*. The functioning of literary conventions and of genre specifically has been discussed in Chapter 4.

2. Emphasis on the *process* of reading, including readers' misinterpretations as later corrected and anticipations as fulfilled or disappointed. The role of the temporal, tentative process of interpretation has been considered in Chapter 5; Louise Rosenblatt's outline may be quoted here as an excellent summary of a process that is far from linear or passive:

In broadest terms, then, the basic paradigm of the reading process consists in the response to cues; the adoption of an efferent or aesthetic stance; the development of a tentative framework or guiding principle of organization; the arousal of expectations that influence the selection and synthesis of further responses; the fulfillment or reinforcement of expectations, or their frustration, sometimes leading to revision of the framework . . .; the arousal of further expectation; until if all goes well . . . the final synthesis or organization is achieved. (54.)

3. The argument that each discourse implies a particular kind of reader. It may be argued that authors habitually imply a reader different from the actual reader, expecting the actual reader to note the disparity, or that the reader is expected to adopt certain implied values, or that the author imagines an ideal reader who will bring certain attitudes, knowledge, and awarenesses to the interpretation of the text. The construction of any of the three will be guided by the same processes that guide readers' interpretations of other authorial intentions.

4. The argument that 'meaning' is created by the reader. Koinonoetic theory vigorously affirms that the active participation of the reader is necessary to interpretation ('meaning' is the imputed

intention of the author, and exists only as someone imputes it). A useful alternative way of phrasing the relationship is that of Louise Rosenblatt: the reader enters into a *transaction* with the text.

> The transactional phrasing of the reading process underlines the essential importance of both elements, reader and text, in any reading event. A person becomes a reader by virtue of his activity in relationship to a text, which he organizes as a set of verbal symbols. A physical text, a set of marks on a page, becomes the text of a poem or of a scientific formula by virtue of its relationship with a reader who can thus interpret it and reach through it to the world of the work. (19.)

However, those critics who have devoted themselves to defending the reader's 'right' to find whatever meaning he or she chooses are attacking a straw man. The reader obviously cannot be denied the 'right' to do whatever he or she wishes to do with a text, but the term 'interpretation' can be denied to many of the quite interesting things readers choose to do with texts.

5. The argument that the culturally induced and largely unconscious perspectives that readers bring to the interpretation of texts (values prescribed by gender roles, or the socio-economic structure, for instance) are of greater importance than the author's intention or achievement. The roles of such values either shared by the author and reader or assumed by the author to be held by the reader as they affect interpretation have been considered in Chapter 5 in the section on the collective dimension. Their importance for the analyst of the culture itself is a matter of the significance rather than the meaning of the text (to be discussed below).

6. The argument that Saussure's description of *langue* as a system of mutually determining signs containing no positive terms authorizes readers to construct any meaning they wish. The possibility of analysing the necessarily inconsistent and whirling senses that attach to words considered outside the dimensional structure in which any *parole* occurs has been granted in Chapter 1 where the term 'interpretation' is denied to that process and the term 'meaning' denied to the result.

7. The argument that the differences between the personal experience and/or the mental conformation of the individual person necessarily produce a different response to a given text in each person (or in each of some set of psychological types). This argument confuses 'response' with 'interpretation': the kinds of variation

described may well produce different mental images and awaken different associations and thus produce different judgements of the aesthetic or other value of the text. These however are matters that have to do with (personal) significance rather than meaning. If a narrator describes a delicately prepared bouillabaisse as part of the representation of a dinner thoroughly enjoyed by one of the characters in a novel, the fact that I dislike seafood may deny me the personal pleasure of thinking of the delights of such a meal (perhaps recalling the best bouillabaisse I've ever tasted or imagining the ideal one), but it will not undercut interpretation of the author's intention.

8. The argument, as set out by David Bleich in *Subjective Criticism*, that it is impossible to define 'a most valid interpretation' (in the Hirschean sense of recovery of the author's meaning that I have adopted) because 'in the vast majority of literature the nominal meaning is already well-known; in cases where the nominal meaning is not known, either it can be discovered with trivial sorts of intellection or it cannot be discovered, so that in either case [*sic*] the acts of understanding or of interpretation are trivial or impossible.' (94.) Therefore interpretation (in Bleich's sense) of aesthetic objects is—like the Freudian interpretation of dreams as he analyses it—the attempt to 'create knowledge on one's own behalf' (93). One 'resymbolizes' the work in a way that will answer one's conscious desires, with the goal of understanding, not the literary text, but one's response to it. Whether regarded as lay therapy or a means of understanding one's evaluative responses, such 'subjective criticism' is by definition not interested in the author's meaning.

3. Extrinsic Commentary

I have given pride of place to interpretation for several reasons. First, it is hardly possible to consider significances of a discourse until one has constructed its meaning. The simplest joke must be interpreted before it can be either enjoyed or deprecated.

> Do you know why rattlesnakes never bite lawyers?
> Because of professional courtesy.

Both those who hold the profession of law in great respect and those who bitterly distrust it must interpret the (indirect) meaning of the dozen words of those two sentences—and they will *interpret* them in the same way—before they address the merits of the humour or the judgement expressed.

Second, interpretation is the only form of commentary on literature that does not make use of frames of reference or norms external to the processes of discourse. Third, there are no evident boundaries to external criticism. No principle limits the number of purposes for which a text may be used or the number of frames of reference against which it may be judged. If interpretation, or intrinsic commentary, is the investigation of the author's intended meaning as expressed through shared dimensions of context, extrinsic criticism is everything else that one might do with or to a literary work.

Though interpretation is the most central activity, readers rarely limit themselves to understanding authorial meaning, nor should they. It is difficult to imagine reading anything other than newspaper stories, instructional manuals, or reference books with minds wholly occupied with interpretation. We respond to associations resulting from quite personal experience; we compare fictional characters to people we know; we mentally file bits of information, phrasing, tropes, or argument for future use in other contexts; we ask ourselves, not about what authors may be expressing, but how they could have held the view of the world we find them to have expressed; we feel pleasure (or the opposite) in the manner in which things are expressed; and we seek theoretical frameworks through which to explain our interpretations.

At theatre performances one is especially conscious of the degree to which spectacular, striking, or simply ingenious staging adds pleasure that has nothing to do with either the interpretation or significance of the action of the play. Of course the acting and staging are part of the total context in which a play is interpreted—acting styles and production techniques affect meanings. At the same time the audience may enjoy fine acting or intriguing stagecraft in and for themselves. To take examples from the 1985–6 London season, there was the cleverness with which the milieu of each scene of the RSC's *The Merry Wives of Windsor* was transposed into the twentieth century, the management of Javert's suicidal drop from the bridge in *Les Misérables* (the audience could not but wonder how Javert could convincingly seem to leap into the water below when the bridge on which he was standing was at stage level), the half-elegant, half-primitive simplicity of the setting of *Yonadab*, the 'doubleness' of the actor Roger Rees at the end of

Double Double, and the inspired *bricolage* of props in the RSC's *The Mysteries*.

More frequently than we may realize, then, meaning *per se* is less important to our response than extrinsic aspects. Indeed *all* evaluation of a text—aesthetic, moral, philosophical—is extrinsic in that it depends on norms of our own choosing. Almost all extrinsic frameworks for considering texts are equally norms whereby we might judge them. There are no literary-critical criteria for ruling out any framework of evaluation. That is, I take it, what those who argue for 'readers' rights' or 'liberty of response' are really saying. They can't be saying that readers must be *allowed* to have certain responses—who is to prevent them? They can't be saying that just any meaning can be imputed to the author as the author's intended one—that is self-contradictory. What is being asserted, and quite correctly so, is that there can be no specifically *literary* norm for ruling out any kind of extrinsic commentary, whether primarily analytical or evaluative. For instance, I may think Marxism hopelessly naïve and Freudianism essentially self-deluding, but I can cite the canons of literary theory against a critic's use of them only to the extent the critic presents extrinsic criticism as interpretation. Beyond this, if I wish to oppose Marxist or Freudian criticism, I must do so by attacking the validity of the Marxist or Freudian framework *qua* framework.

The number of ways in which a text may be used as an example, a critical stalking-horse, or raw material to be mined for information about an author or a culture is countless. However, certain kinds of extrinsic commentary have at present gained especial visibility, not least those like Freudian and Marxist criticism that have developed highly elaborate and sophisticated theoretical structures. The interest of such theories is not here questioned, only the degree of their relevance to interpretation of intended meaning.

1. *For psychological analyses.* One can ask the degree to which Freudian, Jungian, Bloomian, Lacanian, or any other psychological theory explains the author's choice of language, plot, or character, or the language or actions of a character presented in a text, or of the response of readers. Such questions seek the cause of the author's intended meaning rather than the meaning itself (that is, meaning$_3$ rather than meaning$_2$). These extrinsic uses of a text are to be distinguished from implicative situations in which, for instance, an author who could have expected readers to share a knowledge of Freud

constructs a text in which the motivation of a certain character is anomalous until the reader recognizes that the character is mightily influenced by objects of marked convexity or concavity. Such an implicature operates very much like a verbal allusion, for instance like a post-Bloomian use of the term 'belated' that violates our understanding of older uses of the term.

What then of commentary that explains certain portions of a text on the basis of awarenesses that have been explicitly formulated only after the author's time, as in, to take a famous example, commentary on Hamlet's attitude towards Gertrude as an exemplification of the Oedipus complex? How we regard such an explanation depends on what it presumes to explain. A critic who proposes to analyse *Hamlet* on the basis of the claim that the feelings Freud named after the Oedipus myth are common to all human males, and that human beings generally are subconsciously aware of this, is engaged in extrinsic commentary: the author's assumptions and strategies are not involved. Alternatively, it may be claimed that Shakespeare was aware that many (or all) young men experience the Oedipal conflict, but that he did not expect his audience to share this awareness. That is extrinsic commentary to be judged on the basis of the strength of Freud's theory and how it fits with the action of the play. Again, it may be claimed that Shakespeare and his audience shared an inchoate awareness that would have been of service to the audience in interpreting Hamlet's actions. That is an example of intrinsic criticism, to be judged by cultural evidence of the existence of such awareness outside the play as well as its consistency with our understanding of the play as a whole.

In recent years psychoanalytical theorists have increasingly moved from a Freudian preoccupation with a presumably universal structure of the unconscious towards analysis of the way in which the individual mind is structured by the culture around it, and especially by the social experiences of the first few years. This orientation clearly parallels and is easily amalgamated with the recent Marxist, feminist, and 'new historical' criticism mentioned below. Here we must recognize that to the extent such approaches make us aware of cultural values that were accepted by earlier authors and their audiences but which we no longer share, they make the same kind of contribution to interpretation as socio-linguistics, sociology of knowledge, and cultural history.

2. *For Marxist analyses.* 'Marxism is a scientific theory of human

societies and of the practice of transforming them; and what that means, rather more concretely, is that the narrative Marxism has to deliver is the story of the struggles of men and women to free themselves from certain forms of exploitation and oppression.' (*MLC* vii.) This sentence of Terry Eagleton's is as succinct a statement of Marxism, at least as embraced by a literary critic, as one is likely to find. The corollary is that the Marxist critic's role is to explain the literary work as a product of a particular history. Radical fragmentation is of course to be encountered among critics generally accounted Marxist. While pursuing their own specific theses, essays like John Hoyles's 'Radical Critical Theory and English' and Philip Goldstein's 'Humanism and the Politics of Truth' throw into relief the quite major differences between Marxists of 'objectivist' and 'subjectivist' persuasions, and between those influenced by the Frankfurt School and those who have turned to structuralism. Raymond Williams, Terry Eagleton, Louis Althusser, Jacques Lacan, Georg Lukács, Lucien Goldmann, Fredric Jameson, and Pierre Macherey hardly fit comfortably together. None of them is a naïvely reductive Marxist simply seeking to unearth and condemn the bourgeois ideology concealed in literary texts and literary criticism. They raise intriguing questions about the definition of realism, the mechanisms of psychological response, the force of institutions, the successions of modes of conceptualizing. Nevertheless, in Goldstein's words, Marxists 'distrust liberal individualism and construe the author as the voice of his social context or "trans-individual subject" ' (237–8). The assimilation of the history and role of literature to a Marxist concept of historic class struggle is the most general defining characteristic.

Marxist criticism as thus very broadly defined has been attractive to readers troubled by the tendency of New Criticism to discuss texts as though autonomous and in so doing isolate literature from the rest of life. By making literature an aspect of the cultural superstructure that reflects the economic infrastructure which Marxist critics regard as the essential core of society, they seek to reattach literature to the total cultural experience out of which it is produced. The literature of a society becomes a manifestation of its socio-economic health.

The 'correct' understanding of the economic structure that Marxists believe determines (in varying degrees) the cultural superstructure cannot be regarded as part of the collective dimension which author and audience share because, according to Marxists, its enormous influence in human history is largely unrecognized except by the Marxists themselves. From their point of view, all that are consciously shared are the customs, beliefs, and institutions that make up the political, religious, ethical, and aesthetic super-structure. The Marxist critic's primary interests then are almost certain to be wholly extrinsic: not the author's intended meaning, but conflicts and evasions arising out of contradictions in the capi-talist system of which the author is quite unconscious.

The resulting dismissal of the author's meaning is intensified by the Marxist desire to encompass all works in the same descriptive system. Writers, and artists in general, are seen not as creators but as one more class of 'producers' obeying the productive requirements of the economic system. Though many a Marxist critic has urged that the role of literature is to encourage social revolution, the posi-tion can hardly be held with consistency: if the Marxist understand-ing of the relationship between infrastructure and superstructure is correct, it is difficult to see how any portion of the latter could influence the former.

Those who pursue koinonoetic interpretation accept from the beginning that the human experience of reality is a constructed one. They therefore need have no difficulty in accepting a statement like Catherine Belsey's: 'It is argued that what seems obvious and natural is not necessarily so, but that on the contrary the "obvious" and the "natural" are not *given* but *produced* in a specific society by the ways in which that society talks and thinks about itself and its experience' (33). They need have no difficulty indeed in accepting a statement like 'Ideology . . . is *inscribed in* specific *discourses*' (5), though one may question whether a word with the commonly pejorative connotation of 'ideology' or ones as vague as 'inscribed in' are especially useful. (Perhaps what are actually meant are simply aspects of what socio-linguists and discourse analysts call 'the back-ground' of thought or 'cultural grammar'.) They agree with most current Marxist criticism that discourse must be understood within its historical context and that the critique of the historical assump-tions embodied in discourse is an important activity. They further agree that the assumptions made by the literary critic ought to be subject to the same analyses as those of any other discourse.

As I attempted to outline in Chapter 2, any use of language may change our understanding of the contexts of discourse and thus of reality, and changes in our views of reality will alter some of the contexts of discourse. Koinonoetic interpretation thus insists on the intimate and mutual relation between literature and the total social structure and makes use of the insights of socio-linguistics and the sociology of knowledge (both of which owe much to Marxism) while drawing a line between both diagnostic and propagandistic analyses of discourse and interpretation proper.

3. *For structuralist analyses.* The aim of structuralism has been described as the explanation not of the meaning of a given text, but of the source of meaning. In the words of Jonathan Culler, 'Just as the task of linguistics is to make explicit the system of language which makes linguistic communication possible, so in the case of literature a structuralist poetics must enquire what knowledge must be postulated to account for our ability to read and understand literary works.' (*SL* 62.) Structuralism has performed a very valuable service in stressing the importance of explaining how communication (expression and interpretation) is possible in any text, 'literary' or not. However, in practice structuralists have tended to assume an invariant metahuman system which determines what humans can say or think (the high structuralism of Lévi-Strauss, Foucault, or Benoist) or invariant generic forms (low structuralism—as in the investigation by Propp of folk-tales or by Greimas of the structures of narratives in general). In the first case the 'meaning' the structuralist seeks is presumed not to be one consciously intended by a given author in a particular time and place, but one that no author could have avoided since it is somehow innate in the very structure of mind, of language. In contrast, the koinonoetic point of view seeks to explain rather the flexibility of language that makes possible the variety of expression and novelty of thought we actually encounter.

In the second case, the deep structure of the work is presumed to be invariably necessary because it is inherent in the operation of the mind. Examples are Propp's reduction of the roles played by characters in Russian folk-tales to eight or A.-J. Greimas's mapping of the structural possibilities of the key concepts of a narrative through the construction of a semiotic square. The structure of the semiotic square, as explained by Nancy Armstrong more clearly than I have elsewhere encountered it, is this: 'Once any unit of meaning (S_1) is conceived, we automatically conceive of the absence of that meaning ($\bar{S}_1$), as well as an opposing system of meaning (S_2) that correspondingly implies its own absence ($\bar{S}_2$).' (54). One could analyse the concept of 'responsibility' in *King Lear*, it would seem, into the semiotic square shown in Fig. 6.1, and then trace the exemplification of these relations in the play. The interest of such 'low structuralism' is evidently in the possibilities of meaning, not the meaning of the existing work. Genette has summed it up well: such structural criticism 'builds structured sets by means of a structured set, namely *the work*. But it is not at the structural level that it makes use of it: it builds ideological castles out of the debris of what was once a *literary discourse*'. (*FLD* 5.)

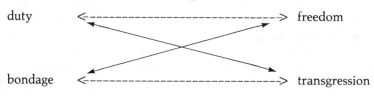

duty   freedom

bondage   transgression

Fig. 6.1

4. *For narratological analyses.* In his Foreword to Gérard Genette's *Narrative Discourse*, Jonathan Culler cites this close study of narrative as 'one of the central achievements of what was called "structuralism" ' (8). While debate is possible over whether structuralism is wholly dead, no one is likely to question the liveliness of what has now come to be called narratology. Whereas structuralism purposed a new concept of the powers of language, certain at least of the mechanisms of thought, and a new understanding of the errors into which uncritical acceptance of language leads us, narratology has followed structuralism's interest in narrative toward a much narrower goal: the refinement of tools for analysing narrative structure. Short stories, novels, and important aspects of drama and the cinema may be much more crisply discussed through sharpened terminology making distinctions like those between 'process' and 'stasis' statements, scenes which are 'kernels' and those which are 'satellites', and the reporting of characters' thoughts through 'direct tagged', 'direct free', 'indirect tagged', and 'free style' constructions. Such distinctions as Genette has made between two kinds of 'perspective' ('mood' referring to 'who sees' and 'voice' to 'who speaks') and such analyses as those of the three categories of temporal relations between the story and the discourse (order, duration, and frequency, the possibilities within each of which he has carefully defined and labelled) are enormously helpful in discussing the

significant elements of form in sophisticated narrative. Narratology has opened a new realm within poetics.

The question of the importance of the narratological distinctions to interpretation is not an easy one. Obviously it is not necessary to be able to assign a technical name like 'analeptic anachrony' to a narrative strategy to be aware of and respond to it. Ancient narrative could hardly have begun *in medias res* if readers were not able to sort out and feel the effects of a narrative return to earlier events, and the special form and implications of the structure of *The Ring and the Book* or *Rashomon* were appreciated long before Genette distinguished 'repeating' from 'iterative' and 'multiple-singulative' kinds of 'frequency' (ND 114–16). One might even argue that while Genette's superb analysis of the structure of *A la recherche du temps perdu* in *Narrative Discourse* gives the reader a much greater appreciation of Proust's art, it adds nothing to the understanding of the book already achieved by the most careful and sensitive of its interpreters. We find it easier to understand indirectly presented meanings than to talk about how they are produced—it is the latter that requires a special vocabulary.

However, Saussurian principles remind us that while the divisions language imposes may mislead us, labelling enables us to take note of differentiations that we might otherwise ignore. Consciousness of the range of narrative possibilities and facility in distinguishing between them cannot but aid the reader in recognizing strategies that carry implicatures. To take a set of progressively more sophisticated examples from Flannery O'Connor's 'Artificial Nigger', the reader who has not been introduced to the concept of symbolism is likely to miss the 'visit to the underworld' motif; the reader not consciously aware of the importance of the degree to which a reader's anticipations are ratified or falsified may fail to notice the unusual number of times the reader's expectations are undercut in this story; and the reader who is innocent of the difference between straightforward third-person narration and the stylistic device of 'indirect free thought' will at times attribute attitudes to the narrator that properly belong to a character. All three kinds of recognition function in the interpretation of the story.

What one must finally say is simply that neither the vocabulary nor a definitive grasp of the technical distinctions labelled by that vocabulary are necessary to interpretation—but on the other hand, structure implies meaning in the same way as selection of actions and choice of words, and anything that increases sensitivity to structure is helpful. The case is similar to that of genre: one need not be able to name or define the relevant genre, or narrative technique, or convention to understand a work, but consciousness of these, and in some cases of the degree of departure from them, is always helpful and in some cases crucial.

5. *For deconstructive analyses.* For deconstructionists the indeterminacy, or undecidability, or infinite regression of the meaning of individual words when regarded as parts of the total system of *langue* leads necessarily to contradictions and indeterminacy in any use of language. The process can easily be made to establish that the meaning of any word is indeterminate, or that its use is in fact self-contradictory, or that the evaluative or hierarchical position it seems to hold in relation to other words is illusory. Alternatively, if one surveys either an extended text or several texts by the same author, it is almost always possible, by lifting out sentences from here and there, to show that an author has used the same word in incompatible senses. If one chooses to bring deconstructive methods to bear on Matthew Arnold's 'culture' for instance, it is easy enough to point out that culture derives from the Latin *cultivare*, 'to cultivate', but if to cultivate means 'to tend, to till, to break up, to bestow attention on', one can ask on what map the dividing lines between these exist. Can we understand 'till' without ascertaining the boundaries between it and say 'dig' or 'scratch'? And are not metaphorical meanings of 'culture', as in 'the rearing of animals' or 'the artificial development of microscopic organisms' possible only because the meaning 'to till' is absent (otherwise the raising of puppies or growth of bacteria must result from the breaking up of soil)?

Or, to take another tack, if culture is the product of cultivation, it alters nature's processes for non-natural purposes. Now plants may evidently be altered for human purposes, but are we not on shifting sands when we talk of altering human beings for human purposes? Or again, if culture is defined by its opposition to anarchy, is not anarchy necessary as the source of that energy that culture would redirect? Is it not indeed the primal, more important member of the pair? Or, to look at Arnold's uses more carefully, do not certain sentences make culture the goal while others make it the means? Is not culture in some instances a synonym for criticism, in others that which is to be achieved by criticism, and then elsewhere the criterion by which criticism judges? What can be done in the deconstructive manner is limited only by the practitioner's ingenuity and energy.

Similarly, rather than seeking consonance one can produce discord by insisting on giving equal importance to direct and indirect meanings. Thus after citing Dryden's lines

> How can the *less* the Greater comprehend?
> Or *finite Reason* reach *Infinity?*
> For what cou'd Fathom GOD were *more* than *He.*

G. Douglas Atkins writes

As rhetorical questions, the first two lines I quoted have both literal and figurative meanings. Rather than different perspectives that may ultimately be reconcilable, these meanings appear mutually exclusive. The figurative meaning of the rhetorical questions does not ask for a positive response, one that would detail the specific ways in which 'the *less*' could comprehend 'the *Greater.*' The figurative meaning, instead, asserts that man *cannot* comprehend God and that it is, in fact, foolhardy even to ask the question since '*finite Reason*' obviously cannot 'reach *infinity.*' But the literal meaning of the lines insists on an answer, one that would deny the assertion of the figurative, describing the ways in which man can come to comprehend God. (100–1.)

But that is rather like finding it undecidable whether 'My love is like a red, red rose' means 'I am in love with a member of the genus *rosa*', an actual red rose, or 'I am in love with a woman whom I compare to a rose' and stubbornly insisting that the literal meaning 'undoes' the figurative one. Or again, where a joker might purposely misinterpret 'Can you pass the salt?' and simply reply 'Yes' without passing it, the consistently deconstructive dinner guest ought perhaps to respond by spending the rest of the evening reaching to pass the salt as the result of interpreting the question as an indirect request and then drawing back and nodding in the affirmative as the literal force 'undoes' the indirect. (For a consideration of a subtler example of deconstructive criticism, see the Appendix.)

Now in fact the system of mutual definitions within language is, again, the source of the flexibility and creativity of language as put to use in discourse. If each word (sign) had a fixed meaning (sense), it would be impossible to think or say anything which required a different way of dividing up the flow of sensation (Saussure's 'vague uncharted nebula' of thought). Even the introduction of new words to express new views of reality would be impossible, for the new concepts or signifieds would clash so totally with the old that there could occur no accommodation.

Once one sees that *langue* is in continued interaction with *parole* and with reality (we experience reality in terms of language but we understand language in terms of reports of reality), language ceases to be a prison-house and becomes the tool common sense assures us it is. The fashionable phrase 'surplus of meaning' now takes on another aspect: rather than describing a necessary burden of unintended meanings, it better describes that probable meaning towards which context aligns otherwise undecidable signs. The flexibility of interpretable expression that ecological criticism finds in the interaction of the contextual dimensions is precisely what makes possible the kind of creativity for which a revisionist critic like Geoffrey Hartman calls. In a world of total flux, creativity has no meaning—indeed the very novelty of revisionist and deconstructive arguments would be impossible. Awareness that the boundaries of our concepts are continually being creatively revised warns against the mechanical use of the word 'coding' so frequently met with among linguists and literary critics: on the one hand, 'coding' too readily suggests a mechanical translation of thought into language whereas thought is partly dependent on language, and on the other hand, it neglects the process by which shifting mental contexts make possible novel thoughts that can only be expressed through novel juxtapositions of the dimensions of discourse. Language is not a code but the possibility of alternative codings.

However, we may happily concede the claim that literary deconstruction is a form of literature: that is, a deconstructive 'reading' proves most rewarding when read aesthetically for the pleasures of paradox, irony, and ingenuity rather than for information about the text which inspires it. The semi-technical language ('technical' because only meaningful within the post-structuralist critical coterie, and 'semi' because intentionally lacking in precise definition) in which deconstructive criticism tends to be written can become a kind of new euphuism or, to pick up an expressive phrase from Christopher Norris, a criticism that 'lives on its wits' (100).

6. *For rhetorical analysis.* The structuralists and deconstructionists who originally sensitized the critical world to the amount of inconsistency and contradiction that can be teased out of significant texts attributed the resulting aporias of logic and chasms of indeterminacy to the very structure of language rather than to the author, whom

they wished to remove as far as possible from the discussion. However more recently critics who accept that texts reflect in large part the intentions or at least the individual modes of thought of their authors have pursued the same kind of search for inconsistencies and hidden assumptions. The result, not surprisingly, is very much a form of the traditional rhetorical criticism which asked not only 'how is this effect achieved?' but 'are the elements of logos, ethos, and pathos achieved in ways that violate logic (not necessarily formal logic) or otherwise open to question?'

What distinguishes many of the contemporary essays in rhetorical criticism is a greater tenacity in searching for inconsistencies and hidden manœuvres; this is in turn encouraged by the belief that not only is all persuasion rhetorical, but all thought is rhetorical in that it can achieve an ordered argument only by suppressing alternative formulations. Exemplary is Stanley Fish's essay, 'Withholding the Missing Portion: Power, Meaning, and Persuasion in Freud's "The Wolf-Man" ':

At the very least we would seem to have a disjunction between Freud's general account of human nature and the claims he makes for his own assertions. The general account says that all knowledge is ultimately rhetorical ('arises from affective sources'); the claim he makes for his own assertions is that they are not rhetorical but true. But were we to fault him for that claim and accuse him of bad faith we would be committing a deep philosophical mistake, the mistake of thinking that our convictions can and *should* be shaken by the knowledge that they are unsupported by anything external to themselves. (WMP 938d.)

Whether or not one regards this as a return to an Aristotelian position depends on whether one believes that Aristotelian rhetoric and dialectic were intended to find and set forth the strongest (most probable) position *or* to make the position one chose seem the strongest. In any case, it chimes well with the fashionable but hardly irrefragable view that all is relative because words do not coincide with an unchanging, ascertainable structure of reality.

7. *For philosophic analyses*. 'Philosophic' is the broadest adjective to describe several kinds of endeavour whose goal is the reconstruction of an underlying structure of thought (ontological, epistemological, or axiological). The most venerable is the method of intellectual history practised by philosophers like A. O. Lovejoy. More recent is what Michel Foucault calls the 'archaeology of

knowledge', which, while abjuring the task of tracking seminal ideas from one period to another (denying indeed the possibility of doing so) exhibits the same interest in understanding how the culture of a particular time and place could have entertained the thoughts it did. It aims to analyse not what is really being said in statements, but what it means for them to have appeared 'when and where they did—they and no others'. One must 'question language, not in the direction to which it refers, but in the dimension that gives it' (109–11). A different approach to rather the same goal, one less eccentric than Foucault's, has developed out of linguistics in recent years. What Roger Fowler calls 'linguistic criticism' analyses texts 'in order to understand how the text constitutes its own theory of reality . . . unpacking the ideology from the linguistic patterns in which it is coded' (21–2).

All three endeavours share with Freudian and Marxist critics the goal of laying bare a deep foundation that determines the cultural pattern which in turn determines how humans relate to (construct a version of) reality. They thus seek a level below that of the shared dimensions of discourse. However, these three 'philosophic' modes of analysis postulate versions of reality that are the product of the activity of mind and that are substantially different in different times and places. They thus differ from the Freudian argument for a universal unconscious structure and from both the Marxist and certain structuralist assertions of a single great historical pattern which fulfils itself independently of human understanding.

8. *For aesthetic analyses.*

The following Treatise is but a small portion of a Volume of Criticism intended to be published in Folio, in which in Treating of the works of the most Celebrated English Poets Deceas'd, I design'd to shew both by Reason and Examples, that the use of Religion in Poetry was absolutely necessary to raise it to the greatest exaltation, of which so Noble an Art is capable, and on the other side, that Poetry was requisite to Religion in order to its making more forcible Impressions upon the Minds of Men. (i. 325.)

That longish apology for Dennis's *The Grounds of Criticism in Poetry* (1704) is interesting in its partial anticipation of Arnold's view of the relation between poetry and religion. However, I cite it here as an example of the way apparently aesthetic qualities are so frequently founded on philosophic, religious, and ethical beliefs.

Few if any critics have actually argued that the value of literature is purely aesthetic. Certainly Matthew Arnold, to whose arguments for the joint importance of literature and criticism we owe the place of vernacular literary studies in the university, defined and practised an essentially ethical commentary. Arnold's 'best' literature offered sovereign standards against which to judge the circumambient culture, but great literature was itself partly defined by ethical qualities. Those who have argued that the value of literature lies in its provision of vicarious experience make a broadening of experience and sympathy the (ethical) norm. Most who have argued that complexity is a criterion of great or important literature assume that complexity is good because complexity in a text mirrors that of reality—in which case it is assumed that it is good for us to be aware of that complexity (for ethical reasons) or that in facing complexity we strengthen our intellects (also ultimately an ethical judgement). Those who argue that the synthesis of opposites, the production of concord among discordant qualities, is the central criterion and that what Bateson calls the Principle of the Semantic Gap (*EPCI* 50) in which the greater the original discordance, the more valuable the synthesis, are either philosophical Parmenideans or aestheticians who accord paradox a special privilege. Perhaps Walter Pater came closest to purely aesthetic judgement: art quickens our sense of life, 'proposing frankly to give nothing but the highest quality to your moments as they pass, and simply for those moments' sake'. Even so the savouring of moments for their own sake becomes the external criterion by which all else is measured. To argue for purely aesthetic judgements would be to argue that certain formal structures are in and of themselves more to be valued than others. Even one who believed that tragedy was the highest genre, symbolism the *sine qua non* of genius, and unrhymed iambic pentameter the pinnacle of prosody would hardly expect to find every highly symbolic blank verse tragedy a stunning success.

'Every critical opinion is an ellipsis; a conditional assertion with the conditonal part omitted,' wrote I. A. Richards (for 'critical opinion' read 'evaluation of a literary text') (*SI* 195). Today we might state the matter in terminology adapted from argument theory. The validity of 'warrants' for assertions (Stephen Toulmin) or 'judgemental standards' (Charles A. Willard) varies across disciplinary and discursive fields. Different standards of demonstration are in force in physics, law, and politics, not to mention on the sports page. Or again we may follow Searle's argument in *Speech Acts* and recognize that descriptive statements become value judgements when combined with institutional facts (or, I would add, any implicit or explicit norm the author assumes the reader shares or can be made to share). But references to single norms are of course simplistic: though a Marxist reader may evaluate texts on the basis of the clarity with which they can be shown to reveal the contradictions in or evils of capitalist society, the same reader may also place a high value on complexity of representation, and/or particular stylistic qualities. That is why honest critics who are too insistent on a single norm often veer round and undercut their own arguments.

What has been said about evaluation to this point is nicely summed up by Northrop Frye: 'When a critic interprets, he is talking about his poet; when he evaluates, he is talking about himself, or, at most about himself as a representative of his age.' (OVJ 39.) However, one may applaud Frye's impatience with claims for the permanence or universality of evaluative judgements without denying their inevitability. We would not trouble ourselves about the correctness of our interpretation, nor be enticed into and pursue aesthetic reading, nor care to comment upon that which we had read, if the text did not appeal to us, that is, if it met none of our criteria of significance. Which brings us to the foundation of the canon of literary works, the never sharply defined mass of texts that are talked about, read, taught, kept in print at any given time. Inclusion is evidence that a text is valued according to one or more of the accepted norms of the time. All analytic commentary, all criticism, is necessarily evaluative. The corollary is that the greater the number of norms a text satisfies, the more likely it is to remain in the active canon.

The fact is that when Stanley Fish writes of different 'interpretive communities', he is confusing interpretation with critical, and especially evaluative, commentary. Interpretation requires reconstruction of the author's intention through awareness of the author's assumptions. Neither assumptions nor intentions change over time (though the difficulty of recovering them may). The changes that occur are in our interests and thus our evaluations. The communities that succeed each other are *critical*, not interpretive. We can be more specific. Fish declared in a characteristic moment of exuberance that there was no necessary bar to the development of an Eskimo critical theory of literature (EDC). He is quite correct. There is no reason that a critic could not look at texts in terms of their attitudes towards Eskimos, or their recognition of the existence of Eskimos, or their recognition of differences between the way Eskimos and the members of the author's cultural group regard the world, or simply in terms of the differences between the world-views stated or assumed in non-Eskimo texts and the world-view of the Eskimo group. The process might not only prove of interest to Eskimo readers but to thoughtful readers in general by illuminating the existence of certain non-Eskimo assumptions about the world of which non-Eskimos are unaware. But however much such readings-of-significance in texts might differ from those to which we are accustomed, readings-of-meaning would not.

9. *For feminist analyses.* Feminist criticism has accomplished a major revolution. Readers have been made infinitely more aware of, and frequently now quite uncomfortable with, the degree to which male assumptions about the relations between and appropriate roles of men and women have manifested themselves in both literature and literary criticism. As Elaine Showalter has made evident in her incisive 'Feminist Criticism in the Wilderness' (1981), this has been accomplished by two major endeavours. One, which she names 'feminist critique', is ideological, concentrating on feminist readings of literature. As examples of its theorists she cites Annette Kolodny and Adrienne Rich. The other, which she names 'gynocriticism', investigates the difference in women's writing: for example, Showalter's *A Literature of Their Own* (1977) and Sandra Gilbert and Susan Gubar's *The Madwoman in the Attic* (1979). Either mode may of course direct attention to women writers whose work has been undervalued.

The whole of feminist criticism powerfully explores questions of significance, demonstrating ways in which both literature and criticism have reflected cultural assumptions. We may well today deny the validity of these assumptions, but we must take them into account in the process of interpretation since they support intended meanings. In addition, our new awareness of the power of masculine chauvinist assumptions has two further implications. First, we ought to recognize that earlier readers who consciously or unconsciously resisted such assumptions are likely to have responded to texts which relied on them in a way different from the majority of readers (the greater the reliance, the greater the difference). However, these readers are almost certain to have been sufficiently aware of the general acceptance of the prevailing assumptions about the nature of sexual differences to have had no trouble in *interpreting* the texts they read. Second, we ought to be alerted to the possibility that we have not fully recognized the degree to which authors who did not share those assumptions incorporated devices to neutralize them. However, either such an author was successful in conveying his or her meaning within the given total context or not. To argue that we are now able to recognize an intended meaning not available to earlier readers is to argue an intention external to the text/total context—to commit the 'intentional fallacy' as Wimsatt and Beardsley meant the term to be understood.

4. Future-oriented Discourse

The point just made requires to be carried a step further. Why, one might ask, can authors not write for a future audience by assuming a different set of shared dimensions in the future and calculating their strategies on those terms? After all it is not unknown for authors to think of themselves as writing more for posterity than for present readers. But in order to make such an argument, we must assume that we know the specific knowledge and beliefs the future sharing of which the author assumed. An author may tell the reader that he expects certain non-standard assumptions to be made in the process of interpretation, but to hope that the author hoped for the application of particular unstated non-culturally-shared awarenesses at a future time simply because we like the interpretation thus possible is to set the basic principles of communication at nought.

In essays of 1983 and 1984, E. D. Hirsch modified his distinction between meaning and significance to accommodate the realization that 'Many texts were authored with intentions toward futurity.' Now there are somewhat curious properties about future-directed utterances, but it is essential that we distinguish between several quite different types. As the first example, in his 1983 Bateson lecture, Hirsch cited a fictitious version of his acceptance of the invitation to give the lecture: 'Dear Bateson Lecture Committee: I am delighted to accept your kind invitation to present the third Bateson Lecture. Yours sincerely, E. D. Hirsch.' (PIPM 84.) If, asks Hirsch, he had intended to give the lecture wearing a dark business suit and found that a sweater and jeans would be more appropriate, would his original intentions include the more informal dress? He concludes that he must answer 'Yes.' But from the position I am setting forth Hirsch is involved in a confusion between the intention in the author's mind and that embodied in the text, which expresses simply his acceptance. What he will wear is not part of the proposition or illocutionary force of his fictitious response. Had he added something like 'I will appear at the appropriate place and time in the appropriate attire,' he would have expressed his intention to be dressed appropriately whatever he thought that attire might be at the time he wrote and whether or not he actually managed to dress suitably by Oxford standards. (Not doing so would be one of those actions which is an implicature.) Had he, in an excess of exactitude, added something like 'I will arrive at 4 p.m. sharp wearing a dark business suit' and subsequently found that a sweater and jeans would be more appropriate, he could not be said to have pursued his announced intention, however good a reason there might be for the change. But the message as it exists in his own example includes no intention as to dress.

As a parallel we may take the quarterback who announces to the local sportswriter, 'I intend to play my best tomorrow.' The quarterback will probably have a game strategy in mind, which may have to be altered in the event. But the quarterback has not expressed *any* strategy, only the intent to follow the principle of playing his best. Now before the game his team-mates may know that a passing game is planned and to them (since the same statement may have different propositional meaning, illocutionary force, and/or perlocutionary effect for different audiences) the statement may well imply playing a good passing game. But they, no more than the newspaper reader, will be surprised or feel misled if the other team's pass defence forces the quarterback to a running game—in such a case had he stuck stubbornly to a passing game, he would probably be judged not to have played his best, even though he intended to; that is, the effect would have differed from his intention just as perlocutionary intent may differ from perlocutionary effect. To fulfil his *expressed* intention, he must alter his unexpressed intention.

Both Hirsch's example and my own illustrate discourse which is directed to a given audience at a given time prior to the events to which the discourse relates. A different case arises when discourse is intended not for the nonce but for interpretation through the ages (or at least through centuries) in which many cultural beliefs and much of the cultural grammar will change. Such of course is the case of most texts in the 'literary' genres. Hirsch's well-chosen example in his 1984 article is Shakespeare's sonnet beginning 'Nor marble, nor the gilded monuments / Of Princes, shall outlive this powerful rhyme'—in which the expectation of something like perpetuity is implicitly expressed. 'Shakespeare intended precisely that his future meaning should *not* be restricted to his own moment,' writes Hirsch (MSR 206). But again, I think, the apparent problem arises out of a confusion. Shakespeare's meaning remains the same; what will change is the difficulty of interpretation. Readers must work harder, must set out consciously to share as much as possible of the cultural grammar Shakespeare assumed in a contemporary audience. If, as a result of a great revulsion against monuments of any sort, not a single one remained on earth in AD 2500, the reader would need to know the historical background to know the sense of 'gilded monuments'. Similarly, readers unaware that in the Renaissance 'to die' could have the sense 'to have sexual intercourse', necessarily missed implicatures. Had this been totally forgotten, so much of an author's meaning, when such an implicature was intended, would have been lost.

This is not the case when we turn to such other of Hirsch's examples as Stowe's *Uncle Tom's Cabin* or Homer. When Hirsch asks if *Uncle Tom's Cabin* can be 'salvaged', the question is about significance, our evaluation of human nature, not meaning. When Hirsch asks about continued enjoyment of Homer despite disbelief in his gods, the question again is one of significance; we need to know something of Zeus or Athene to grasp Homer's meaning (indeed it is always possible that there is vital information we are missing which causes us to misinterpret) but we do not need to believe in the Greek Pantheon to interpret. Questions of the degree to which *we* can find meaning in the Greek gods are questions of significance. Hirsch's succeeding argument in his 1983 article is that 'allegorical referentiality' is the principle that keeps us interested in older literature. Here, I think, he enters especially dangerous ground through failure to distinguish between allegory intended by the author and allegory imputed by the audience. The difference is arrived at through a version of our constant koinonoetic principle. If the features of a story that imply allegory are ones that we believe would have been recognized as such by author and audience, we have intentional allegory; if not, imputed. Leaving aside divine revelation, authors cannot know whether or what contexts may have changed so much that their works can only be accepted as allegories by later audiences. To allegorize because one does not approve of the values apparently embodied in an author's text, that is, to disagree because of significances one discovers, leads to such quaint allegorizings of Homer as that which transmogrifies Odysseus's dalliance with Calypso (how could he, with faithful Penelope waiting!) into a homily in which Odysseus belatedly repudiates lust. The kind of allegorizing Hirsch defends in the 1983 article in *Essays and Criticism* seems precisely 'the Gadamerian mode of interpretation [in which] meaning is *made* to conform to the critic's view of what is true' that he condemns in the 1984 *Critical Inquiry* essay (*MSR* 218).

The process of interpreting laws is yet a different case, for, unlike most other uses of language, laws present principles whose application is expected to change with circumstances. Here those who frame them intend that they assimilate unforeseen contexts. Hirsch's example is the *Brown* v. *Board of Education* case in which the American Constitution's enunciation of the principle of equality, which had previously been regarded as satisfied by equal educational facilities for blacks and whites, was 'reinterpreted' as requiring the integration of facilities. Here (unlike the case of the quarterback who enunciates a principle applicable to a single event) we have a principle intended to be applied according to any number of future contexts. Such open-ended, future-directed intentions are a special genre. The courts called upon to apply the principle of equality in the collective context of, for instance, 1904 assumed equality to be achievable by separate but equal facilities; those applying it in 1954 could not. I have used the word 'apply' rather than 'interpret' intentionally. Though we speak of interpreting the law, actually the *situation* is being interpreted in terms of the *principle* of the law. The situation had changed by 1954—it had become clear that equal educational facilities for blacks and whites had not in fact been achieved in such a way as to provide equal opportunity, and that indeed it was impossible to create truly equal facilities. The principle of equality had not changed, the context in which its application was interpreted had.

7

Conclusion

The speech-act can exist only in anticipation of a contextually defined interpretive act; the interpretive act looks back to the strategically incorporated context of the speech-act. That is the model of koinonoetic or ecological interpretation. So many definitions, distinctions, and exemplifications have been trotted out in the course of my presentation, however, that the outlines of the whole may have been obscured by the dust of detail. By way of amendment, let me summarize the general principles I have tried to develop before concluding with some remarks on the complementarity of interpretation and criticism.

1. Interpretive Principles

1. Though we cannot expect language to express *what* or *how* brute reality exists, that it does exist is assumed in all discourse. Though we can never get outside or beyond that interaction of sense reports, language, and experience we call thought, we do not seriously doubt the existence of a 'brute' physical reality. We do not discount it in ordinary life (at this moment, I am aware that there is a physical distance between the library desk at which I am writing and a particular theatre, and that if I do not allow sufficient time to traverse it I will be late for the performance), and we do not forget it when formulating our utterances or interpreting those of others. When we read that a man 'leaps tall buildings at a single bound' or that Gregor Samsa awoke one morning with the body of an insect, we know that we are asked to imagine a contrived, a fantastic, world. The world, wrote I.A. Richards, 'is a fabric of conventions which for obscure reasons it has suited us in the past to manufacture and support' (*PR* 41-2). More accurately, our conceptualization of reality is a fabric of conventions, but these conventions have been called into being by the interaction of human purpose and an insistent physical reality.

2. *Langue* is the abstraction that explains the possibility of meaning in language; discourse (*parole*) expresses meaning. Though we know that the words we use are drawn from a system of *langue* made up of words that are mutually defining, we never in fact forget that words are always used (uttered or written) in relation to a set of contexts all of which can be described in language and influenced by language but most of which require the existence of extralinguistic objects, feelings, and institutions. The existence of a *langue* depends on *parole*; *parole* exists only in the total context of discourse.

3. Discourse occurs in a complicated and interactive environment or context: meaning is dependent on the author prospectively and the reader retrospectively sharing the context. 'Part of what we know is what others know and what they know that we know.' What others know and know we know are shared contexts. Aware of what elements of each context are shared or are likely to be shared by an assumed audience, an author estimates what contextual elements readers will assume he or she assumed when the text was constructed.

4. That authors intend consonance of discourse as the means of expressing their intended meanings and that readers will attempt to discover the intended meaning by seeking consonance in their reconstructions can only be assumptions, but they are constitutive assumptions: they constitute the possibility of meaning by defining it. It is true that the assumption of consistency or unity will always be self-fulfilling (a designedly un-unified text will be regarded as intended to be consistently inconsistent and thus unified) just as the assumption of inevitable inconsistency and contradiction will always be self-fulfilling. The question becomes, which model do we believe is assumed by the users of language in the immeasurably overwhelming proportion of instances?

5. When we note an apparent anomaly, violation, ambiguity, or resistance disturbing the set of contexts we expect, we pursue reconciling implicatures by seeking less immediate contexts. The interpretive presumption does not require that we consciously assure ourselves that every word, sentence, and section of a text can be shown to have a purpose consistent with our total construction: the degree to which we should be alert to anomalies and ambiguities is suggested first by the genre and then by our experience of the text itself. We discover how a text is to be read in the process of reading it.

Since it is always possible for a reader to have failed to note an implicative anomaly and therefore to have constructed an incorrect, or inadequate, or incomplete interpretation, competent readers may well disagree over whether some feature of a text is an anomaly. If reader *A* cannot convince reader *B* that an anomaly exists, *A* and *B* will differ at least slightly in their interpretations. But the difference is often slight indeed—readers who disagree over the illocutionary force or perlocutionary intent of a sentence here and there may well agree on the illocutionary force of the whole. Hedging as it may seem, what we seek is sufficient probability, sufficient unity, sufficient accuracy in interpretation. Since readers can never be sure what an author has assumed, obviously the broader their knowledge in each of the dimensions, the less likely they are to fail to recognize an anomaly, or fail to discover the implicature that resolves the anomaly. We recognize intuitively that (1) the more we know, the better readers we are likely to be; and (2) the further removed the text is from us in time and culture, the more information we require.

At the same time, we realize that much of what we do know about even the linguistic, collective, and specific dimensions obtaining when the text was written will *not* be essential to interpretation. For example, in *Bleak House* in the opening joint description of the London fog and the Court of Chancery, the Lord High Chancellor is described as 'outwardly directing his attention to the lantern in the roof, where he can see nothing but fog'. Now though one always speaks under correction in these matters, I cannot see that it makes much difference for the interpretation of the narrator's intent whether the reader knows that 'lantern' here refers to an architectural feature of the building or thinks it a hanging glass case with a flame inside. It is true that the image is more effective if one visualizes the fog filling the highest point in the chamber. But the redundancy of such a passage is sufficient so that a reader who had no knowledge of English court proceedings and could make next to nothing of references to 'silk gowns', 'solicitors', or 'goat-hair and horse-hair warded heads', nor of the allusion to truth at the bottom of a well found in the same paragraph, would, while finding the passage heavy going, still emerge with an accurate enough understanding of the total proposition, the illocutionary force, and perlocutionary intent of the narrator of the passage.

6. The processes by which indirect and non-literal meanings are

expressed and interpreted in discourse are the same as those by which we interpret many an action. Some actions are intended to be expressive: they are intentionally employed signifiers. Putting one's arm around a friend's shoulders expresses camaraderie or sympathy, refusal to shake hands expresses anger or contempt (which of these, in each case, depends as usual on context). We also regard a quick glance over a shoulder, or a sudden huskiness of voice, or a staggering gait as signifiers, usually unintentional ones.

7. Tropes—that is, 'figures of thought' like metaphor, irony, litotes, metonymy, and hyperbole—are cardinal examples of implicature. The recent efflorescence of interest in metaphor has pretty well established that metaphor can be recognized only in context. To take standard examples, 'Richard is a fox' is a metaphor only if Richard is not a member of the genus *vulpus*; 'Sally is a block of ice' is not a metaphor in the circumstance for instance that the name 'Sally' has been given to an ice-sculpture. Tropes in fact always depend on context. Take the following sentence from a newspaper description of the Queen's procession at the opening of Parliament: 'The crown will occupy the first coach.' That could be metonymic, a way of saying 'the Queen will occupy the first coach', as well as the literal statement that the actual crown alone will occupy that coach.

8. Interpretation can never rise from probability to certainty; but then certainty is appropriate only to the realm of Plato's ideas. One of E. D. Hirsch's most cogent comments on the business of criticism is that 'It is a logical mistake to confuse the impossibility of certainty in understanding with the impossibility of understanding.' (*VI* 17.) We may also say that it is an error to confuse the impossibility of demonstrating the relation of every sentence to the author's total intentions with the impossibility of there being an interpretable intent. The koinonoetic view of interpretation aligns it closely with developments in the area of argumentation theory, which, since the seminal works of Stephen Toulmin and Chaim Perelman (both 1958) has recognized that all argument about substantive issues must necessarily accept argument based on probable premises rather than apodictically certain ones and thus can never be logically necessary. Validity differs from logical necessity. Though certain revisionist critics are fond of sayings like Paul de Man's 'Interpretation is nothing but the possibility of error' (141), the appropriate analogue would be that 'food is nothing but the possibility of poison'.

Much post-structuralist criticism relies on the impossibility of a stable centre, or first principle, or ground of judgement. But it is once again essential to hold to the difference between that which can be proved true and that which can be understood. It may not be demonstrably true that 'haste makes waste', or 'reading makes a full man', or that 'ripeness is all', or that 'God is no deceiver', or that 'one should always act as though the principle of one's act were to become a universal maxim', or that 'all syllogisms may be reduced to the figure *Barbara*', or that 'there exists a realm of noumena we cannot know'—but we can understand the meaning of each of these statements. There is no novelty in asserting that there is no absolute truth, no final ontological or epistemological explanation of how things 'really' are, not even a reliable set of practical rules. Robert Louis Stevenson said that as well as anyone in the final three paragraphs of 'Crabbed Age and Youth', of which I quote the last:

I suppose it is written that anyone who sets up for a bit of a philosopher must contradict himself to his very face. For here I have fairly talked myself into thinking that we have the whole thing before us at last; that there is no answer to the mystery, except that there are as many as you please; that there is no centre to the maze because, like the famous sphere, its centre is everywhere; and that agreeing to differ with every ceremony of politeness, is the only 'one undisturbed song of pure concent' to which we are ever likely to lend our musical voices.

But such scepticism, the very waxing and waning of which may attest to the relativity of all human opinion, is one thing, and the interpretation of meaning is another. While we may not believe that Stevenson is right, we can feel reasonably sure that we know what he meant (which is the first step towards considering whether he is or is not correct).

9. Perlocutionary intentions are on the far boundary of interpretation simply because an author may or may not intend that they be correctly understood. In any case, the intended perlocutionary effect may well not be achieved. Even when it is, there will very likely be additional perlocutionary effects as the reader relates the text to his or her interests; criticism of a text's significance as viewed from one or more external framework is almost certain to be part of a reader's response.

10. Changes in cultural knowledge and awareness (which lead to changes in intellectual interests as well) are of course changes in the collective dimension. As E. D. Hirsch has pointed out in other

terminology, since readers' interpretations of others' interpretations of literature generally depend on the collective dimension, modes of explaining the meaning of a text will change as the
collective dimension changes (*VI* 129 ff.). Hypothetical constructs
or models unknown to the author—drawn for example in the twentieth century from psychoanalysis, or physics, or Heideggerian
philosophy—are often extremely useful in explaining or clarifying
an author's meaning, so long as they are recognized as heuristic
parallels and not assumed to be part of that meaning. Such illustrative models are however likely to date much more quickly than the
meanings they are used to elucidate. For instance, David Masson
cast his 1874 explanation of the Romantic revolution in terms of
current scientific speculation: 'From the mineral core of the vast
world, outwards to the last thoughts . . . there runs, as science
teaches, a mystic flow of intercourse and affinity . . .' (6–7.) One
would hardly find it useful to begin an essay on Wordsworth in that
way today. As in all discourse, different strategies are appropriate
to different contexts.

11. The mind, the physical circuitry of the brain, allows for the
constant comparison of what our senses report with our knowledge
of (mediated) reality, language, conventions, other persons, what
other persons know, which other persons have told us what, our conjectures, our beliefs, our present interpretations. This process makes
possible not only judgements which bring together enormous quantities of information, but the corrections of judgements already made.

Each of the above principles opposes a fashionable fallacy:

(1) That there is no reality for language to refer to since we can't
know what reality really is.
(2) That all the possible meanings of a word are necessarily part of
its meaning in every use.
(3) That the author and audience are hermetically sealed from each
other.
(4) That meaning must be defined by a single and objective structure of language, not by the many and subjective intentions
embodied in its use.
(5) That if the external context of discourse is once evoked as a
means of interpretation, all possible contextual information
becomes relevant.
(6) Linguistic expression and interpretation are *sui generis* among
human activities.

(7) That, all language being tropic, meaning flees from trope to trope for ever.
(8) That that which is not certain is not.
(9) That interpretation is identical with closure.
(10) That continual changes in modes of explaining a text's meaning evidence the instability of meaning.
(11) That all attempts at interpretation are necessarily wrecked by the Scylla of the relativity of words or the Charybdis of the hermeneutical circle.

These are all varieties of a single master fallacy, the fallacy of absolutism, or, more colloquially, or all-or-nothingism.

2. *Another Look at the Value of Critical and Interpretive Commentary*

Arnold's famous answer to the question of the function of criticism—which he was almost the first to ask and thus to answer—was to propagate the best that has been known and thought or, what is really an alternative phrasing, to see things in themselves as they really are. Arnold's formula proved powerful enough to carry the study of literature in English to a prominent place in the schools and universities of England and the United States (which was *not* his primary intent). For a good three-quarters of a century various versions of it have continued to provide justification for academic criticism and college-level study of literature (activities now inextricably intertwined). Essential weaknesses in these formulations have of course become more and more evident over time. *How* are we to know what is the best? *How* is it possible to see things as they really are, and *how* would we be sure we were doing so? Thus they have been translated or transmogrified into such forms as 'the most interesting expression of what has been thought', or the most interesting thoughts', or 'seeing the text as it really is', or 'seeing things in a new way'. So apologetic have become those who still owe intellectual allegiance to Arnold that the *breadth* of his argument has been neglected.

We can preserve that breadth by a different kind of modification. The critic's purpose is to direct attention to what he or she thinks belongs to the best known and thought, and is of most value in seeing things as they are. Now Arnold would not have approved of any such dilution, but given the relationship between language, thought, and reality with which I began and the externality of all evaluative criticism, it is not so toothless as it may sound. It does not deprecate the fact that different critics make different evaluative judgements but recognizes that these different judgements largely arise from the fact that there are many norms against which literature can be, has been, is, and will be judged. That literature can be judged in terms of diverse criteria results from its ability to serve many functions—a fact to be celebrated rather than deplored by those who love it. What Arnold could not recognize was that no one critical framework or evaluative criterion is adequate. Contention between multiple uses and norms does not imply anarchy. What will be convincing depends partly on society's knowledge, beliefs, and experience that provide the warrants and backing for assertions of significance and evaluation. Critics must take account of the continuing critical dialogue, even if they wish to alter its conventions, assumptions, or principles.

Further, the role of context in making interpretation of the critic's own discourse possible and determining what arguments will be judged valid does not imply that critical commentary simply reproduces socially determined structures of thought. Critics are like other authors: by bringing to bear individual experience and unique combinations of information and mental energy they are able to move to new points of view and construct novel arguments to support them. Indeed a critic's commentary is likely to be interesting only to the extent that it provides new insights or states older ones in fresh ways. Nor does the view of extrinsic criticism here sponsored imply that it is merely a continually shifting whirl—there *is* a brute reality, and there *are* institutional facts that not only guide us in interpreting language, but resist conceptual follies and reward conceptual salience. Brute reality may not be what we think it, institutional facts may be misunderstood because the categories by which we try to assess them do not adequately fit, but both continually demand that we take account of their existence.

In saying that extrinsic criticism uses a text to exemplify an external conceptual framework or to give evidence of its validity, I do not mean that extrinsic commentary never illuminates the text itself. By offering a perspective other than that intended by the author, it may cause the reader to see the text afresh and notice new aspects. It is by no means unprofitable or illegitimate to say 'let us look at the text *as if*': as if Shelley's overwhelming motivation had been to escape the influence of Wordsworth, as if *Paradise Lost* were an apologia for male supremacy, as if Dickens's sentimentality resulted from an unconscious understanding of a necessarily vicious capitalism.

Finally, to say that extrinsic criticism is essential to human interest in literature is not to say that readers can make a text mean anything they wish. They can argue for any significance, any evaluative norms, they wish, and so far as extrinsic criticism goes Stanley Fish is correct: the proper model is persuasion rather than demonstration (*ITT* 356 ff.). When, however, we are concerned with interpretation rather than criticism, the author's presumptions about the possibilities of interpretation constitute the rules that must be reconstructed and adhered to in pursuing the intended meaning of the text. We are free of course to stipulate different presumptions and derive different rules, but then we have entered the realm of extrinsic criticism.

Having adhered as strongly as possible to the distinction between interpretation and extrinsic criticism to this point, we can now recognize that it is essentially a heuristic one. Though it is possible to find both purely interpretive and purely extrinsic examples, most commentary is mixed. Frequently elucidation of meaning is combined with praise for the artistry with which the author conveyed his intent or for the profundity or value of that which the author has (intentionally or unintentionally) conveyed or revealed. In such cases, the praise, or the norms on which the praise is based, or both, may be more implicit than explicit. Such a mixture is natural since we read for meaning, significance, and aesthetic qualities at the same time. Elaine Showalter has done good service in pointing to the fact of 'double reading,' that is, our ability to recognize (and keep separate) the author's meaning and the degree to which the sequence of thoughts or actions presented by the text accords or clashes with, exemplifies or challenges conceptual structures and frames of reference in which we have a particular interest or investment. In addition, however, we also respond aesthetically. We find pleasure in implication (especially tropes) and unexpectedly apt choices of words in all discourse, and in piquant characterizations and clever turns of plot in narrative. We take pleasure in following novel modes of argument, thought that turns down fresh pathways, the sense of increasingly intertwined implication in deft plotting. There is as much pleasure in understanding Iago's machinations as in listening to Touchstone's wise foolery. We find delight in participating in the meanings we reconstruct: Wordsworth's response to Tintern

Abbey, Faulkner's description of a bear hunt, Lamb's irreverent response to melancholy tombstone warnings.

It may seem perverse to call 'extrinsic' the sources of the pleasure we take in our reading: surely the author intended that the reader should have such pleasure? But our basic principles continue to hold. To recognize that authors intended turns of phrase, tropes, images, characterizations, descriptions, witty twists of argument, or meditation to be enjoyed is part of interpretation; but to evaluate the success of these intentions, to praise the work and recommend it to others for those qualities is extrinsic criticism. We have little doubt that we are expected to take pleasure in the diction of *Euphues*, or the savage satire of Swift's 'A Beautiful Young Nymph Going to Bed', or Dickens's idealized portraits of children and hero- ines, but few readers will now be found who do so. The disparity is more readily acknowledged between the intended and our actual aesthetic response in the case of the legions of novels, poems, and essays never praised by anyone for their literary value. Most must have been read with enjoyment by someone at some time and the most unimaginative and predictable of Harlequin romances, the dullest of Westerns, the most derivative of detective stories are being read in their thousands today. They offer whatever is necessary for some readers to read aesthetically: there are many 'evaluative com- munities' existing at any given time. It is also true that the less sophisticated of these undergo metamorphosis as well as those of accredited critics. What portion of the 1860 holdings of Mudie's Select Library are read, or would be read willingly, by those wishing to pass an idle hour today?

Much commentary thus mixes interpretation of meaning, analy- sis of significance, and/or evaluation of aesthetic qualities (the latter two both constitute extrinsic criticism, but since they appeal to different kinds of norms, it is useful to distinguish them). Commen- tators who are clear about the difference will be explicit about it in their writing; where they are not, the reader must warily sift the commentary. Each is legitimate so long as it does not pretend to be other than it is.

Why then does so much commentary on literature seem unsatis- fying or trivial? One must grant from the beginning that a great deal of it has been written by academics because they were expected to do it. The Liberal Arts, emulous of the sciences (driven by what Maxine Hairston has so happily referred to as 'physics envy'), capitulated to a largely inappropriate model of research and publication; English departments, that had been intentionally staffed with faculty who liked the challenge of leading undergraduates to enjoy literature, aped research universities in requiring that their members find new things to say—in print—about literature.

It is not that most of those who profess literature don't enjoy discussing what they have read. The problem is that what may be eminently suited for intimate discussion is not necessarily suited for professional publication. When we read a text we especially enjoy or think especially significant, we want to share that enjoyment or sense of worth, to enter into a more active relationship with it. If we have found portions difficult to interpret, we wish to share the meaning we have discoverd. We may, let us admit, even wish to boast that we have achieved a more complete understanding of its meaning than others. These things the academic profession offers its members the opportunity to do—but only if done in conformity with certain, largely generic, conventions. One of the most important of these is that, with certain exceptions, commentary should have point, specifically that it should represent the solution of a problem or correction of an error. Whether or not what commentators have to say originated in recognition of such a problem or error, they therefore cast it into that mould, formulating as a problem the question to which what they wish to say would be the appropriate answer, or pointing to interpretations which ignore or treat unsatisfactorily one or more aspects of the text so that they can make good the defect.

The result has too often been superfluous interpretations of the sufficiently interpretable, usually presented as further adjustments to multiply extant interpretations. Alternatively, commentators search for external structures of thought that might suggest as yet unnoticed significances in well-worn texts. Where the critic is genuinely interested in the relationship between the text and an external system, illuminating criticism results; too often the exercise is carried out merely because no one has done it before.

That may sound as cynical as the straightforward assertion that most members of the profession write books and articles only because they are told by provosts, deans, and colleagues that they should or must. But the original impulse is honest enough, though our awareness of disciplinary conventions distorts the process by which we proceed. Here by the way is an illustration of the difference between discussing the author's intention in terms of an external framework and interpreting the intention expressed in a text. The *meaning* of the seventeenth essay one has read on *The Turn of the Screw* is just what a competent writer of an abstract would say it was: perhaps, say, a setting forth of additional reasons for believing that the governess is subject to hallucinations. That is the author's intended meaning as embodied in the essay, though his (probably somewhat pinched and ill-used) muse would know that his intention was more generous, if more vague, in the beginning.

Of course the best of commentary rises far above these dreary exercises. It may offer quite new information that, by altering one of the dimensions of interpretation, will lead to a genuinely fuller interpretation. It may use the resources of language, trope, and structure in such a way as to make aesthetic reading of the argument itself worthwhile, in which case it acquires one of the characteristics by which we define literature. It may even give sufficient pleasure by the process of setting forth a sufficiently intriguing 'as if' theory: 'Let us read Henry James as if it were inevitable that his meaning would prove undecidable.' Or, and here we enter the realm of neo-Arnoldian criticism, it may throw new light on what we believe or have believed, or how we live or have lived, or it may call the reader's attention to a text that offers one or another kind of aesthetic pleasure.

But what is worth publishing and what is worth presenting in the classroom, though contiguous, are not congruent. If we wish to justify our 'mystery', we of the guild of academic scholarship and criticism must demonstrate two overriding principles. The first is that an author's intended meaning *can* be understood with reasonable probability and accuracy, but only through knowledge of as much of the context assumed by the author as possible. The corollary is of course that interpretation requires knowledge of historical events, cultural attitudes, linguistic usages, and biographical fact— in short, of what, in the broadest sense of the term, used to be called philology. The necessity for such knowledge and the means of discovering and relating it to the discourse to be interpreted are of equal exigence.

The second is that extrinsic criticism is quite another thing from interpretation. Why should not undergraduates who encounter a Marxist 'interpretation' of *Tom Jones* in one classroom, a feminist 'interpretation' in another, a psychoanalytical in another, and a deconstructive in yet another conclude that they have fallen among ignorant armies clashing by night, and either seek to escape the darkling plain of literary study altogether, or else immerse themselves in a protective Pyrrhonism? Students of literature need to understand from the beginning that, on the one hand, Fielding's intended meaning is not by definition indeterminable and, on the other, that multiple analyses of any discourse are not only possible but may be of great value. We read with two purposes: to understand what the author means, and to relate that meaning to what we know, believe, seek to know, or might believe.

The two are not wholly separate enterprises: the very process of mastering the historical context may well suggest the value of critical analysis of cause-and-effect relationships. As a minor instance, the reader of nineteenth-century novels must recognize the convention by which the eldest unmarried sister is referred to by the family name while younger sisters are referred to by their first names. (Thus in *Cranford* we have the sisters Miss Brown and Miss Jessie, as also Miss Jenkyns and Miss Mattie.) Now though this bit of cultural knowledge is applied in interpretation simply to keep track of who is being referred to, it says a great deal about the orderly way society presumed daughters would be presented to society and married ('married off' in the tell-tale phrase), and about the way in which the principle of primogeniture, so important for assuring male succession, led to a hierarchy among sisters as well as brothers. As Marxist criticism, for instance, has become more sophisticated, it has given more and more attention to the context of utterances, both to better understand their meaning and better evaluate their significance. (Excellent examples are to found in *Re-Reading English*, edited by Peter Widdowson.)

Since the koinonoetic or ecological approach is applicable to all discourse, it overcomes the fatal distinction between a narrow poetics, whether conceived as the study of mimesis, or literariness, or literary structure, and a narrow rhetoric conceived as the study of the techniques of argument. It equally overcomes the fatal distinction between the study of literature conceived as commentary on the best others have said or written, and instruction in composition conceived as practice in saying what the individual student can find to say under artificial conditions. To understand the process of interpretation is to understand not only how to interpret others as adequately as possible but how to get others to interpret our own meaning with similar adequacy.

A final question must be faced. If extrinsic criticism is the use of a literary text to argue the validity or universality of a conceptual framework that attempts to explain some aspect of the world or delineate some norm, why is not the interpretive scheme here set forth just such an external framework? It may be—but the challenge falls to those who would deny it a privileged status as the only acceptable explanation of the interpretation of meaning. Is there an explanation that more fully accords with what we do when we seek to convey a particular meaning? Is there an explanation that more fully accords with what we do when we seriously seek to understand what another's discourse means?

Appendix: A Closer Look at Deconstruction at Work

Deconstructive critics can rightly point out that those who challenge the validity of deconstructive commentary more often attack its theoretical statements than analyse specific examples of its practice. The same demurrer can be lodged against the assessment I have made in this volume that deconstruction is simply one of many significative frameworks. The difficulty of looking closely at instances is that deconstructive strategies are so diffuse and import so many externally motivated constructions that analysis quickly becomes tangled and tedious.

J. Hillis Miller's 'Walter Pater: A Partial Portrait' has become a standard seminar example of the American variety of deconstruction viewed with fascination by avid proponents and irritated foes alike. Miller's article in fact exemplifies how assumptions and terminology taken from the philosophical arguments of Jacques Derrida can motivate deconstructive essays in which Derrida is never mentioned and force one to choose between humanistic criteria of unity and order on the one hand and necessary chaos on the other without being directly confronted with the philosophical ramifications of such a choice. I will therefore indicate in a number of places where Miller's argument is illuminated by Derridean parallels, though to critique Miller's manœuvres in themselves it is necessary only to recognize that they are illegitimate extrapolations from Saussure. Thus if possible associations, meanings, and uses of a word within the total language (*langue*) are assumed always to be available—that is, if the given text (*parole*) and situation of utterance (situation within extralinguistic reality) are not granted the capacity to control associations and possible meanings, one may revel limitlessly in associations and analogies. Miller pursues this direction one step further: if neither reference nor immediate context can determine meaning, all use of language will eventually fall into contradiction. Hence the role of the critic is to demonstrate the necessary self-contradiction of each text.

Although Miller comments on a rich variety of Pater's personal and literary characteristics, I will concentrate on the way the major thesis unfolds in answer to the question, 'Is Pater's work centered or acentered, and if centered, what is its center, its origin, ground or end?' (99.)

Miller begins to move towards his central thesis by remarking:

> Pater's writing offers the same fascination to the reader as that of any author, the fascination of a complexity which *works*, which hangs together, which may be 'figured out' or resolved. His work has that consonance, those unexpected echoes of this passage with that passage, those hidden resonances and harmonies which Pater saw as the ideal of a musical form that would have absorbed all its matter into that form. (101.)

But it is not the unity and coherence of Pater's writing that primarily fascinate Miller. The transition to quite the opposite interest is made quietly, and one might think, curiously. 'Nevertheless, if, as Charles Rosen affirms, the basis of muscial expression is dissonance, the critic must, in Pater's case, take note also of disharmonies, contradictions, omissions, hiatuses, incongruous elements which precisely do not "work".' (Miller's reference is to Rosen's 'Schoenberg and Atonalilty'.) Despite the fame of Pater's dictum that 'all art constantly aspires towards the condition of music', this is a slim kind of authorization for leaving the pursuit and contemplation of the consonance of Pater's thought to search for dissonances, especially given the 'if' that introduces the assertion that musical expression is based in dissonance. And why the phrase 'in Pater's case'? One must assume that while many of the early readers of the 1976 essay might have accepted the logic of that transition at face value, the critical *cognoscenti* would have seen that the real source of authorization for this proceeding was not Charles Rosen but Jacques Derrida. Derrida's *De la grammatology* (1967) had just appeared in Gayatri Spivak's English translation (1976), accompanied by Spivak's impressive 87-page preface. The recipe for such a deconstructive reading is summarized, for instance, in that preface:

> If in the process of deciphering a text in the traditional way we come across a word that seems to harbour an unresolvable contradiction, and by virtue of being one word is made sometimes to work in one way and sometimes in another and thus is made to point away from the absence of a unified meaning, we shall catch at that word. If a metaphor seems to suppress its implications, we shall catch at that metaphor. We shall follow its adventures through the text and see the text coming undone as a structure of concealment, revealing its self-transgression, its undecidability. (*OG* lxxxv.)

Significantly, Miller avoids introducing Derrida's larger philosophical rationale for searching for the flaw or rift through which the apparently unified text may be dismantled. Having prepared us for the pursuit of dissonances and contradictions, Miller enters upon a beautifully ordered, concise tracing of the meaning of the 'moment', 'the intense and wholly individual instant of experience' for Pater (101). The analysis moves from the significance of the moment to Pater's search for the 'virtue' or unique power to be found in a moment, whether the moment is an instant of experience, a work of art, or an author or artist. Miller then points out that the 'virtue' of a writer is transmitted by 'style' and further that such virtue is in fact the writer's consciousness or personality, that is, his or her subjectivity. Then, in a move that appears gratuitous but the reason for which would be clear enough to a reader coming to Miller's essay from *Of Grammatology*, Miller comments that 'in Pater's work, as in one important strand of the Western tradition generally, subjectivity is the name given to the Logos, paternal origin, goal, and supporting ground' (100). The uses of the word 'logos' have a long and complex history, but what is being put before us is the Logos that, to use a voguish term, 'inhabits' Derrida's 'logocentrism', or, in his words, 'the infinite creative subjectivity in medieval theology' (*OG* 13).

Miller then announces what seems to him a different, incompatible aspect of Pater's view of the moment and its peculiar virtue: 'The uniqueness of each momentary impression is a result not of its singleness but of its special combination of contradictory forces.' (101.) Certainly one must agree that the vision of human life, and all other existence, as 'but the concurrence, renewed from moment to moment, of forces parting sooner or later on their ways' is central to the famous 'Conclusion'. For Pater, each experience observed is 'a design in a web, the actual threads of which pass out beyond it'. Miller's comment on this Paterian vision of existence, however, is curious:

> Pater's materialist notion of impersonal forces underlying each personality involves a specific theory of repetition. This theory denies the possibility of finding any fixed origin for any person or impression . . . Whatever the critic reaches as an apparent beginning, a solid ground on which to base an interpretation, dissolves on inspection into a repetition . . . As in Nietzsche, so in Pater, a sense of vertigo is generated by this infinite regression into the past . . . (104.)

Though one can understand what Miller means by 'repetition'—each force has played a part in an infinity of moments—it's an odd word to use precisely because Pater seems rather to say that the uniqueness of each moment is the result of an unrepeatable collocation of forces, unrepeatable because those particular forces are not moving in parallel but passing through the 'moment' from a variety of previous moments on their way to different destinations. And, so far as I know, Miller is the first to experience 'vertigo' in reading Pater. The source of that vertigo is less Pater than the Derrida who can regard thinking as 'what we already know we have not yet begun' (*OG* 93).

At this point one encounters another gratuitous interpolation. 'In place of the subject as *Logos*, Pater seems to put another equally traditional idea of the metaphysical ground. . . The *Logos* is a ubiquitous and multiple force, energy, *energeia.*' (104.) But it is Miller, not Pater, who is here feeling the compulsion to identify a Logos or ground. Miller's next move is to make, in his own way, the point I raised as an objection to his earlier unqualified use of the term 'repetition': since the forces that combine and part continue for ever (and thus have no origins), what is new, for instance in Plato's thought, is nothing but the form in which old speculations, or thoughts, or intellectual forces come together. Thus, 'In Pater's doctrine of recurrence, repetition is always with a difference.' (105.) The difference is the form in which the old material coheres.

Miller is now ready to move to an exposition of a third formulation of Pater's thought which he finds irreconcilable with the first two: '. . . the full exploration of Pater's concept of form will deconstruct once more the apparent end point reached in the interpretation of his work. Such an exploration puts in question both the notion that for Pater subjectivity is the *Logos* and the notion that for him material energy is the *Logos.*' (106.) We note that what we are actually promised is that Miller's third way of looking at Pater's thought will undercut *Miller's* notion 'that for Pater subjectivity is the *Logos*' and *Miller's* notion 'that for him material energy is the *Logos*'. Here is the key paragraph that transports us into the third way of thinking of Pater:

> Meaning or significance in a personality, in a gem, a song, a painting, a piece of music, is always defined by Pater as a force, as the power to make an impression. This power is not single, nor is it a harmonious collocation of energies making a unity. A 'virtue' always results from antagonistic forces, sweetness against strength in the case of Michelangelo, strangeness against the desire for beauty in Leonardo, and so on. The meaning is in neither of the two forces separately, nor in their sum. It arises in the space between them, out of the economy of their difference. (106.)

This again is an odd passage. Though the meaning, or power, or virtue of anything that makes an impression is the result of a conjunction of forces for Pater, and he does like to find formulas for virtues that emphasize the pressure of two forces against one another, the virtue of a moment is never the result of only two forces even though we may choose to single out an opposition that seems especially prominent. The next paragraph begins with a *non sequitur*: 'The sign thus constituted by two enemy forces does not draw its meaning solely from its own internal differentiation. It also carries within itself the echo, across the gap of a further difference, of earlier similar gatherings or forces.' (106.) Whence the 'thus'? And whence the 'sign'? Personalities, gems, songs, paintings, pieces of music *can* be called signs—one can divide each into a signifier and a signified—but the unexplained, unprepared-for introduction of the term 'sign' here seems to serve no purpose—except to allow the importation of a semiotic analogy to a portion of Pater's thought.

The mystery of what is going on here further increases in the next paragraph, which begins, 'Another discontinuity in each sign or virtue is the relation of meaning to its material embodiment.' (107.) 'Sign or virtue'? How have we arrived at this identity, or even parallelism, between virtue and sign? However, the point being made here, which Miller goes on to develop even more fully, is Pater's recognition that the material of expression, the word, or paint, or marble, is never reduced wholly to form. So forced seems Miller's comment, or transmogrification of, the impossibility of transforming the material wielded by the writer or artist into pure form, that I must ask indulgence to quote a lengthy passage:

> A remnant of non-saturation is always present, a part of the body left over, some matter not wholly absorbed into form. Its existence leads to the recognition that art for Pater is generated only in the interval between forces. This is not that other kind of Logocentrism which sees the Logos as energy rather than as subject. It involves a different notion, more difficult to grasp, in fact ungraspable. It is the ungraspable as such, an ungraspable which for Pater, with his sense for nuance, is essential to literature and to art generally. The notion is ungraspable because it cannot be thematized or conceptualized. It can only be glimpsed fleetingly, out of the corner of the eye, in the interplay between images. This non-conceptual insight, perpetually in flight, is the notion of meaning constituted by difference. Such meaning is not a correlate of force, whether that force is subjective or objective, self or matter. Such meaning is always in excess of the material substratum that embodied it. It appears momentarily in the openings between, and it is always in league with death. Such a notion might be called the uncanny, but it is not the uncanny as the occult presence of some *ur*-force which has differentiated itself and works as fate. It is the uncanny as the absence of origin. (108.)

Full analysis of those sentences would require the sort of hundred-fold magnification to which Derrida is fond of submitting brief passages, but a sampling of the difficulties they raise can be suggested by half a dozen questions. Why does the fact of 'non-saturation' lead to a view that art 'is generated only in the interval of forces'? What in fact could such a statement mean? Does not the sentence beginning 'This is not that other kind of Logocentrism' beg the question of whether 'this', if 'this' refers to Pater's description of art as aspiring towards becoming nothing but form, is *any* kind of logocentrism? The chain of presumed synonyms with which Miller presents us seems to be: a kind of logocentrism = the ungraspable = a non-conceptual insight = the notion of meaning constituted by difference = something which is always in excess of the material substratum that embodies it = something always in league with death = the uncanny as the absence of origin. But why, for instance, is the notion of meaning constituted by difference 'ungraspable'? Saussure seems to have been able to grasp the notion well enough. How did we get from the concept of material unabsorbed into form to meaning in excess of the material? And how do death and the uncanny find their way in—except as part of the constant Freudian accompaniment to that Derridean mode of thought which has been brought in with the announcement of 'the absence of origin'?

What Miller regards as the necessary contradictoriness of the three aspects of Pater's thought that he has outlined is exemplified in his analysis of the following passage from Pater's 'The Myth of Demeter and Persephone':

> Symbolism as intense as this, is the creation of a special temper, in which a certain simplicity, taking all things literally, *au pied de la lettre*, is united to a vivid pre-occupation with the aesthetic beauty of the image itself, the *figured* side of figurative expression, the *form* of the metaphor. When it is said, 'Out of his mouth goeth a sharp sword,' that temper is ready to deal directly and boldly with that difficult image, like that old designer of the fourteenth century, who has depicted this, and other images of the Apocalypse, in a coloured window at Bourges. Such symbolism cares a great deal for the hair of *Temperance*, discreetly bound, for some subtler likeness to the colour of the sky in the girdle of Hope, for the inwoven flames in the red garment of *Charity*. (*GS* 99.)

The meaning of this passage is 'undecidable', writes Miller:

> The passage, in its insistence that only a 'special temper' is capable of the 'real illusion' of allegory *au pied de la lettre*, can be taken as reaffirming Pater's subjectivism. In its suggestion that the stratum below the play of allegorical representation is material forces, flame, or sky, the passage may be seen as congruent with Pater's objectivism, his materialism of 'inwoven' forces. In its recognition that both of these notions are generated by a play of language, the passage may be taken as congruent with the third reading I have proposed. (111.)

It may be taken in those ways—if one has already set up three opposed 'aspects' of Pater's thought. However, unless one is committed to exemplifying an 'undecidability' produced by the oppositions between three 'aspects', one is likely to find something a good deal less dramatic. That is, one is likely simply to recognize that Pater often describes the 'virtue' of a moment, or work of art, or text because of the fascination of its complex of forces, or the complex of responses one might feel, *without evaluation*. Pater's own response is thus often left ambiguous: whether he found the window beautiful, or quaint, or bizarre, we do not expect to be told. That the curiousness of the window results from the literal visualizing of the vehicle of the metaphor is unquestionable, but Pater's recognition of the results of literalization of the play of language is conventional enough; wits of the Renaissance had their own fun with a literal reading of sonnets to a mistress with hair of gold, cheeks of roses, and lips of cherries. But for Miller, the 'undecidability' of the passage given, and of Pater's texts as a whole, authorizes his well-known assertion that 'Pater's writings, like those of other major authors in the Occidental tradition, are at once open to interpretation and ultimately indecipherable, unreadable. His texts lead the critic deeper and deeper into a labyrinth until he confronts a final aporia.' (112.)

I have suggested questions and objections to Miller's deconstructive analysis at a number of points in my admittedly tendentious, but I hope not inaccurate, summary; I now turn to the larger strategies of the essay. What we find there will, I think, also provide an answer to the truly imperious question: are the texts of 'major Occidental writers' (all? most? some? a few?) finally merely indecipherable, finally merely invitations to descend to an aporia which we know beforehand we will discover if we go far enough? The key strategy that produces Miller's reading is, I would argue, the arbitrary truncation of lines of thought. The supporting strategy is the importation of analogues, parallels, or associations unauthorized by anything in the text, in effect denying that the structure of the text constitutes an internal context that limits possible meanings and relationships. Let me exemplify both in Miller's discussion of what he offers as the first aspect of Pater's thought, the identification of subjectivity with the Logos.

The argument, we recall, moves from the importance of the individual moment, to the virtue of the moment, to the style which expresses that virtue, to the personality behind the style. However, all that exists— material objects, including the human body, and the combination of memory, thought, and present perception in the human mind—are the result of momentary confluences of certain forces. Moreover, though it is on the intense, brief moment of rare quality that Pater forcuses, any congruence of forces that hangs together in a way that seems to sustain an identity may on Pater's terms be regarded as a moment (though of course there will be changes from instant among the forces that make up the moment in the more sustained sense). Thus a personality is a moment. My point is that there is no reason arbitrarily to cease one's analysis of what follows from Pater's concentration on the moment when one arrives at personality and to announce it as the 'ground'; the next step is to make clear that the 'virtue' of a personality, or natural scene, or work of art, is the result of the same play of forces. 'Like the elements of which we are composed, the action of these forces extends beyond us: it rusts iron and ripens corn' Pater continues, 'Far out on every side of us those elements are broadcast, driven in many currents; and birth and gesture and death and the springing of violets from the grave are but a few out of ten thousand resultant combinations.' The ceaseless weaving and unweaving of such forces should lead naturally to what Miller regards as the second aspect, the ubiquitousness of energy. But he terminates his analysis of the first aspect by identifying

subjectivity with the Logos regarded as 'paternal origin, goal, and supporting ground'.

Miller then begins over with an analysis of the second aspect of Pater's
thought, and, after having developed the role of this restless play of forces,
terminates his exploration of this second aspect by identifying it with
another conception of the Logos: energy as envisioned by Heraclitus or
Lucretius. To repeat, Pater's sense that both material and intellectual
energies continue on beyond any given moment, and that the moment is in
fact the form taken at a point of time, actually fits well into the framework
of what Miller has taken as the first aspect of Pater: the virtue of the moment
is the result of the form we discover among the forces at play (forces that
come together in a formless way have little power or virtue). Thus only
Miller's own assertion that Pater identified first 'subjectivity' and then
'energy' with the Logos creates an opposition between the two 'aspects'.

The third aspect of Pater's thought that Miller announces seems essentially to revolve around the production of meaning and significance from
difference and discontinuity, arising 'in the space between' forces, 'out of the
economy of their difference' (106). Whether Miller regards Pater as having
also identified the play of differences with the Logos is not clear, but certainly the semiotic terminology is an importation into Pater's discourse. The
differences that Miller develops are between the past moment and the present, between meaning and its 'material embodiment'. However, rather
than developing the idea of difference as a separate aspect and aligning it
with currents of thought in ways for which there is little warrant in Pater,
one might merely note that the way in which past moments become forces in
the mind, and in which the material forces observed at any moment of
experience always exceeds the significance or form which we read into
them, follows quite naturally from Pater's total vision of forces endlessly
interacting. Pater's essay on 'Style' makes manifest that while material
which we use creatively to embody intellectually grasped form and significance always exceeds that form, at the same time the form grasped or
thought always exceed the form expressed.

I have tried to show that the aporia at which Miller arrives is created in
part by choosing to ignore links that can easily be made between various of
Pater's key concepts, and in part by the wholesale importation of systems of
thought Miller thinks analogous to some portions of Pater's thought. As
discussed in Chapter 3, the ordinary answer to whether such importations
are valid or not is provided by the principle that allusions, analogues,
symbolic interpretations, and parallels are admissible only to the extent that
they prove congruent with the total pattern of the work. Until quite
recently, unquestioned critical methodology ruled out possible interpretations that could not be assimilated to a consistent pattern.

What an argument such as Miller's does is deny that unity and coherence
are guiding principles for the interpretation of a text in order not only to

deny that unity *is* to be found in the text under analysis, but to make possible the critic's own choice of associations and partial parallels as interpretive tools, models, and goals. Circular as this strategy is, Miller would point out that the usual mode of interpreting texts by the criterion of coherence is equally circular, since it is the assumption of unity that allows us to rule out extrapolations from and interpretations of particular passages that do not fit comfortably with what seems the most certain or likely meanings of the whole. (One might also expect the objection associated with the 'hermeneutic circle' to be raised against pursuers of unity, but a moment's thought will show that to the extent it is valid, it tells equally against those for whom the 'whole' they discover is coherent and those for whom it is internally dissonant.)

The very statement of the crux implies one resolution. If the world is in fact incoherent and chaotic, the search for chaos, aporia, and contradiction is neither interesting nor profitable. If the world is, on the other hand, a nicely adjusted and generally intelligible structure, the constantly repeated labours of artists and philosophers to represent its unity seem on the one hand redundant and on the other strangely unsuccessful. What is left is the paradox that in a problematic and frequently perverse world, order, literary or other, takes part of its value and interest from the very difficulty and ephemerality of its achievement.

To the extent that the study of vernacular literature has been justified by Arnoldian arguments, the belief or faith in organic unity has been bound up closely with it. In the background is Arnold's ever-lively sense of disorder and chaos; 'culture', 'criticism', and 'the best known and thought' are the antidotes to a chaos continually reasserting itself. It is hardly surprising that one encounters frequent ambiguities and at times direct contradictions in just those texts the world has judged most interesting and valuable.

References

ALTIERI, CHARLES, *Act and Quality: A Theory of Literary Meaning and Understanding* (Amherst: University of Massachusetts Press, 1981).

ARMSTRONG, NANCY, 'Inside Greimas's Square: Literary Characters and Cultural Restraint', in *The Sign in Music and Literature* (Austin: University of Texas Press, 1981).

ARNOLD, MATTHEW, *The Complete Prose Works of Matthew Arnold*, ed. R. H. Super (Ann Arbor: University of Michigan Press, 1960–77).

ATKINS, G. DOUGLAS, *Reading Deconstruction: Deconstructive Reading* (Lexington: University of Kentucky Press, 1983).

AUSTIN, J. L., *How to Do Things with Words* ed. J. O. Urmson and Marina Sbisá (Cambridge, Mass.: Harvard University Press, 1975).

BACH, KENT and HARNISH, ROBERT, *Linguistic Communication and Speech Acts* (Cambridge, Mass.: MIT Press, 1979).

BANFIELD, ANN, *Unspeakable Sentences: Narration and Representation in the Language of Fiction* (Boston: Routledge and Kegan Paul, 1982).

BARTHES, ROLAND, *Image-Music-Text*, trans. Stephen Heath (New York: Hill and Wang, 1977).

—— *S/Z*, trans. Richard Miller (New York: Hill and Wang, 1974). Originally published in French in 1970.

BATESON, F. W., *English Poetry: A Critical Introduction* (London: Longmans, Green, 1950).

—— *English Poetry and the English Language*, (Oxford: Clarendon Press, 1934).

—— 'The Function of Criticism at the Present Time', *Essays in Criticism*, 3 (Jan. 1953), 1–27.

BELSEY, CATHERINE, *Critical Practice*, (London: Methuen, 1980).

BERGER, PETER, and LUCKMAN, THOMAS, 1966, *The Social Construction of Reality* (Garden City: Doubleday Anchor, 1967).

BLEICH, DAVID, *Subjective Criticism* (Baltimore: The Johns Hopkins University Press, 1978).

BLOOM, HAROLD, *The Anxiety of Influence: A Theory of Poetry* (New York: Oxford University Press, 1973).

BROOKS, CLEANTH, *The Well Wrought Urn* (New York: Harcourt, Brace, 1947).

BROOKS, CLEANTH and WARREN, ROBERT PENN, *Understanding Poetry* (New York: Henry Holt, 1938).

BROWN, GILLIAN and YULE, GEORGE, *Discourse Analysis* (Cambridge: Cambridge University Press, 1983).

BURKE, KENNETH, *A Grammar of Motives*, 1945 (Cleveland: World Publishing Company, 1962; with *A Rhetoric of Motives* (Meridian Books)).

—— *The Philosophy of Literary Form*, 1941 (New York: Vintage Books, 1957).

CARNAP, RUDOLF, 'The Elimination of Metaphysics Through the Logical Analysis of Language', trans. Arthur Pap, in *Logical Positivism*, ed. A.J. Ayer (Glencoe, Ill.: The Free Press, 1959).

COULTHARD, MALCOLM, *An Introduction to Discourse Analysis* (New York: Longman, 1977).

CRANE, R.S., 'Critical Inquiry: or, the Perils of the "High Priori" Road', in *The Idea of the Humanities*, ii (Chicago: University of Chicago Press, 1967).

—— 'History versus Criticism', in *The Idea of the Humanities*, ii (Chicago: University of Chicago Press, 1967). First published *English Journal*, 23 (1935), 740–58.

CULLER, JONATHAN, *Structuralist Poetics* (Ithaca: Cornell University Press, 1975).

—— 'Structuralism and Literature', in *Contemporary Approaches to English Studies*, ed. Hilda Schiff (New York: Barnes and Noble, 1977).

CUNNINGHAM, J.V., *Woe or Wonder* (Denver: Denver University Press, 1951).

DAVIE, DONALD, *Purity of Diction in English Verse* (London: Chatto and Windus, 1952).

DE MAN, PAUL, *Blindness and Insight* (New York: Oxford University Press, 1971).

DENNIS, JOHN, Preface to *The Grounds of Criticism in Poetry*, in *The Critical Works of John Dennis*, ed. Edward Niles Hooker, (Baltimore: The Johns Hopkins University Press, 1939–43).

DERRIDA, JACQUES, *Of Grammatology*, trans. Gayatri Spivak (Johns Hopkins University Press, 1976).

—— 'Limited Inc a b c . . .', trans. Samuel Weber, *Glyph*, 2 (1977), 162–254.

—— 'Signature, Event, Context', trans. Samuel Weber and Jeffrey Mehlman, *Glyph*, 1 (1977), 172–96.

DIJK, VAN, TEUN A., and KINTSCH, WALTER, *Strategies of Discourse Comprehension* (New York: Academic Press, 1983).

DILLON, GEORGE, *Language Processing and the Reading of Literature* (Bloomington: Indiana University Press, 1978).

DUMITRIU, ANTON, *History of Logic* (Tunbridge Wells: Abacus Press, 1977).

EAGLETON, TERRY, *Literary Theory: An Introduction* (Minneapolis: University of Minnesota Press, 1983).

—— *Marxism and Literary Criticism* (London: Methuen, 1976).

ELIOT, T. S., *On Poetry and Poets* (London: Faber and Faber, 1957).

EMPSON, WILLIAM, *The Structure of Complex Words* (London: Chatto and Windus, 1951).

FISH, STANLEY, English Department Colloquium, Pennsylvania State University, October 1980.

—— *Is There a Text in This Class?* (Cambridge, Mass.: Harvard University Press, 1980).

—— 'Literature in the Reader: Affective Stylistics', *New Literary History*, 2 (Autumn, 1970, 123–62). Reprinted in *Is There a Text in This Class?*

—— 'Withholding the Missing Portion: Power, Meaning and Persuasion in Freud's "The Wolf-Man" ', *TLS*, 29 August 1986, pp. 935–8.

FOUCAULT, MICHEL, *The Archaeology of Knowledge*, trans. A. M. Sheridan Smith, 1969 (New York: Harper Torchbooks, n.d.).

FOWLER, ALASTAIR, *Kinds of Literature: An Introduction to the Theory of Genres and Modes* (Cambridge, Mass.: Harvard University Press, 1982).

FOWLER, ROGER, *The Language of Literature* (New York: Barnes and Noble, 1971).

—— *Literature as Social Discourse: The Practice of Linguistic Criticism* (Bloomington: Indiana University Press, 1981).

FREGE, GOTTLOB, 'On Sense and Reference', trans. Max Black, in *Translations from the Philosophical Writings of Gottlob Frege*, ed. Peter Geach and Max Black (Oxford: Basil Blackwell, 1952). First published in German in 1892.

FRYE, NORTHROP, *Anatomy of Criticism* (Princeton: Princeton University Press, 1957).

—— 'On Value Judgements', in *Criticism: Speculative and Analytical Essays*, ed. L. S. Dembo (Madison: University of Wisconsin Press, 1968).

GARDNER, HELEN, *The Business of Criticism* (Oxford: Clarendon Press, 1959).

GENETTE, GÉRARD, *Figures of Literary Discourse*, trans. Alan Sheridan (Oxford: Basil Blackwell, 1982). First published in French in 1966.

—— *Narrative Discourse: An Essay in Method*, trans. Jane E. Lewin (Oxford: Basil Blackwell, 1980). First published in French in 1972.

GOLDSTEIN, PHILIP, 'Humanism and the Politics of Truth', *Boundary 2*, xii. 3/xiii. 1 (Spring/Autumn 1984), 235–55.

GOMBRICH, E. H., *Art and Illusion*, 1960 (Princeton: Princeton University Press, 1969).

GOUDGE, THOMAS A., *The Thought of C. S. Peirce* (Toronto: University of Toronto Press, 1950).

GRAFF, GERALD, *Professing Literature: An Institutional History* (Chicago: University of Chicago Press, 1987).

GREGG, RICHARD, *Symbolic Inducement and Knowing* (Columbus, SC: University of South Carolina, 1984).

GREIMAS, A.-J., *Structural Semantics: An Attempt at a Method*, trans. D. McDowell, R. Schleifer, and A. Velie (Lincoln: University of Nebraska Press, 1983). Originally published in French in 1966.

GRICE, H.P., 'Logic and Conversation', in *Syntax and Semantics*, 3 (New York: Academic Press, 1975).

—— 'Meaning', *The Philosophical Review*, 66 (1957), 377–89.

—— 'Utterer's Meaning, Sentence-Meaning, and Word-Meaning', *Foundations of Language*, 4 (Aug. 1968), 225–42.

GRIMSHAW, ALLEN, *Language as Social Resource* (Stanford: Stanford University Press, 1981).

HAIRSTON, MAXINE, 'Breaking our Bonds but Reaffirming Our Connections', Chairman's address, 1985 Conference on College Composition and Communication.

HALLIDAY, M.A.K. and HASAN, RUQUAIYA, *Cohesion in English* (London: Longman, 1976).

HARRIS, WENDELL V., 'Adam Naming the Animals: Language, Context, and Meaning', *Kenyon Review*, n.s. viii (Winter 1986), 1–13.

—— 'Toward an Ecological Criticism: Contextual versus Unconditioned Literary Theory', *College English*, 48 (Feb. 1986), 116–31.

HARTMAN, GEOFFREY, 'Words, Wish, Worth: Wordsworth', in *Deconstruction and Criticism*, ed. Harold Bloom (New York: Continuum, 1979).

HIRSCH, JR., E.D., 'Meaning and Significance Reinterpreted', *Critical Inquiry*, 11 (Dec. 1984), 202–24.

—— 'Past Intentions and Present Meanings', *Essays in Criticism*, 33 (April 1983), 79–98.

—— *Validity in Interpretation* (New Haven: Yale University Press, 1967).

HOEY, MICHAEL, *On the Surface of Discourse* (London: George Allen and Unwin, 1983).

HOFMANNSTHAL, HUGO VON, 'The Letter of Lord Chandos', trans. Tania and James Stern, in *Hugo von Hofmannsthal: Selected Prose* (London: Routledge and Kegan Paul, 1952). First published in German in 1902.

HOLLOWAY, JOHN, *Narrative Structure: Exploratory Essays* (Cambridge: Cambridge University Press, 1979).

HOYLES, JOHN, 'Radical Critical Theory and English', in *Re-Reading English*, ed. Peter Widdowson (London: Methuen, 1982).

HUSSERL, EDMUND, *Cartesian Meditations: An Introduction to Phenomenology*, trans. Dorion Cairns (The Hague: Martinus Nijhoff, 1977).

HUXLEY, T.H., *Science and Education*, vol. iii of *Collected Essays* (New York: Appleton, 1899). First published 1880.

HYMES, DELL, *Foundations in Sociolinguistics: An Ethnographic Approach* (Philadelphia: University of Pennsylvania Press, 1974).

JAKOBSON, ROMAN, 'Closing Statement: Linguistics and Poetics', in *Style in Language*, ed. T. A. Sebeok (Cambridge, Mass.: MIT Press, 1960).

JAUSS, HANS ROBERT, 'Literary History as a Challenge to Literary Theory' in *Toward an Aesthetic of Reception*, trans. Timothy Bahti (Minneapolis: University of Minnesota Press, 1982).

KATZ, JERROLD, *Propositional Structure and Illocutionary Force* (New York: Crowell, 1977).

KEAST, W.R., 'Imagery and Meaning in the Interpretation of *King Lear*', *Modern Philology*, 47 (Aug. 1949), 45–64. Reprinted as ' "The New Criticism" and *King Lear*', in *Critics and Criticism*, ed. R. S. Crane (Chicago: University of Chicago Press, 1952).

KERMODE, FRANK, *The Sense of an Ending* (London: Oxford University Press, 1967).

KUHN, THOMAS, *The Structure of Scientific Revolutions*, 1962; second edition (Chicago: University of Chicago Press, 1970).

LANGER, SUSANNE K., *Philosophy in a New Key* (Cambridge, Mass.: Harvard University Press, 1942).

LEAVIS, F. R., *English Literature in Our Time and the University* (London: Chatto and Windus, 1969).

—— 'The Responsible Critic, or The Function of Criticism at Any Time', *Scrutiny*, 19 (Spring 1953), 162–83.

LENNEBERG, ERIC, *Biological Foundations of Language* (New York: John Wiley, 1967).

LÉVI-STRAUSS, CLAUDE, *The Raw and the Cooked*, trans. John and Doreen Wrightman (New York: Harper and Row, 1969). Originally published in French in 1964.

MAILLOUX, STEVEN, *Interpretive Conventions: The Reader in the Study of American Fiction* (Ithaca: Cornell University Press, 1982).

MASSON, DAVID, 'Wordsworth', in *Wordsworth, Shelley, Keats and Other Essays* (London: Macmillan, 1875).

MILLER, J. HILLIS, 'On Edge: The Crossways of Contemporary Criticism', *Bulletin of the American Academy of Arts*, 32 (Jan. 1979), 12–32.

—— 'Stevens' Rock and Criticism as Cure', *Georgia Review*, 30 (Spring/Summer 1976), 5–31, 330–48.

—— 'Walter Pater: A Partial Portrait', *Daedalus*, No. 105 (Winter 1976), 97–113. (This article was incorrectly paginated; I cite pages by the numbers as printed.)

MONTROSE, LOUIS, 'Renaissance Literary Studies and the Subject of History', *English Literary Renaissance*, 16 (Winter 1986), 5–12.

OGDEN, C.K. and RICHARDS, I.A., *The Meaning of Meaning*, 1923 (London: Kegan Paul, Trench, Trubner, 1927).

OLSEN, ELDER, 'An Outline of Poetic Theory', in *Critics and Criticism*, ed. R. S. Crane (Chicago: University of Chicago Press, 1952).

PARRISH, STEPHEN MAXFIELD and PAINTER, JAMES ALLAN, *A Concordance to the Poems of W. B. Yeats* (Ithaca: Cornell University Press, 1963).

PATER, WALTER, *Greek Studies* (London: Macmillan, 1910). (I have silently changed Miller's quotation from 'The Myth of Demeter and Persephone' to agree with the Macmillan edition.)

—— 'Style', in *Appreciations*, Library Edition (London: Macmillan, 1910).

PEIRCE, C. S., *Collected Papers of Charles Sanders Peirce*, ed. Charles Hartshorne and Paul Weiss, vols. i–vi, and Arthur W. Burks, vols. vii–viii (Cambridge, Mass.: Harvard University Press, 1931–5, 1958).

PERELMAN, CHAIM and OLBRECHTS-TYTECA, L., *The New Rhetoric: A Treatise on Argumentation* (Notre Dame, Ind.: University of Notre Dame Press, 1969).

PRATT, MARY LOUISE, *Toward a Speech Act Theory of Literary Discourse* (Bloomington: Indiana University Press, 1977).

REICHERT, JOHN, 'Making Sense of Interpretation', *Critical Inquiry*, 6 (Summer 1980), 746–8.

—— *Making Sense of Literature* (Chicago: University of Chicago Press, 1977).

RICHARDS, I. A., *Coleridge on the Imagination* (New York: Harcourt, Brace, 1935).

—— 'How Does a Poem Know When It Is Finished?' in *Poetries and Sciences* (London: Routledge and Kegan Paul, 1970).

—— *Interpretation in Teaching* (New York: Harcourt, Brace, 1938).

—— *The Meaning of Meaning.* (See Ogden.)

—— *The Philosophy of Rhetoric*, 1936 (New York: Oxford University Press, 1965 (Galaxy Book Edition)).

—— *Principles of Literary Criticism*, 1925 (New York: Harcourt Brace Jovanovich, n.d. (Harvest Book Edition)).

—— *Speculative Instruments* (London: Routledge and Kegan Paul, 1955).

RICŒUR, PAUL, *The Conflict of Interpretations* (Evanston: Northwestern University Press, 1974).

—— *Interpretation Theory: Discourse and the Surplus of Meaning* (Fort Worth: Texas Christian University Press, 1976).

RIFFATERRE, MICHAEL, 'Describing Poetic Structures: Two Approaches to Baudelaire's "Les Chats",' *Yale French Studies* (1966) 36–7.

ROSEN, CHARLES, 'Schoenberg and Atonality', *Georgia Review*, 29 (Summer 1975), 298.

ROSENBLATT, LOUISE, *The Reader, The Text, The Poem: The Transactional Theory of the Literary Work* (Carbondale: Southern Illinois University Press, 1978).

SAUSSURE, FERDINAND DE, *Course in General Linguistics*, ed. Charles Bally and Albert Sechehaye, trans. Wade Baskin (New York: McGraw-Hill, 1966). First published in French in 1915.

SEARLE, JOHN, *Expression and Meaning: Studies in the Theory of Speech Acts* (London: Cambridge University Press, 1979).

—— *Speech Acts* (London: Cambridge University Press, 1969).

SHOWALTER, ELAINE, 'Feminist Criticism in the Wilderness', *Critical Inquiry*, 8 (1981), 179–205.

SMITH, BARBARA HERRNSTEIN, *On the Margins of Discourse: The Relation of Literature to Language* (Chicago: University of Chicago Press, 1978).

STEVENSON, LAURA C., *Praise and Paradox: Merchants and Craftsmen in Elizabethan Popular Literature* (Cambridge: Cambridge University Press, 1984).

STUBBS, MICHAEL, *Discourse Analysis: The Sociolinguistic Analysis of Natural Language* (Chicago: University of Chicago Press, 1983).

TODOROV, TZVETAN, *Mikhail Bakhtin: The Dialogical Principle*, trans. Wlad Godzich (Minneapolis: University of Minnesota Press, 1984).

—— *Symbolism and Interpretation*, trans. Catherine Porter (Ithaca: Cornell University Press, 1982).

TOULMIN, STEPHEN, *The Uses of Argument* (Cambridge: Cambridge University Press, 1958).

TUVE, ROSAMUND, *Elizabethan and Metaphysical Imagery* (Chicago: University of Chicago Press, 1947).

VALERY, PAUL, 'Poetry and Abstract Thought', in *Essays on Language and Literature*, ed. J. L. Hevesi (Port Washington, NY: Kennikat Press, 1967). First published in French in 1939.

WATSON GEORGE, 'The Stacked Deck of Language', *Sewanee Review*, 93 (Summer 1985), 412–27.

WELLEK, RENÉ and WARREN AUSTIN, *Theory of Literature* (New York: Harcourt, Brace, 1949).

WIDDOWSON, PETER, ed. *Re-Reading English* (London: Methuen, 1982).

WILLARD, CHARLES, *Argumentation and the Social Grounds of Discourse* (University, Ala.: University of Alabama Press, 1983).

WIMSATT, W. K., Jr. and BEARDSLEY, MONROE, 'The Affective Fallacy', *Sewanee Review*, 54 (Summer 1946), 468–88. Reprinted in Wimsatt's *The Verbal Icon* (Lexington: University of Kentucky, 1954).

YEATS, W. B., *W. B. Yeats: The Poems*, ed. Richard J. Finneran (London: Macmillan, 1984).

Index

The abbreviation *illus.* indicates that reference is to a literary work used as an illustrative example.